G.B. Army Royal Engineers, G.B. Royal Engineers' Institute

Professional Papers of the Corps of Royal Engineers

Royal Engineer Institute, occasional papers

G.B. Army Royal Engineers, G.B. Royal Engineers' Institute

Professional Papers of the Corps of Royal Engineers
Royal Engineer Institute, occasional papers

ISBN/EAN: 9783337282042

Printed in Europe, USA, Canada, Australia, Japan

Cover: Foto ©Andreas Hilbeck / pixelio.de

More available books at **www.hansebooks.com**

PROFESSIONAL PAPERS

OF THE

CORPS OF ROYAL ENGINEERS.

EDITED BY

MAJOR R. H. VETCH, R.E.

ROYAL ENGINEERS INSTITUTE

OCCASIONAL PAPERS,

VOL. VIII.

1882.

London:
PUBLISHED FOR THE ROYAL ENGINEERS INSTITUTE,
BY EDWARD STANFORD, 55, CHARING CROSS,
1883.

PREFACE.

THE present volume and Vol. VII. were put in hand together, but as the latter volume was entirely devoted to Permanent Fortification, and as it was most desirable that no further time than was absolutely necessary should be allowed to elapse in bringing it out, precedence was given to it and Vol. VIII. somewhat delayed in consequence. It may be some compensation, however, for the delay that Officers receive for last year two volumes instead of one, while those papers in the present volume which were likely to be of immediate practical use were printed separately in pamphlet form and issued to Officers who wished for them.

While, we believe, all the papers in the present volume will be found to be valuable contributions to our knowledge, there is one on "Railways for Military Communications in the Field," by Colonel J. P. Maquay, R.E., which, at the present time, when railway work in the field has been brought into such prominence, is of peculiar interest. The present paper has been entirely recast and revised from a report that he made in 1881 to the Inspector General of Fortifications, who submitted it to the Secretary of State for War and to H.R.H. the Field Marshal Commanding-in-Chief.

That there will be some who will differ from Colonel Maquay's conclusions we do not doubt, and we trust that his paper will lead to other contributions, so that the subject may be thoroughly investigated in the *R.E. Professional Papers*.

ROBT. H. VETCH, MAJOR, R.E.,

Secretary, R.E. Institute, and Editor.

December, 1882.

CONTENTS OF VOL. VIII.

LIST OF PLATES AND TABLES.

SUBJECT OF THE PAPER.

ERRATA.

In "List of Plates," in Paper 1, the number of Plates should be 10 instead of 8.

ERRATA.

Page 34, line 28, *for* " junctions " *read* " junction "
,, 44, ,, 16, *after* " Khán " *insert* comma
,, 54, ,, 14, *after* " Álam " *insert* comma
,, 60, ,, 4 from the bottom, *dele* " been "
,, 65, ,, 6 and 7, *for* " Aligrah " *read* " Aligarh "
,, 68, ,, 4 from the bottom, *for* "and now completely " *read* " was now completely "
,, 68, ,, 2 from the bottom, *for* " Álbm " *read* " Álam "
,, 69, ,, 16, *for* " scimatars " *read* " scimitars "
,, 71, ,, 2, *after* " Mysoreans " *insert* comma
,, 77, ,, 3, *for* " Ruperat " *read* " Ruparel "
,, 80, ,, 8, *for* " depredation " *read* " depredations "
,, 80, ,, 25, *after* " time " *dele* inverted commas
,, 80, ,, 29, *after* "August " *insert* inverted commas
,, 97, ,, 13, *for* " Márathás " *read* " Maráthás "
,, 97, ,, 17, *for* " below " *read* " between "
,, 97, ,, 22 and 23, *for* " circutious " *read* " circuitous "
,, 103, foot note ‡, *for* " 811 " *read* " 181 "
,, 104, line 19, *for* " right " *read* " regret "
,, 110, ,, 10, *for* " of Chambal " *read* " of the Chambal "
,, 110, ,, 26, *for* " advantage " *read* " advantages "
,, 113, ,, 10, *for* " Káhupúr " *read* " Káhupúr "
,, 113, ,, 9 from the bottom, *for* " Berá " *read* " Berár "
,, 113, ,, 16 from the bottom, *for* " Colonel Harcourt marches " *read* " General Lake marches "
,, 113, ,, 3 from the bottom, *for* " Fot " *read* " Fort "
,, 114, ,, 18, *for* " Judúr " *read* " Indúr "
,, 114, ,, 26, *for* " Farukábád " *read* " Farakhábád " .
,, 115, last line, *for* "was Serai " *read* " was the Serai "
,, 120. lines 16 and 17, *for* " Pilhannah " *read* " Pilhaunah "
,, 121, ,, 27, 28 and 29, *for* " Sker Kot " *read* " Sherkot "
,, 121, ., 33 and 34. *for* " Chandausé " *read* " Chandausi "

PROVISIONAL FORTIFICATION.

(2nd Paper.)

By Captain G. S. Clarke, R.E.

In a previous paper* it was sought to direct attention to a branch of fortification, which is at present receiving considerable development at the hands of continental Military Engineers, has won enhanced importance from the experiences of the Russo-Turkish War, and which appears in some respects particularly adapted to our own defensive requirements.

The term 'provisional' was deliberately chosen, in preference to its competitors 'position' and 'semi-permanent,' to distinguish the branch in question. The first of the two latter terms was rejected as being insufficiently comprehensive, and rather referring to a special use than affording a true technical distinction. The second appeared inadmissible as being somewhat unmeaning. 'Permanent' being assumed to mean work the destruction of which by natural agencies is not taken into consideration, 'semi-permanent' would seem to possess no very clearly defined significance. On the other hand, 'provisional,' which denotes work as efficient and highly finished as time allows, but capable of improvement and development to any extent compatible with contemporary possibilities, appears to be just the word to express the subject of this and the previous paper.

While the ordinary fortification of the field of battle might almost be evolved on the spot from first principles, it is evident that on the design of a provisional work much labour and thought would have to be bestowed. An ideal provisional fort must in fact be fully thought out at leisure, and it seems of great importance that we

---

* Paper XIII., Volume III. (page 253), *Professional Papers of the Corps of Royal Engineers*, R.E. Institute Occasional Papers.

should possess some really good standard designs, with complete estimates of time, labour, and material. Colonel Schaw, R.E., in a lecture delivered at Chatham on the 6th September, 1876, states "the question of a really efficient field redoubt, is one which may well engage the attention of the Corps, at present we have no good type" and though the typical examples given in Part I. of *Instruction in Military Engineering* meet the ordinary requirements of the field, there has, it is believed, been no attempt to give us a well considered and fully worked out design for a provisional work of a much higher class. Such a work, requiring perhaps for its execution more than as many weeks as the field redoubt would need days, may, nevertheless, come into play in the wars of the future, and may even in some cases supersede permanent fortification.

Broadly speaking, provisional works may be divided into two classes according to the conditions under which they may be expected to be employed.

1st. Works constructed after the beginning of a campaign on sites not previously strategically considered, or which have become important in consequence of strategic developments not anticipated. In such cases neither the topographical nor geological conditions might be fully known and, which is also of much importance, the extent of the resources of the neighbourhood in labour and material might be more or less undetermined.

2nd. Works constructed at the declaration of war, or its approach, for a well defined and previously considered object, on sites perfectly well known, and under conditions accurately ascertained beforehand.

As an instance of works of the first class, Plevna may be cited; as instances of the second, Adrianople and Tschataldscha; as an instance of the possible demand for the second class, London.

The former class would usually have to be carried out by Military Engineers capable of adapting standard designs to varying conditions and full of resource, so as to be able to make the best use of the time available, and the material and labour forthcoming. On the other hand, works of the latter class could be designed in the fullest sense during the calm of peace. Their requirements in labour and material would be exactly known. The resources of the neighbourhood would have been accurately gauged, and the how and the whence to supply deficiences would have been considered. Moreover, if a properly elaborated design existed, the execution might safely be left to civil labour under civil supervision.

In the defence of England, both classes of fortification would probably come into play. Certain strategic, commercial, or manufacturing centres would appear to need protection under any circumstances, others would call for fortification as soon as the landing place of the invader, or his subsequent plan of operations, had declared itself.

A method of fortification, in which forethought and brain power applied in advance may save enormous and possibly useless, because misdirected, expenditure, appears to be worth very careful study. And there are circumstances which make provisional fortification particularly applicable to our own country. The sea secures us time and a fair warning. Our resources in labour and the very ordinary materials required are practically unlimited. Our great railway system facilitates the rapid concentration at any spot of labour and material. Moreover, England possesses in her Civil Engineers a very powerful force, which could at a time of need be applied to the defence of the country. There is a very considerable body of young and able Engineers who, if provided with proper designs, are perfectly well able to carry out all the work necessary to fortify a position, and who have great experience in dealing with, and organising civil labour on a large scale. In any time of real necessity the *personnel* of the Corps would have demands made upon it which its strength could scarcely meet, and it is no small advantage to have this very real 'reserve force' to fall back upon. The same may be said of many of our colonies, and it remains for us to prepare in peace time a complete system of provisional defence, and by modifying it from time to time to keep it abreast of the advancing power of the attack. A paper army is rightly held up to contempt as a species of deception, which no great nation, jealous of the management of its affairs, should tolerate ; but a paper system of fortification may, it is contended, form a very real defence. Only this paper system must be thorough, and the brain power applied to it unstinted.

A very little reflection serves to shew that the design of a provisional work is a task of considerably greater difficulty than that of a field redoubt. The restriction to two or three days, or less, in the case of the latter, introduces a very sharp limitation to the possibilities of design. Extend the time to three or four weeks, or even longer, postulate an ample supply of timber, of railway bars, and even perhaps of bricks and cement, and it will be evident that these possibilities have enormously widened, and that very considerable variations of trace, profile, and general arrangement will present themselves for consideration. It is even contended

4

that the design of a good provisional work is more difficult than
that of an analagous permanent structure, and that it affords more
scope for clever and resourceful engineering. Granting the importance of the whole question of provisional defence, it becomes
desirable to consider carefully what has been already either proposed, or actually carried out, in other countries, and it is believed
that from the designs now selected for description some valuable
suggestions may be gleaned.

In the previous paper a provisional fort for Infantry defence, designed by Captain von Wittenburg of the Prussian Engineers was
described. *Plates* I. and II., accompanying the present paper, give
the plan and sections of a work for Infantry and Artillery designed
by the same Officer. This work is unprovided with caponiers, but
the ditches are all more or less defended; that of the right flank by
fire from the parapet; that of the left flank by fire from an exterior
trench; those of the gorge by fire from the gorge parapet which is
broken outwards to form a species of tambour, as shewn on plan.
The flanking of the ditches of the front faces is secured by a special
arrangement. The salient is flattened off, its crest having a command of 14' 9", and in front of the main parapet a second line of fire
is obtained over a crest whose command is 5' 6". The trace of this
lower parapet is of the form of a bastioned front reversed, and it
provides a fire line of about 160' 0" run—say 53 rifles. The ditches
of the front faces are swept by the fire from the flanks of this lower
line of parapet, and the front line of the latter brings a fire to bear
on the glacis-like escarp (section on AB, *Plate* II.), and the ground
beyond. The defenders of this species of outwork are protected
from enfilade fire on the front face and reverse fire on the flanks by
a long traverse carried on the line of the capital nearly the whole
depth of the work, and affording a covered communication, or postern, from the casemates under the two large interior traverses.
(See sections on A B and C D, *Plate* II.).

A ditch of the usual form is not provided round the outwork at
the salient, nor on the right flank. In these cases the escarp slopes
gently down, terminating in a steep counterscarp covering an
abattis. The glacis-like escarp is swept by Infantry fire from the
crest of the main parapet on the flank, (section on E F, *Plate* II.),
and at the salient by fire from the parapet of the outwork, (section
on AB, *Plate* II.). At the foot of the exterior slope of the right
flank there is a very broad berm, and on it a second or interior line
of abattis (section on E F, *Plate* II.). The escarp at the salient and
on the left flank, together with the bottom of the gorge ditch, are

covered with wire entanglement, or strewn with obstacles of the usual class.

This form of profile, by which the exterior line of abattis and the obstacles on the escarp are well covered, while the latter are swept by fire from the work, seems good, but on the other hand the abattis on the berm is particularly exposed, and extremely liable to damage from the distant Artillery fire of the attack.

The outward splay of the exterior line of the berm of the right flank (*Plate* I.), whereby the line of the ditch is not parallel to that of the flank, appears to be designed so as to give a greater length to the flanked ditch of the right front face, and also to ensure the escarp of the flank towards its front end being swept by fire from the parapet, which here has a greater command than at the rear end. A different profile (probably intended to be alternative) is given to the ditch of the left front face and left flank, which, though not shewn in the drawing, is easily recognised from the plan.

The principle by which a species of glacis is substituted for an escarp, is adopted in most of Captain von Wittenburg's designs. It seems based on a tendency to trust at the last stage of the attack mainly to the deadly effect of breach-loader fire over an obstacle-strewn field, and less to the ditch, and particularly the escarp as a physical obstacle. It appears to be assumed that an attack can thus be effectually stopped. And on the whole the experiences of Plevna go to prove that, even if this view is not wholly correct, a work of this class properly defended could only be taken at a very heavy sacrifice. The Germans distinguish between works which are *sturm-frei*, and those which are not, meaning by the word works which require special appliances—such as scaling ladders—to enable their actual physical obstacles to be surmounted—works in short which could not be carried by a rush even if there were no active defence. Provisional works can rarely be made absolutely *sturm-frei*, but modern breechloaders in the hands of steady troops very largely compensate for the want of storm-freedom.

Turning to the interior arrangements, it will be noticed that an Infantry banquette runs completely round the work, interrupted only by the eight lateral traverses. It is of great importance that, at the moment preparatory to the final rush, it should be possible to man the parapet everywhere with Infantry; but it is by no means clear that, as is sometimes stated, the action of this arm would commence only when the Artillery was silenced. Under easily conceivable circumstances, long range Infantry fire, up to at least 2 500 yards, might be employed with effect at an earlier period.

The standing Infantry garrison—200 men—would of course be quite insufficient to man a line of parapet of about 310 yards, but supposing the fort to belong to a line of defences, there would be towards the closing stages of the attack, a gradual drawing in of men from intervening shelter trenches to the closed works, which, independently of reinforcement from the rear, would render a dearth of men at the last moment unlikely to occur.

In rear of the Infantry banquette, the gunbank also runs round the work except at the gorge. The space between two adjacent traverses is supposed to contain only one gun, except at the shoulders where two might be employed, by which means the whole armament—12 guns—can be brought into action. In rear of the gunbank a slope leads down to the terreplein. This facilitates the withdrawal and interchange of guns according to requirement. It may be assumed that if the enemy had established batteries bringing an overwhelming converging fire upon the work, the guns of the latter would have to be withdrawn under cover, and only brought into action again when a favourable opportunity occurred. It might even be advisable in some cases to withdraw the guns temporarily out of the work altogether, and employ them behind epaulments in the line of adjacent shelter trenches. In fact a considerable amount of movement of guns may be expected to take place, affording scope for much skill and judgment in the direction of the Artillery defence.

The construction of the shell-proof casemates under the traverses, and of the main postern, or covered central communication, calls for no special remark, but it may be noticed that brickwork is employed in the walls of the main magazine (section on A B, *Plate* II.), and also, apparently, in a few other cases where a traverse cut off short to afford communication needs steep revetment. A more extended use of brickwork might in some cases be both possible and desirable. Since bricklayers, placed 4 feet apart, and working continuously, could build about 6 feet in height, of 4-brick wall, in 24 hours, it is not unreasonable to expect in provisional works the employment of bricks for many purposes. It may, in fact, be laid down as a general rule that, if by the use of brickwork for any purpose the progress of the earth-movement is not delayed, bricks whenever available should unhesitatingly be employed.

The work is unprovided with a covered way, which, if practicable, should always be constructed, but the value of such a covered way will depend on whether it can give a real second line of fire—a line of fire, simultaneous, at moderate ranges, with that from the work itself. Whether this can be secured will usually depend on the lie of the ground, since the command which can be given to the crest of the parapet of a provisional work will rarely be great.

In *Plates* III. and IV., the plan and section of a fort (B) designed for a similar garrison and armament are given. In this work the ditches are all unflanked (by the work itself at least) except that at the gorge which is defended as in fort A, *Plate* I.

The gunbank is interrupted at the shoulders, which are prepared only for Infantry defence. There are a few other points of difference apparent from the drawing. For the front faces and flanks alternative sections (A B and C D, *Plate* IV.) are proposed, of which the latter would seem preferable, since it not only presents no exposed abattis, but provides a covered way with a line of fire.

Captain von Wittenberg estimates the time required for these works at about six weeks, employing an average working party of 500 'day labourers,' and 100 carpenters. Night work does not seem to be taken into consideration and the work might probably be carried out in little more than four weeks by continuous labour.

It is proposed now to turn to some examples of design actually carried into practice during the course of the Russo-Turkish war. The credit of the works surrounding Adrianople, and those forming the lines of Tschataldscha, is very generally ascribed to Bluhm Pasha, a Turkish Engineer officer of Prussian extraction, but he was probably not without very able assistance.

These works would fall into the second category. It was sufficiently clear that Constantinople would need land defence and strategic and geographical conditions alike indicated Adrianople and the Tschataldscha position—the former as what may be termed a strategic advanced work, the latter as a main line of defence. The precise time of commencement of the work cannot be stated, but the latter probably received its first real impetus at the time of Gourko's crossing the Balkans and subsequent exploration of the Tundscha Valley. The first appearance of the Russians across the Balkans took place on the 14th July, 1877, and the arrival of their cavalry in front of Adrianople on the 20th January, 1878; there was, therefore, a period of 27 weeks, which the Turks could devote to the work of fortification.

Adrianople is situated at the confluence of the Maritza, the Tundscha and the Arda (or Arta) (*Plate* V.), three considerable rivers. The railway lines from Jamboli and Philippopolis, uniting at Tirnova, pass less than three miles from the town and, branching near Dimotika, lead to Constantinople and to Dedeagatch on the Marmora, near the mouth of the Maritza. Roads lead North-West to

Philippopolis, North along the Tundscha Valley to Jamboli, North-East to Burgas, East to Kirk-Kilissa, South-East to Constantinople, South along the Maritza Valley to Dimotika and Peridjik, and West along the Arda Valley.

Thus commanding the railway and numerous roads, and placed nearly midway between the two seas, Adrianople is a position which, if fortified and strongly held, no invader advancing on Constantinople, and not possessing the command of the sea, could ignore. Unfortunately for the Turks, Suleiman Pasha's force was drawn into a series of engagements near Philippopolis, as the result of which the last Turkish army was practically dispersed, and on the 20th January Stroukoff's Cavalry occupied the town, followed on the 22nd by Skobeleff's Infantry Division. The Turkish garrison of about 4,000 men—10,000 according to some accounts—retired on Constantinople without firing a shot. Had Suleiman, who early in January disposed of an army of 50,000 to 60,000 men with more than 100 guns, retired in time on Adrianople, the strength of the new works would probably have been thoroughly tested.

The defences consist of a chain of redoubts, 24 in number (*Plate* V.), situated on heights surrounding the town. This chain completely encloses the latter, its suburb Ilderim, the villages of Karagatch and Arnantkioy, and the Railway Station. The perimeter of the whole line of defence is about 28 miles, and the average interval between the works about 2,200 yards.

In *Plate* VI. details of two of the most considerable of the redoubts (Nos. 1 and 22) are given. No. 1 on a well defined hill top has a commanding position. It consists of an elliptical main parapet with an interior elliptical cavalier, but no ditch, and a large ravelin-like outwork. Cavalier, ravelin, and main parapet mount guns, the two former being designed for overbank fire: the latter has three embrasures at each side. The major axis of the trace of the redoubt at the crest is 88 yards : the minor axis 66 yards. The parapet is 26' 3" thick, reduced to 19' 9" at the gorge. The length of side of the ravelin is about 98 yards and the salient is rounded off, forming a gunbank raised above those of the sides. The ravelin has also provision for six overbank guns, protected by four lateral traverses. The gorge of the ravelin is nearly closed by the head of a large T-shaped traverse, the body of which protects the sides of the ravelin from reverse fire. This traverse also covers a large casemate, the sides of which, and the steps which lead down to the floor, are formed in brickwork, and which is roofed over by railway sleepers covered by a layer of fascines, and about 16' 6" of earth. The roof is further supported by intermediate uprights of squared oak, each carrying a transverse sill. The redoubt itself has four lateral traverses, two of which contain casemates. A banquette for Infantry runs round the work and is interrupted only at the gorge, the traverses, and the gun portions. The gorge is covered by a traverse of elliptic trace, provided with an Infantry banquette. About 55 yards in rear of the work and on the reverse slope of the hill, there is a sunken covered barrack, with brick end and rear walls and staircase. The roof is supported as described above, and has about 6' 6" of earth over it. Most of the Adrianople works had barracks of this description built in sheltered positions in rear, and usually linked to them by covered communication. The principle of keeping the Infantry garrisons of their works well sheltered in rear and bringing them up only when actually required was largely acted upon by the Turks at Plevna.

Redoubt No. 22 (*Plate V.*) also presents some distinctive features. The trace of the crest is the segment of a circle (diameter 70 yards), but that of the ditch is polygonal, a very usual arrangement in the works attributed to Bluhm Pasha. This work mounts 12 guns, firing through embrasures and protected by six small traverses and one large traverse. The latter and two of the former contain casemates with brick side-walls. The parapet is 26' 3" thick except at the gorge, where it is 19' 9" only. The trace of the ditch is an irregular pentagon: at the shoulders the angles are thrown outwards, as shown in the plan. There is a glacis and covered way for Infantry fire running round the work, and the two flank faces have small bonnettes (see section on C D, *Plate* VI.) which afford some protection against enfilade fire. Two steps, cut in the counterscarp, serve to give a resting place to men not actually manning the covered way. The gorge is covered by a semi-circular defensible traverse, with an Infantry banquette and one gunbank. There is a covered communication leading to a barrack in rear.

The Adrianople trench-work, was carried out mainly by Bulgarian peasants, and, at the time of their evacuation, the works are said to have been nearly all completed and to have been partially connected by a line of telegraph. About 200 guns were mounted and a large stock of provisions and ammunition had been collected. In tactical features the ground resembles that of Plevna, but the soil is somewhat lighter. The works were far more solidly built than those of Plevna, and were capable of much greater individual defence. Supplemented as they could have been by any number of dependent trenches and rifle pits, the Adrianople works might easily have repelled better planned and better executed attacks than those directed against Plevna.

The more celebrated lines of Tschataldscha, or Boyuk Tchekmedje, are about 25 miles from Constantinople. The Peninsular is here about 24 miles from sea to sea, but the broad lake of Derkos on the North, and a deeply indented bay on the South, narrow this distance to about 12 miles. A nearly continuous ridge, about 700 feet high, running almost North and South spans this distance (*Plate* VII.), and the ground slopes thence gently to the West. The ridge was intended to be defended by 37 closed works, of which the greater number were finished at the time of the armistice. They were disposed, roughly speaking, in two lines and may be classified according to their trace as follows—large, medium, and small, circular, elliptic and segmental elliptic. The ridge was almost without tree growth ; the ground in front afforded little cover and the soil was very favourable. The position was in fact admirably fitted for defence, but the garrison at the end of January, about 30,000 men, was hardly sufficient. With the dispersion of Suleiman's army and the loss of the Schipka force, the Turkish resistance completely collapsed, and by the terms of the armistice signed on the 31st January the Tschataldscha lines were evacuated.

The works were all constructed on the general principles ascribed to Bluhm, and are alike in their main features. Redoubt No. IV. (*Plate* VIII.) has an elliptic trace, major axis about 87 yards, minor axis 55. The work has six gun-banks, protected by eight lateral traverses. There is also one gunbank in the elliptic traverse covering the gorge. The Infantry banquette runs round the work but is interrupted at the gun portions. Five of the traverses contain casemates with brick side and end walls. Those used as barracks have a brick chimney and a ventilating shaft, as shown in the section. There is an unflanked polygonal ditch surrounding the work (except at the gorge-traverse), with a glacis and a covered way for Infantry fire. The terreplein of the work is drained into the ditch, and the latter is drained on to lower ground in front.

Redoubt No. V. (*Plate* VIII.) is very similar in general features. The trace of the work is the segment of an ellipse, major axis at the crest about 65 yards, minor axis about 54 yards. The chord of the segment forms the gorge and is broken up, forming a bastioned front covered by a semi-elliptic defensible traverse. There are five lateral traverses protecting the gun-banks and three of them contain casemates.

At the time of the armistice almost the whole of the works in first line were completed and armed. Nearly all the earth and brick-work of these redoubts, as of those around Adrianople, was carried out by civil labour, and the execution and general finish are universally pronounced to have been excellent. In all, nearly 300 guns are said to have been either mounted or in readiness; of these from 70 to 80 were Krupp siege guns of 5·91″ and 5·12″. Here also, as at Adrianople, the works were connected by a line of telegraph, and provisions and ammunition in large quantities had been accumulated.

The Tschataldscha lines would have been attacked by Skobeleff if the armistice had not been signed. It is certain that after the many experiences gained at Plevna and more recently at Shenovo, the attack would have been well planned and probably no finer body of men than the seasoned Russians of that period could have been found to undertake it, so that as a test of the relative powers of attack and provisional defence the operation would have been almost crucial.

Since the peace, the original works have been completed and new ones added. Lieut. Greene is probably not beyond the mark in stating of the Constantinople of to-day, "no other capital in the world posseses such a line of defence." Unless turned by an enemy possessing command of the sea, the Tschataldscha lines would seem to be almost impregnable.

In *Plates* IX. and X., the plan and sections of a typical provisional work for the defence of a hill-top are given. This design was furnished by Bluhm Pasha to Colonel Ott of the Swiss Engineers, from whose report these a nd the four preceding plates have been taken.

The work is in trace a circular segment (diameter about 60 yards) and four sides of the polygonal ditch are flanked by caponiers (*a, a, a, a,*) with two tiers of fire, formed in the counter-scarp at its front ends. These caponiers are well placed for protection from distant Artillery fire, but in the event of the enemy gaining and maintaining possession of the ditch their defenders would be sacrificed. Accommodation is provided for eight over-bank guns in the work and one in the gorge traverse. The latter is really a segmental lunette partially enclosing a traverse containing a shell proof casemate. A covered way affording a line of Infantry fire runs round the work, and the front line is broken so as to form two bastioned fronts and also two places of arms at the shoulders, defiladed by four traverses (*c, c, c, c*) containing casemates. Brickwork is employed in all the casemates and also in the steps leading from the ditch down into the caponiers and up to the covered way.

The total length of the line of fire is about 650 yards run, and to man it, therefore, at least an equal number of men would be needed. Casemate cover for 200 men is provided, and magazine accommodation to the extent of about 645 square feet.

The most salient features of the works attributed to Bluhm are thus:—

1. The curved trace of the crest of the main work.

2. The polygonal trace of the ditch; the latter usually unflanked.

3. The combination of Artillery and Infantry fire from the work itself; the employment of the latter only from the covered way.

4. The curved defensible traverse to cover the gorge; the large lateral traverses containing casemates for men and magazines.

5. The employment of brickwork as much as possible for the walls of the casemates and for stepped approaches..

The works appear to have several merits. The circular, or elliptic trace cannot well be enfiladed: it affords a maximum of interior space with a minimum of parapet: there are no undefended angles. The old objection to circular redoubts—that they tend to too great a dispersion of fire—has now less weight, since a smaller number of breachloaders is as effective as a comparatively large number of the old rifles. Nor has the other objection—that the circular trace is suited only to direct defence, and that works so designed have no self-flanking power—quite its old force, since the increased range of Artillery enables works belonging to a line to afford each other more effective mutual flank defence than formerly. Moreover redoubts would frequently be flanked by detached batteries in rear of the general line of their positions.

On the other hand, it may perhaps be said that the works above described provide insufficient cover for their garrisons, that the broad berm at the angles of the ditch affords a good resting place for an assaulting party to accumulate prior to the final rush for the parapet, and that there is on the whole too little storm-freedom. The latter objection may however be partially met by a liberal use of obstacles. It will be noticed that none of the works above described have any reduits, since the cavalier in redoubt No. 1 (*Plate* VI.) can hardly be so regarded.

In conclusion, and in connection with the question of the importance of providing good type drawings, it is suggested that there is a want (easily supplied) of a somewhat different field *Aide*

Mémoire from those at present existing. Few can securely commit to memory a mass of dimensions, although broad principles once mastered are rarely lost. What is needed is, it seems, a book of type drawings only, letter press to be omitted and all necessary notes written on the drawings themselves. The latter should be printed on waterproof calico, and with a limp waterproof cover should form a small roll easily carried in the pocket and available for reference *on the ground in any weather*. The drawings should be perfect in execution and in convenience for purposes of reference. In the selection of subjects, care should be taken to include nothing superfluous. Thus, while a text book should include everything needful and should presuppose no knowledge, the field *Aide Mémoire* should assume a previous engineering education. Such a matter as the preparation of a hedge, or wall, for defence might therefore safely be omitted. It could not be necessary to give to a trained Engineer a picture of a banquette on planks and casks, since to suppose that, casks and planks being at hand, it would not occur to him to use them, is surely to condemn him as destitute of elementary engineering resource. The same might be said of a considerable number of other matters which find their proper place in a text book. On the lines above indicated an eminently handy and portable book, embodying typical profiles, traces and general details of field, siege, and provisional works might be compiled which would, it is believed, prove a real boon in the field.

G. S. C.

PLATE I.

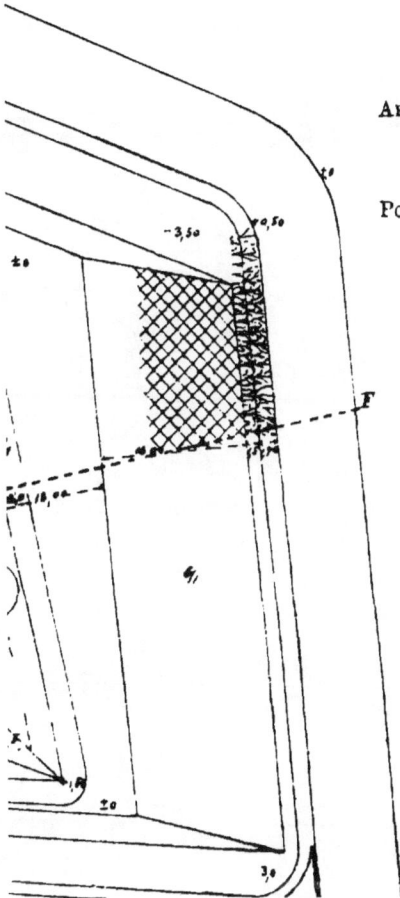

NOTE.

GARRISON, Infantry, 200
Artillery, 100
_____
Total. 300 { 2/3 Accommodated
in Casemates.

ARMAMENT, 15 C.M. Guns, 4
,,   12   ,,   8
_____
Total. 12

POWDER MAGAZINES, 2 Expense Magazines,
each 50 tons = 100 tons.

2 General Magazines,
each 200 tons = 400 tons.
_____
Total. 500

AMMUNITION, 15 C.M. Shells, 2,800
12   ,,   5,600
_____
Total. 8,400

PROVISIONAL FORT A.

Scale 1/32

REFERENCES.

1 a Express Powder Magazine
1 b Shell Shed
1 c Drilled

2 a Gunners' Quarters
2 b Shell filling Room

3 Provision Store
4 Hospital
5 Commandant's Quarters
6 Officers' Quarters
7 Latrine
8 Guard Room
9 9 Main Powder Magazine

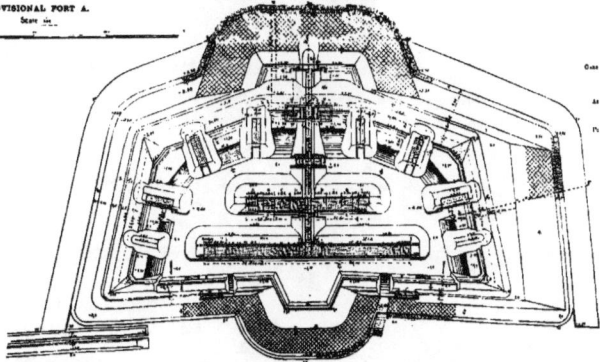

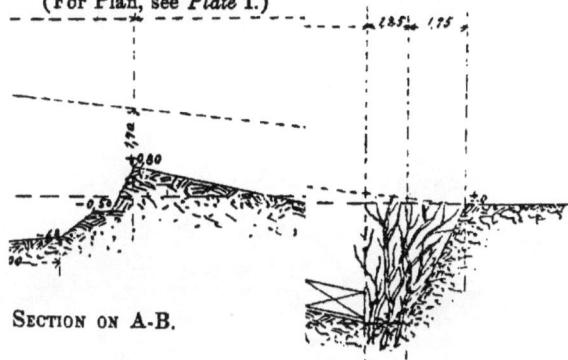

SECTION ON A-B.

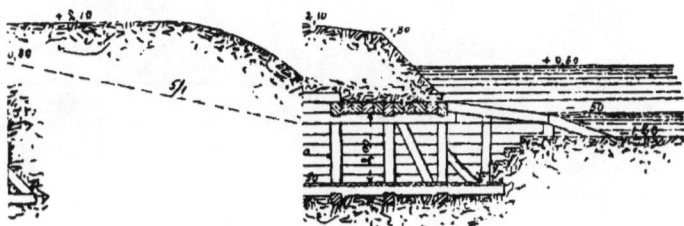

TION ON G-H.

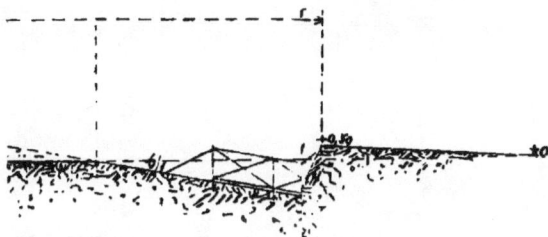

N ON E-F.

Scale $\frac{1}{200}$

PLATE II.

PROVISIONAL FORTIFICATION.
PROVISIONAL FORT A.
(For Plan, see Plate I.)

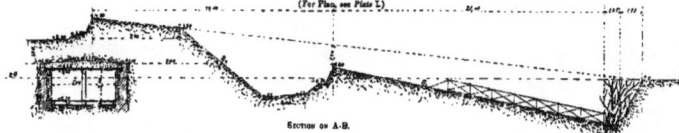

SECTION ON A-B.

SECTION ON C-D.

SECTION ON G-H.

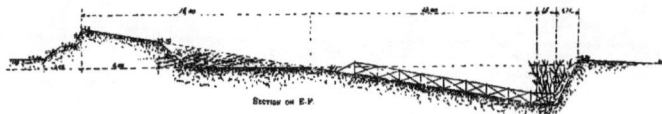

SECTION ON E-F.

Scale 1/80

PLATE III.

NOTE.

GARRISON, Infantry, 200
         Artillery, 100

    Total. 300 { all Accommodated in the Casemates.

ARMAMENT, 15 C.M. Guns, 4
    ,,   12   ,,   8

    Total 12

POWDER MAGAZINES, 2 Expense Magazines,
        each 50 tons = 100 tons.
        2 General Magazines,
        each 200 tons = 400 tons.

        Total. 500

AMMUNITION, 15 C.M. Guns

PROVISIONAL FORTIFICATION.

PROVISIONAL FORT B.

PLATE III.

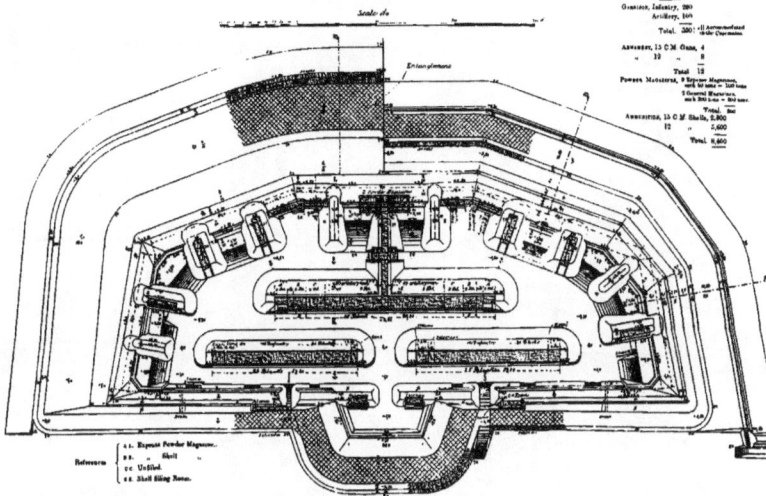

References
a a. Express Powder Magazine.
b b. ,, Shell
c c. Unfilled.
d d. Shell filling Room.

PLATE IV.

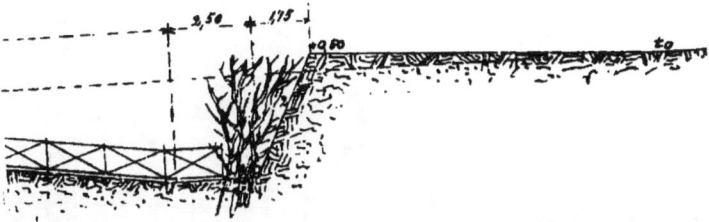

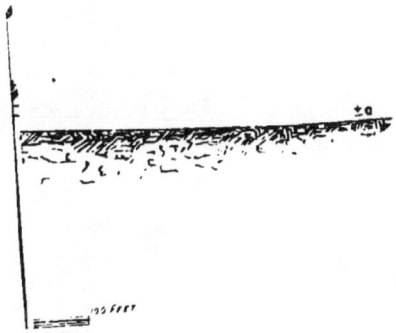

PLATE IV.

PROVISIONAL FORT B.

(For Plan, see Plate III.)

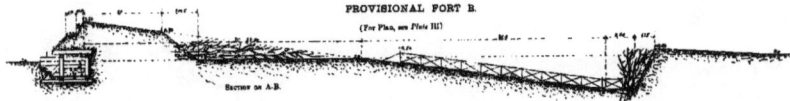

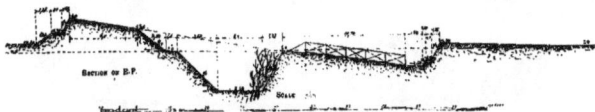

Section on A.B.

Section on C.D.

Section on E.F.

Scale

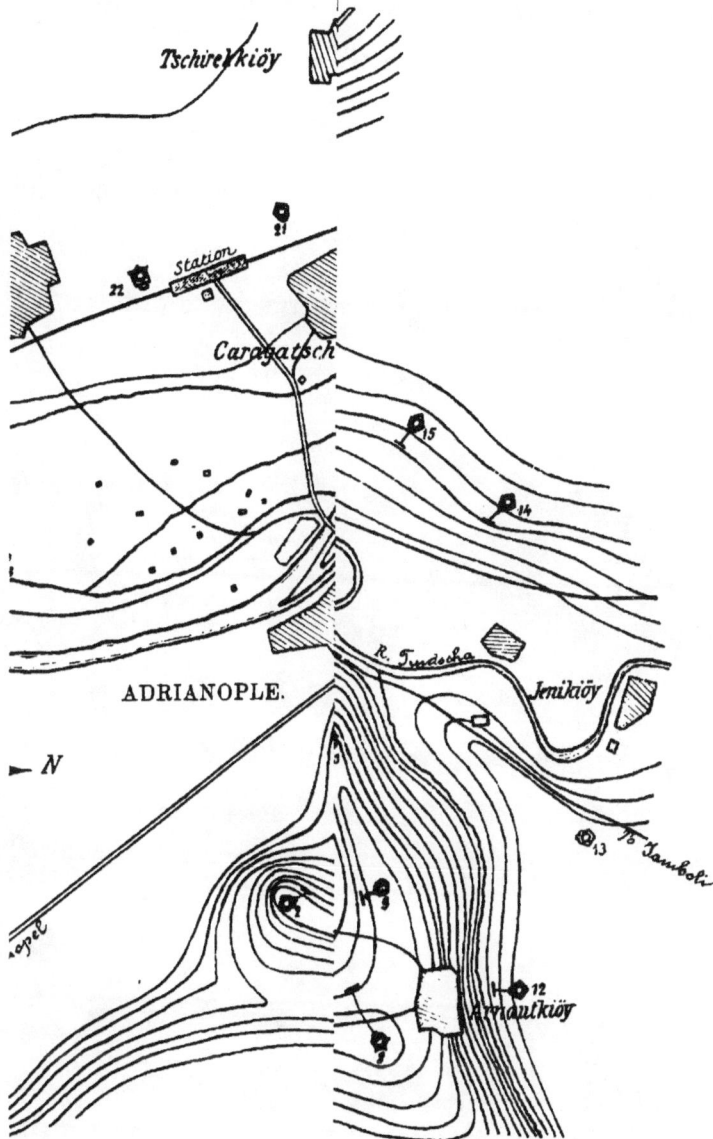

PLATE V.

PROVISIONAL
ADRI

Tschirelkiöy

Station

Caragatsch

ADRIANOPLE.

N

R. Tundscha

Jenikiöy

Jamboli

Arnautkiöy

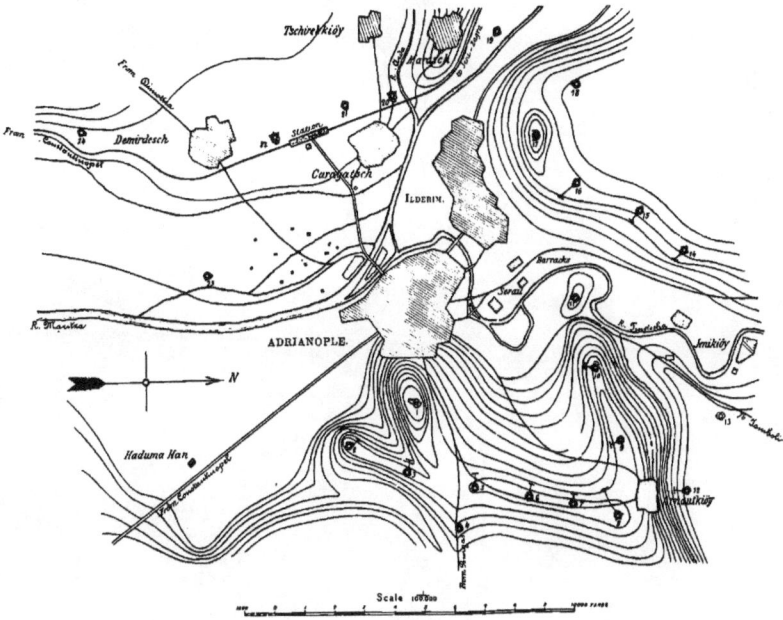

PLATE VI.

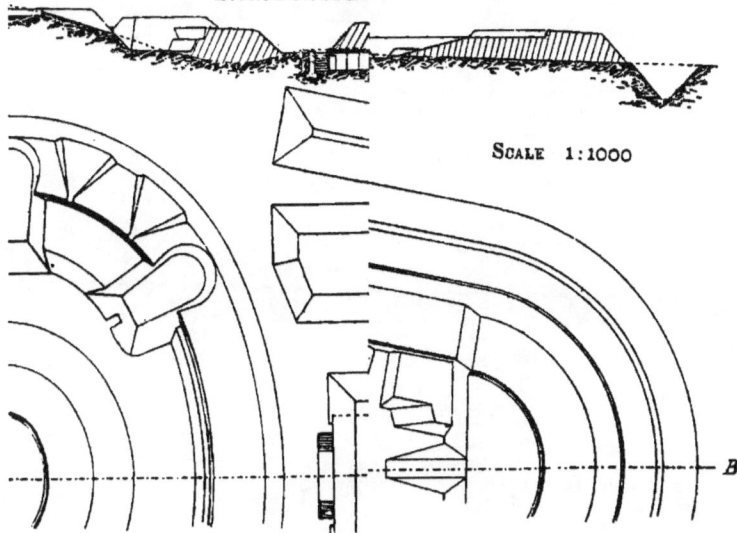

SCALE 1:1000

B

REDOUBT No. 22.

'RAVERSE T.

nal Section.

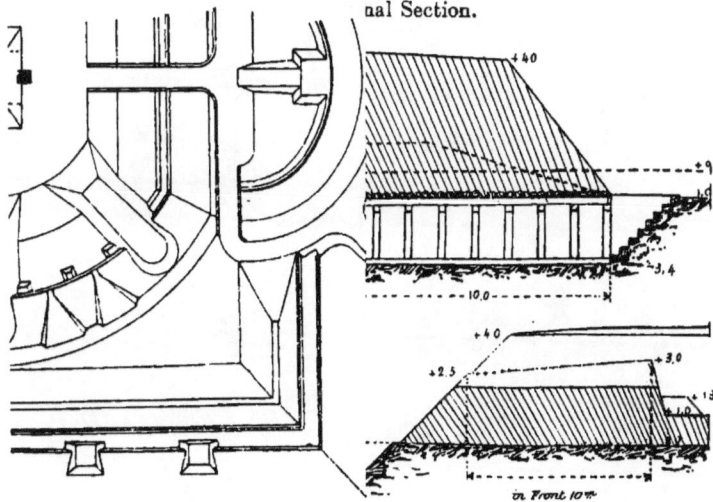

PROVISIONAL FORTIFICATIONS.
REDOUBT No. 1 (Dörtkioy Tabia).
Section on A B.

PLATE VI.

Covered Barrack Section.

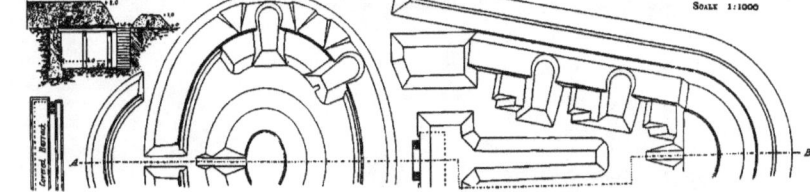

SCALE 1:1000

Covered Barrack.

A — — — — B

Distance 20—50 Metres.

REDOUBT No. 22.

HOLLOW TRAVERSE T.
Longitudinal Section.

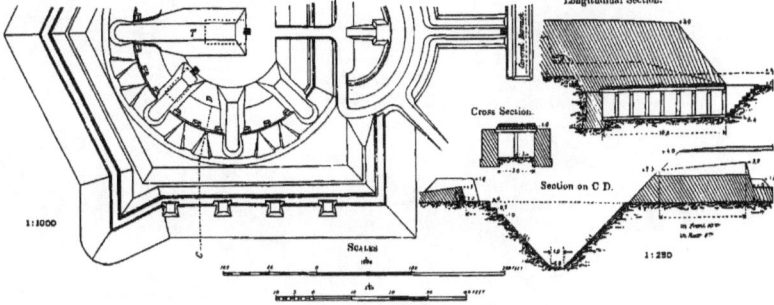

Cross Section.

Section on C D.

1:1000

Covered Barrack.

SCALES

1:250

PLATE VII.

PROVISIONAL FORTIFICATION.
TSCHATALDSCHA LINES.

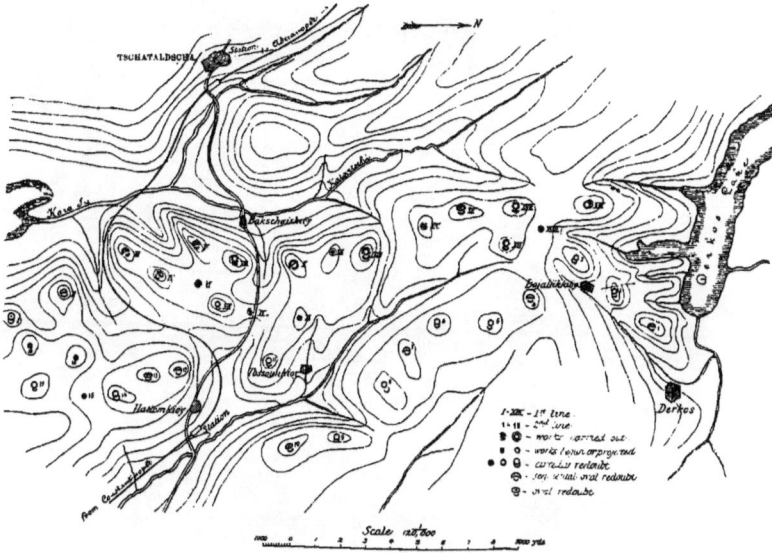

REDOUBT V.

HOLLOW
Gos.

Long

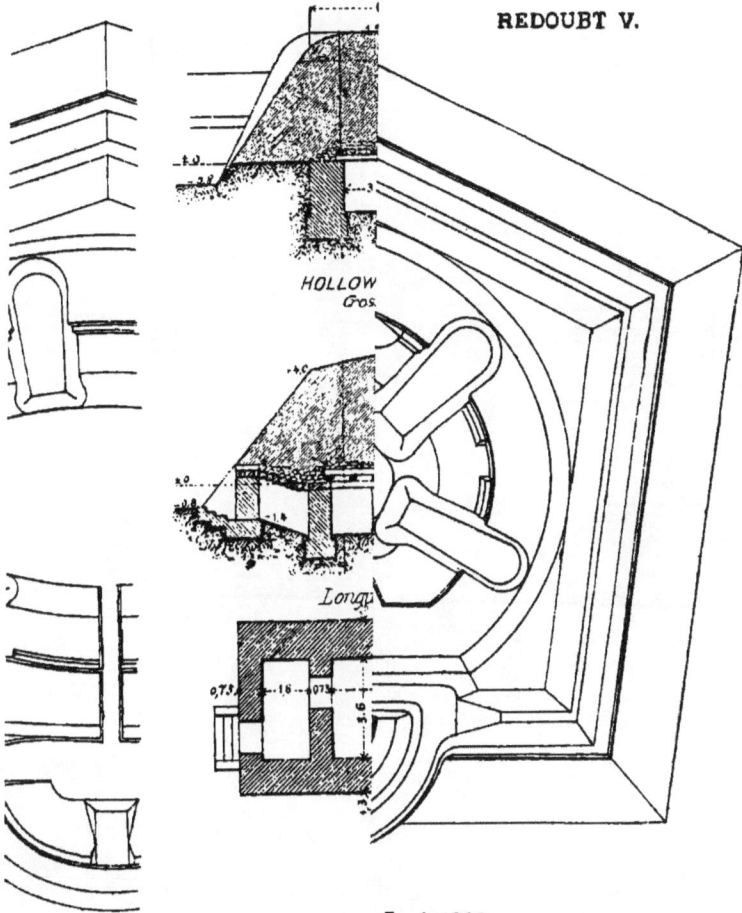

NORMale 1:1000

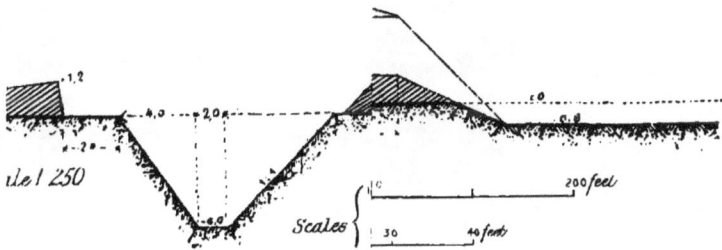

ile 1 250

Scales

200 feet

30   40 feet

REDOUBT IV.

REDOUBT V.

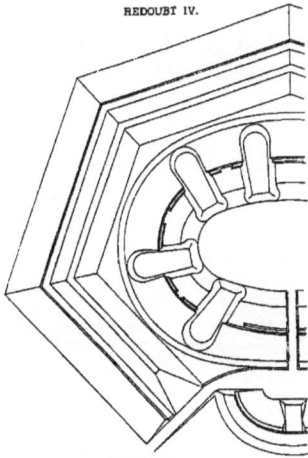

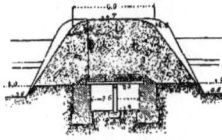

HOLLOW TRAVERSE
Cross Section

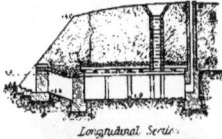

Longitudinal Section

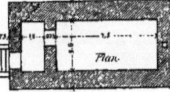

Plan

1:250

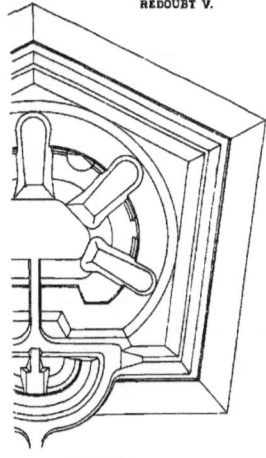

Scale 1:1000

NORMAL SECTION

Scale 1:1000

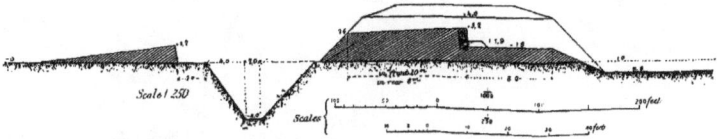

Scale 1:250

Scales

CATION OF A HILLTOP.

7ISiONAL REDOUBT

aponiers for Defence of Ditches)

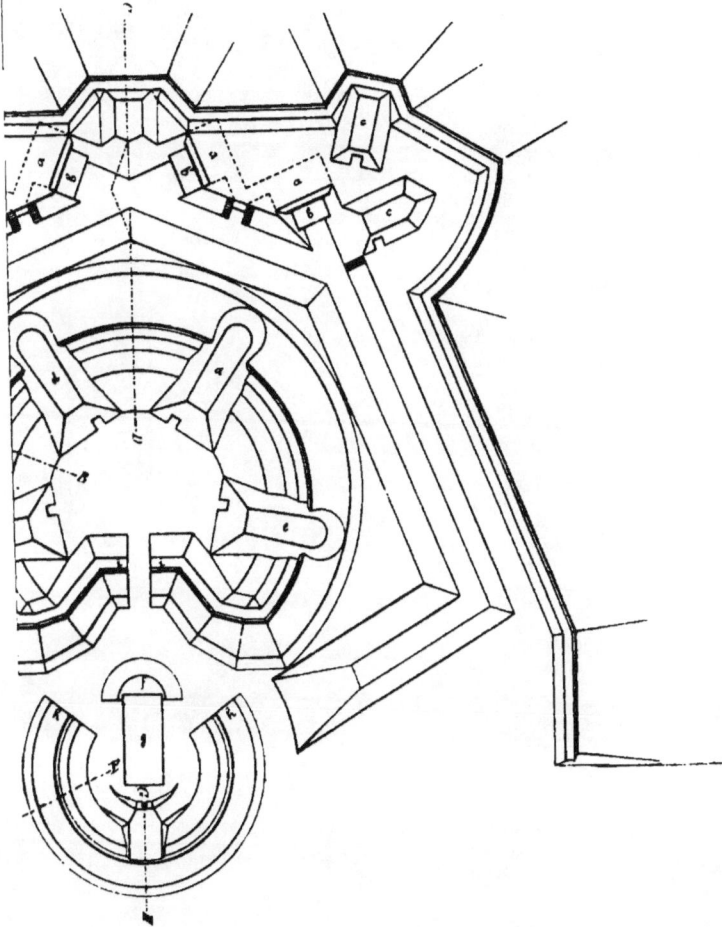

FORTIFICATION OF A HILLTOP.

PROVISIONAL REDOUBT

(With Caponiers for Defence of Ditches)

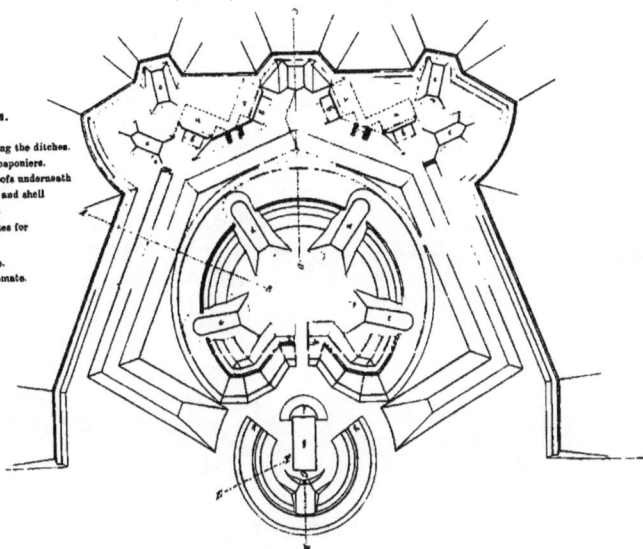

REFERENCES.

a. Double caponiers flanking the ditches.
b. Excavation in front of caponiers.
c. Traverses with shellproofs underneath
d. Traverses with powder and shell
   magazines underneath.
e. Traverses with casemates for
   garrison underneath.
f. Small powder magazine.
g. Sunken shellproof casemate.
h. Latrines.
i Casemates.

Scale 1000

PLATE X.

t A-B.

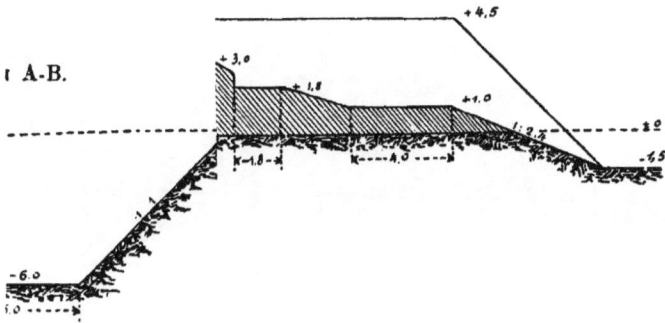

)N ON C-D.

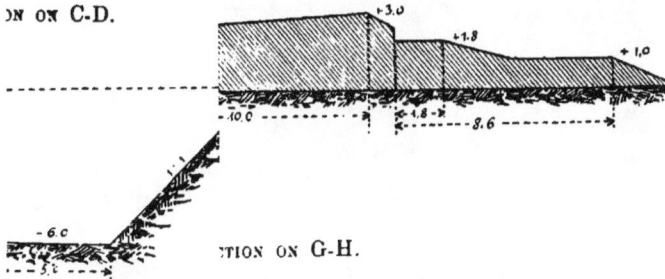

TION ON G-H.

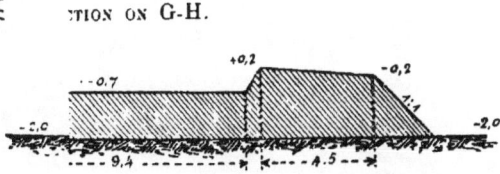

SCALE

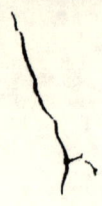

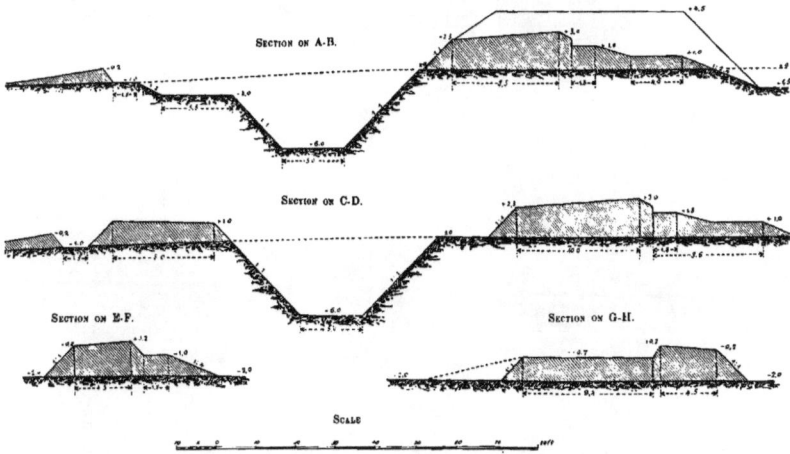

SECTION ON A-B.

SECTION ON C-D.

SECTION ON E-F.

SECTION ON G-H.

SCALE

PAPER II.

GRADUATED ARCS FOR HEAVY GUNS.

BY

CAPTAIN M. H. G. GOLDIE, R.E.

ERRORS in length have been discovered in the-graduated arcs supplied for heavy guns. If the centre of gun pivot be also the centre of a graduated arc of erroneous length, the angles through which the gun passes will differ from the angles given on the arc : thus, if it were desired to traverse the gun through an angle, A, and accordingly the gun were traversed until the pointer reached A, then since the arc length is erroneous, the gun will not really have been traversed through the angle A, and conversely if the gun be actually traversed through A, the pointer will not indicate A, but a greater or less angle.

Let P (*Plate* I., *Fig.* 1), be the gun pivot, A″ D″ the graduated arc with centre P. Let $\angle$ A″ P D″ = θ ; θ is the greatest angle the arc ought to read. This, however, is not always the case, as the arcs sometimes read greater angles, and may also read less. Let D″ P A be the greatest reading of the arc, = a, suppose. Produce D″P to O. Make D″O A = θ. Draw A″A parallel to D″O. With radius O A = P A″ = r, describe the arc A D. Then the arcs A D, A″ D″ are precisely similar, since each has the same radius, and subtends an angle θ. In this position of the arc errors in length almost disappear, but it can be shown that they are not wholly compensated.

Manifestly there is no error at D or A, for at these points the arc reads 0, a, and the angles of traverse are 0, D P A, that is 0, a. Let P C bisect the angle D P A ; then if all error has disappeared throughout the arc, D C would be equal to C A. Join A D, A C,

C D, C O. Suppose C A equal to C D; then in the triangles C P A, C P D, since the sides A C, C P are equal to the sides D C, C P, and the angle C P A is by construction equal to the angle C P D, the angles C A P, C D P must be equal or supplementary. But they are not supplementary, for if, as before supposed, C A be equal to C D, the triangles A C O, D C O are equal in every respect, therefore $\angle$ C O D = $\frac{\theta}{2}$. But O C = O D, therefore $\angle$ O C D = $\angle$ O D C; therefore $\angle$ O C D = $\frac{\pi}{2} - \frac{\theta}{4}$; similarly $\angle$ O C A = $\frac{\pi}{2} - \frac{\theta}{4}$; therefore $\angle$ A C D = $\pi - \frac{\theta}{2}$; therefore the angles A C D, A O D are together equal to $\pi + \frac{\theta}{2}$, that is, the angles A C D, A O D are together greater than two right angles, and, therefore, the angles C A O, C D O are together less than two right angles; *à fortiori*, the angles C A P, C D P are together less than two right angles, that is C A P, C D P are not supplementary as long as C A is supposed equal to C D.

Nor are they equal; for since A P, P O are greater than A O, they are greater than D O; that is, A P is greater than D P; therefore $\angle$ A D P is greater than $\angle$ D A P. But if C A be equal to C D, $\angle$ C D A is equal to $\angle$ C A D; and therefore, $\angle$ C D P is greater than $\angle$ C A P. Therefore, if C A be equal to C D, the angles C A P, C D P are neither equal nor supplementary, which is an absurdity; therefore C A and C D are unequal, that is the arcs C A, C D are unequal, and all error has not disappeared throughout the arc. The amount of error remaining has not here been indicated, but there is no difficulty in finding a general expression for it, nor in determining its maximum amount.

Suppose C P D = x, any angle through which it is desired to traverse the gun. In order to traverse the gun through x, the pointer would be brought to some point B, where B reads x degrees. Evidently B C would represent the amount of error corresponding to x. Assume, for the present, that B D is greater than C D, and let B C = u, A D = l, the length of the arc.

Then u = B D − C D.

By hypothesis, whatever fraction $\angle$ C P D is of A P D, that fraction B D is of A D;

$$\text{that is, } B D = \frac{xl}{a}.$$

Also, $CD : AD = \angle COD : \angle AOD$.

Therefore,

$$u = \frac{xl}{a} - \frac{l}{\theta}\, COD$$

$$= \frac{xl}{a} - \frac{l}{\theta}\, (x - OCP)$$

$$= xl\left(\frac{1}{a} - \frac{1}{\theta}\right) + \frac{l}{\theta} \sin^{-1}\left(\sin x \,\frac{OP}{r}\right)$$

$$= xl\left(\frac{1}{a} - \frac{1}{\theta}\right) + \frac{l}{\theta} \sin^{-1}\left\{\sin x\, \frac{\sin(a - \theta)}{\sin a}\right\} \quad \cdots \quad (1)$$

an expression for the error at any point in A D.

In order to determine the value of x which makes u a maximum, differentiate (1), then

$$\frac{du}{dx} = l\left(\frac{1}{a} - \frac{1}{\theta}\right) + \frac{l}{\theta} \cdot \frac{\cos x \dfrac{\sin(a - \theta)}{\sin a}}{\left\{1 - \sin^2 x \dfrac{\sin^2(a - \theta)}{\sin^2 a}\right\}^{\frac{1}{2}}}$$

Put $\dfrac{l}{\theta}\left\{\dfrac{\cos x \sin(a - \theta)}{\sin^2 a - \sin^2 x \sin^2(a - \theta)}\right\}^{\frac{1}{2}} = l\left(\dfrac{1}{\theta} - \dfrac{1}{a}\right)$

then, $\dfrac{\sin^2(a - \theta) - \sin^2 x \sin^2(a - \theta)}{\sin^2 a - \sin^2 x \sin^2(a - \theta)} = \dfrac{(a - \theta)^2}{a^2}$

$$\sin^2 x \sin^2(a - \theta)(2\theta a - \theta^2) = a^2 \sin^2(a - \theta) - \sin^2 a (a - \theta)^2$$

$$\sin^2 x = \frac{a^2 \sin^2(a - \theta) - \sin^2 a (a - \theta)^2}{\sin^2(a - \theta)(2\theta a - \theta^2)}$$

$$\sin x = \pm \frac{\left\{a^2 \sin^2(a - \theta) - \sin^2 a (a - \theta)^2\right\}^{\frac{1}{2}}}{\sin(a - \theta)(2\theta a - \theta^2)^{\frac{1}{2}}}$$

$$x = \sin^{-1} \pm \frac{\left\{a^2 \sin^2(a - \theta) - \sin^2 a (a - \theta)^2\right\}^{\frac{1}{2}}}{\sin(a - \theta)(2\theta a - \theta^2)^{\frac{1}{2}}}$$

$$\frac{d^2u}{dx^2} = \frac{l}{\theta}\left[-\left\{1 - \sin^2 x \frac{\sin^2(a - \theta)}{\sin^2 a}\right\}^{\frac{1}{2}} \sin x \frac{\sin(a - \theta)}{\sin a}\right.$$

$$+ \cos x \frac{\sin(a - \theta)}{\sin a} \frac{\sin x \cos x \dfrac{\sin^2(a - \theta)}{\sin^2 a}}{\left\{1 - \sin^2 x \dfrac{\sin^2(a - \theta)}{\sin^2 a}\right\}^{\frac{1}{2}}}$$

$$\left. \div \left\{1 - \sin^2 x \frac{\sin^2(a - \theta)}{\sin^2 a}\right\}\right]$$

$$= \frac{l}{\theta}\left[(\sin x - \sin^3 x)\frac{\sin^3(a - \theta)}{\sin^3 a} - \sin x \frac{\sin(a - \theta)}{\sin a}\right.$$

$$\left\{ 1 - \sin^2 x \; \frac{\sin^2 (a - \theta)}{\sin^2 a} \right\}^{-} \div \left\{ 1 - \sin^2 x \; \frac{\sin^2 (a - \theta)}{\sin^2 a} \right\}^{\frac{3}{2}}$$

$$= \frac{l}{\theta} \; \frac{\sin x \left\{ \dfrac{\sin^3 (a - \theta)}{\sin^3 a} - \dfrac{\sin (a - \theta)}{\sin a} \right\}}{\left\{ 1 - \sin^2 x \; \dfrac{\sin^2 (a - \theta)}{\sin^2 a} \right\}^{\frac{1}{2}}} \quad \ldots \ldots \quad (2)$$

Now, for arcs too short, a is always greater than θ, hence a is greater than $a - \theta$, that is $\sin a$ than $\sin (a - \theta)$; therefore $\dfrac{\sin (a - \theta)}{\sin a}$ is a proper fraction, and $\dfrac{\sin^3 (a - \theta)}{\sin^3 a} - \dfrac{\sin a - \theta}{\sin a}$ is negative. Therefore, the numerator of (2) is negative if $\sin x$ is positive: but the denominator of (2) is always necessarily a positive proper fraction, hence (2) is negative when $\sin x$ is positive; that is, u is a maximum when $\sin x$, and therefore x, takes the positive sign. That is u is a maximum when

$$x = \sin^{-1} \frac{\left\{ a^2 \sin^2 (a - \theta) - \sin^2 a (a - \theta)^2 \right\}^{\frac{1}{2}}}{\sin (a - \theta) (2 \, \theta a - \theta^2)^{\frac{1}{2}}} \quad \ldots \ldots \quad (3)$$

An assumption has been made that in this case B D is greater than C D: this must be examined. It is true, so long as a is not greater than a right angle, that is, if the whole arc be less than 180°, and truly divided so that the gun reads correctly on its central line of fire. To greater arcs the following investigation would not apply.

Call an error at any point in the arc positive when the actual angle traversed by the gun in reaching that point is greater than the arc-reading at that point; and negative when the angle traversed is less than the arc-reading. Then in the position A" D" (see *Plate* I., *Fig.* 2) all errors are clearly negative, and the maximum is $A'' K' = D'' K' - l = \dfrac{l \, a}{\theta} - l = l \dfrac{a - \theta}{\theta} \quad \ldots \quad (4)$

Throughout A" D" then B D is less than C D; but in A D the error at A has vanished, and a little consideration will show that negative errors have become positive, that is, in A D, B D is greater than C D, which may be proved thus :—

As long as $x = b$, $\dfrac{\sin a \sin x}{\sin b} = \sin \dfrac{a \, x}{b}$. But when x is diminished, since the sines of angles diminish less rapidly than the angles themselves, where those angles are less than 90°, therefore $\dfrac{\sin a \sin x}{\sin b}$ is greater than $\sin \dfrac{a \, x}{b}$ so long as $\dfrac{a}{b}$ and $\dfrac{x}{b}$ are proper fractions: that is

$$\sin^{-1}\left(\frac{\sin a \sin x}{\sin b}\right) \text{ is greater than } \frac{ax}{b}.$$

Now, as long as a is greater than θ, $\frac{a - \theta}{\theta}$ is a proper fraction;

therefore, if x be less than a, $\sin^{-1}\left\{\sin x \frac{\sin (a - \theta)}{\sin a}\right\}$ is

greater than $x \frac{a - \theta}{a}$.

But in the case under consideration, a is always greater than θ; therefore, in this case the right hand term of (1), which is positive, is greater than the left hand term, which is negative; therefore (1) is positive, that is B D is greater than C D.

Since in passing from A″ D″ to A D, it is found that negative errors have become positive, the error at each point in the arc has changed its sign and must have passed through zero. Hence the maximum negative error in A″ D″ is greater than any negative error to the right; the maximum positive error in A D is greater than any positive error to the left. For the maximum negative error is always the intercept between A A″ and A K′ of the arc produced, and this can never be greater than A″ K′.

Let A′ D′ be any third position of the arc in which take a point, B′. Make B D = B′ D′, and let x' be the angle of traverse corresponding to the reading at B′.

Then $\frac{x}{a} = \frac{BD}{DA} = \frac{B'D'}{D'A'} = \frac{x'}{a}$ therefore $x' = x$ and C′ D′ is

greater than C D, that is B C than B′ C′. But the position of B is unrestricted so long as it lies in the arc, and is so placed that the error is positive; and the position of the arc A′ D′ is unrestricted so long as it lies between A D and A″ D″; therefore, wherever B′ may be, the positive error at B′ is less than the positive error at a point B in A D. There must then be some position of the arc, such as A′ D′, where the maximum error, whether positive or negative is the least possible. In A′ D′ the maximum positive and negative errors are equal to each other, for in any position of the arc to the left of A′ D′, the maximum negative error is greater, and in any position to the right the maximum positive error is greater. Therefore, the best possible position of the arc is A′ D′ where the maximum positive error is equal to the maximum negative error.

Produce D′ A′ to K. A′ K is the maximum negative error

Take C′ P D′ so that B′ C′ is the maximum positive error in A′ D′. Then A′ K = B′ C′.

But A′ K = D′ K − A′ D′.

$$= \frac{l}{\theta}\,D'\,O'\,K - l = \frac{l}{\theta'}\,(a - P\,K\,O') - l$$

$$= \frac{l}{\theta'}\left\{ a - \sin^{-1}\left(\frac{O'\,P}{r}\sin a\right) \right\} - l \quad \ldots \ldots (4^a)$$

And B′ C′ = B′ D′ − C′ D′

$$= l\frac{x'}{a} - l\frac{C'\,O'\,D'}{\theta'} = \frac{l\,x'}{a} - \frac{l}{\theta'}\,(x' - O'\,C'\,P)$$

$$= l\,x'\left(\frac{1}{a} - \frac{1}{\theta'}\right) + \frac{l}{\theta'}\sin^{-1}\left(\frac{O'\,P}{r}\sin x'\right)$$

$$= l\,x\left(\frac{1}{a} - \frac{1}{\theta'} + \right)\frac{l}{\theta'}\sin^{-1}\left(\sin x'\frac{O'\,P}{r}\right)$$

Therefore

$$\frac{l}{\theta'}\left\{ a - \sin^{-1}\left(\frac{O'\,P}{r}\sin a\right) \right\} - l = l\,x'\left(\frac{1}{a} - \frac{1}{\theta'}\right) +$$

$$\frac{l}{\theta'}\sin^{-1}\left(\sin x'\frac{O'\,P}{r}\right)$$

But the right hand side of this equality is a maximum when

$$x' = \sin^{-1}\frac{\left\{ a^2\,O'\,P^2 - r^2(a - \theta')^2 \right\}^{\frac{1}{2}}}{O'\,P\,(2\,\theta'\,a - \theta'^2)^{\frac{1}{2}}}$$

Therefore,

$$\left(\frac{1}{a} - \frac{1}{\theta'}\right)\sin^{-1}\frac{\left\{ a^2 \cdot O'\,P^2 - r^2\,(a-\theta')^2 \right\}^{\frac{1}{2}}}{O'\,P\,(2\,\theta a - \theta'^2)^{\frac{1}{2}}} +$$

$$\frac{1}{\theta'}\sin^{-1}\frac{\left\{ a^2 \cdot O'\,P^2 - r^2\,(a-\theta')^2 \right\}^{\frac{1}{2}}}{r\,(2\,\theta'a - \theta')^{\frac{1}{2}}} + \frac{\sin^{-1}\left(\frac{O'\,P}{r}\sin a\right)}{\theta'}$$

$$= \frac{a}{\theta'} - 1. \quad \ldots \ldots \ldots \ldots (5)$$

An awkward expression, but less so than it seems, for O′ P cannot be greater than O P, that is than $r\,\dfrac{\sin (a - \theta)}{\sin a}$ nor can it be less than $\dfrac{r}{\sin a}\sin\left\{ a - (\theta + \dfrac{\theta}{l}\,B\,C) \right\}$ (*Fig. 2*). These values lie close together, and leave little choice in finding O′ P by trial: moreover the separate terms of (5) being to a great extent constant, can be found by logarithms and tabulated, so that not much additional labour is involved in trials after the first. Thus $\left(\dfrac{1}{a} - \dfrac{1}{\theta'}\right)$,

$r^2 (a - \theta')^2$, $(2 \theta' a - \theta'^2)^{\frac{1}{2}}$ .... can be found once for all and tabulated.

From the above expressions can be found :—

I. The error at any point in the arc.

II. The maximum error in any position of the arc from A D to A″ D″.

III. The best general position of the arc.

IV. Also, having determined the error in the best general position, these expressions give a means of determining in what arcs, however placed, the maximum errors are appreciable, and, therefore, of deciding what arcs to reject. It will be found that to cause an appreciable maximum error in its best position an arc must be very considerably out in its length.

It might be desired to place an arc so that at any particular reading there should be no error at all in the angle of traverse. Thus, suppose the reading y on the arc is to be precisely correct, so that the gun with pointer at y shall have exactly passed through an angle y. To secure this O′ P must be laid down with the value

$$r \; \frac{\sin (y - \dfrac{\theta}{a} y)}{\sin y} \; \text{as may be easily shown.}$$

Case II. (see *Plate* I., *Fig.* 3).—Arcs too long, and not greater than 180° Using the same nomenclature, let A″ D″ be the arc with centre at P, the pivot of the gun: A″ P D″ $= \theta$; let A P D $= a$ the highest reading of the arc.

As before, let the arc be symmetrically placed about D P, so that the gun reads correctly on its central line of fire. Then the errors in A″ D″ are evidently positive, and the maximum error A″ K greater than any positive error to the left. Take the arc to the position A D ; then the errors have become negative—that is, C D is always greater than B D, as may be shown in precisely the same way as before.

Therefore,

$$u = \text{B C} = x \, l \left(\frac{1}{\theta} - \frac{1}{a} \right) + \frac{l}{\theta} \; \sin^{-1} \left\{ \sin x \, \frac{\sin (\theta - a)}{\sin a} \right\}$$

And this is a maximum when

$$x = \sin^{-1} \left\{ \frac{a^2 \sin^2 (\theta - a) - (\theta - a)^2 \sin^2 a}{\sin (\theta - a) (2 \theta a - \theta^2)^{\frac{1}{2}}} \right\}^{\frac{1}{2}}$$

and is then greater than any negative error to the right. There must, therefore, be an intermediate position, such as A′ D′, where the maximum error is the least possible. In this position $A' K = B' C'$, that is

$$l - \frac{l}{\theta'} \left\{ a + \sin^{-1} \left(\frac{O' P}{r} \sin a \right) \right\} =$$

$$l \left(\frac{1}{\theta'} - \frac{1}{a} \right) \sin^{-1} \frac{\left\{ a^2 O' P^2 - r^2 (\theta' - a)^2 \right\}^{\frac{1}{2}}}{O' P (2 \theta' a - \theta'^2)^{\frac{1}{2}}} + \frac{l}{\theta'} \sin^{-1}$$

$$\frac{\left\{ a^2 O' P^2 - r^2 (\theta' - a)^2 \right\}^{\frac{1}{2}}}{r (2 \theta' a - \theta'^2)^{\frac{1}{2}}} \text{ from which } O' P \text{ can be found as}$$

before.

Finally, if it be desired to place the arc so as to make both arc reading and angle of traverse correct at any angle, as y', then the arc must be placed so that

$$O' P = \frac{r}{\sin y'} \sin \left(\frac{y \, \theta}{a} - y' \right)$$

Case III. Arcs of 180°, (see *Plate* I., *Figs.* 4 and 5).—This is a a particular case. Here $\angle$ C O D $= x \mp$ O C P $= x \mp \sin^{-1} \left(\frac{O P}{r} \sin x \right) = x \mp \sin^{-1} \pm (\cos \theta \sin x)$: therefore C D $= \frac{l \, x}{\theta} \mp \frac{l}{\theta} \sin^{-1} \pm (\cos \theta \sin x)$. And B D $= \frac{l \, x}{a}$.

As long as $x = a = 90°$, $\sin \frac{90° - \theta}{90°} x = \cos \theta \sin x$. But if x be diminished, $\sin \frac{90° - \theta}{90°} x$ is less than $\cos \theta \sin x$, since $\frac{90° - \theta}{90°}$ is a proper fraction, and the sines of smaller angles diminish more rapidly than those of greater angles. Therefore $x \left(\frac{1}{a} - \frac{1}{\theta} \right)$ is never so great as $\frac{1}{\theta} \sin^{-1} (\cos \theta \sin x)$ and C D is less than B D.

Conversely, when the arc is too long, B D is less than C D. The general expressions can be easily found. Thus in *Fig.* 4 u is a maximum when $x = \sin^{-1} \frac{\left\{ a^2 \cos^2 \theta - (a - \theta)^2 \right\}^{\frac{1}{2}}}{\cos \theta (2 \theta a - \theta^2)^{\frac{1}{2}}}$ and the best position of the arc is found from

$$\left(\frac{1}{a} - \frac{1}{\theta} \sin^{-1} \right) \frac{\left\{ a^2 O' P^2 - r^2 (a - \theta)^2 \right\}^{\frac{1}{2}}}{O' P (2 \theta a - \theta^2)^{\frac{1}{2}}}$$

$$+ \frac{1}{\theta} \sin^{-1} \left\{ \frac{a^2 O' P^2 - r^2 (a - \theta)^2}{r (2 \theta a - \theta^2)^{\frac{1}{2}}} \right\}^{\frac{1}{2}} + \frac{1}{\theta} \sin^{-1} \frac{O' P}{r} = \frac{a}{\theta} - 1.$$

Case IV. Arcs exceeding 180°. Arc too short (see *Plate* II. *Fig.* 6).—A″ D″ is the arc, P its centre. The error at any point $= \dfrac{l}{a} x \curlyvee \dfrac{l}{\theta} x$, that is, the error is always negative and a maximum when $x = a$; whence $u = A'' K' = D'' K' - l = \dfrac{l a}{\theta} - l = \dfrac{l (a - \theta)}{\theta}$ as before. This is the greatest negative error in any position up to A D. A D is a second position of the arc, so that A P D $= a$.

Error in A D $=$ B D $\curlyvee$ C D $= \dfrac{l x}{a} \curlyvee \dfrac{l}{\theta}$ C O D.

$$= \dfrac{l x}{a} \curlyvee \dfrac{l}{\theta} \left\{ x - \sin^{-1} \sin x \, \dfrac{\sin (a - \theta)}{\sin a} \right\}$$

To ascertain which of these terms is the greater is to ascertain which is the greater of $x \left(\dfrac{1}{\theta} - \dfrac{1}{a} \right)$ and $\dfrac{1}{\theta} \sin^{-1} \sin x \dfrac{\sin (a - \theta)}{\sin a}$ that is, of $x \dfrac{a - \theta}{a}$ and $\sin^{-1} \sin x \dfrac{\sin(a-\theta)}{\sin a}$. But $\sin a = \sin$ $(\pi - a)$, and as long as x is $> \pi - a$, $\dfrac{\sin x \sin (a - \theta)}{\sin (\pi - a)}$ is $> \sin$ $(\theta - a)$, while x being $< a$, $\sin \dfrac{x}{a} (a - \theta)$ is $< \sin (a - \theta)$. In this case,

$$\sin^{-1} \sin x \ \dfrac{\sin (a - \theta)}{\sin a} \text{ is } > x \dfrac{a - \theta}{a}.$$

When $x = \pi - a$, $\dfrac{\sin x \sin (a - \theta)}{\sin (\pi - a)} = \sin (a - \theta)$ and $\sin x$ $\dfrac{a - \theta}{a}$ is $< \sin (a - \theta)$, since $a > \pi - a$ by hypothesis; therefore when x is $=$, or $> \pi - a$,

$$\sin^{-1} \sin x \ \dfrac{\sin (a - \theta)}{\sin a} \text{ is } > x \dfrac{a - \theta}{a}.$$

But x may be less than $\pi - a$. In that case

$$\sin \dfrac{a - \theta}{a} x \text{ is always } < \dfrac{\sin (a - \theta)}{\sin (\pi - a)} \sin x,$$

because $\dfrac{a - \theta}{a}$ is a proper fraction, x is less than $\dfrac{\pi}{2}$, and therefore sines of fractional values of x diminish more rapidly than sines of x. Hence in all cases

$$\sin^{-1} \dfrac{\sin (a - \theta)}{\sin a} \sin x \text{ is } > \dfrac{a - \theta}{a} x;$$

24

therefore C D is < B D, and the error is positive. The maximum values of x, and therefore of u, are the same as before, and the position of the arc corresponding to least error is found from the same formula as for arcs less than 180°.

Case V. Arcs exceeding 180°. Arc too long (see *Plate II.*, *Fig. 7.*)—The figure is given. From it it is evident that the errors in A″ D″ are positive, and that the maximum is $A'' K'' = l\ \dfrac{\theta - a}{\theta}$.

Also, it can be shown that the errors in A D are negative, and $=$

$$x\, l \left(\frac{1}{\theta} - \frac{1}{a} \right) + \frac{l}{\theta}\ \sin^{-1} \left\{ \sin x\, \frac{\sin\,(\theta - a)}{\sin a} \right\}$$

the maximum being as before.

Likewise the best position of the arc may be found as in Case II.

The following practical example illustrates the application of the above expressions :—

Chord of arc of 120° measures............... 8′·277
Versin.................................... 2′·3

Whence, by calculation, $r = 4'·873$, $l = 4·944$, $\theta = 58° 7' 32''·6$ or 58·1257, $a = 60°$, $a - \theta = 1° 52' 27''·4$ or 1·8743.

I. To find x, the angle giving maximum error in A D (*Fig. 2*).

$$2 \log \sin a\quad = 19·8750612$$
$$2 \log (a - \theta) =\quad ·5456782$$

$$20·4207394$$
$$20$$

$$\log 2·6347497 =\quad ·4207394$$
$$\therefore\ \sin^2 a\ (a - \theta)^2 = 2·6347497.$$
$$2 \log a\quad\quad = 3·5563026$$
$$2 \log \sin (a - \theta) = 17·0292586$$

$$20·5855612$$
$$20$$

$$\log 3·8508903 =\quad ·5855612$$
$$\therefore\ a^2 \sin^2 (a - \theta) = 3·8508903.$$

And
$$\left\{ a^2 \sin^2 (a-\theta) - \sin^2 a\,(a-\theta)^2 \right\}^{\frac{1}{2}} = \left\{ 3·8508903 - 2·6347497 \right\}^{\frac{1}{2}}$$
$$= 1·1028.$$

Again,
$$(2\,\theta a - \theta^2)^{\frac{1}{2}} = 59\cdot96237.$$

$$\log\,(2\,\theta a - \theta^2)^{\frac{1}{2}} = 1\cdot7778788$$
$$\log\sin\,(a - \theta) = 8\cdot5146293$$

$$\begin{array}{c} 10\cdot2925081 \\ 10 \end{array}$$

$$\log\,1\cdot9611378 = \cdot2925081$$
$$\therefore\ \sin\,(a - \theta)\,(2\,\theta a - \theta^2)^{\frac{1}{2}} = 1\cdot9611378.$$

By (3) $x = \sin^{-1}\dfrac{1\cdot1028}{1\cdot9611378}$ $\log\,1\cdot1028 = \cdot0424968$
$\log\,1\cdot9611378 = \cdot2925081$

$$= \sin^{-1}\,\cdot5623266 \qquad \log\,\cdot5623266 = \overline{1}\cdot7499887$$
$$= 34^\circ\,13'.$$

II. To find the maximum error in A D (*Fig.* 2).
$$\frac{x\,l}{a} = 2\cdot81945;\quad \frac{x\,l}{\theta} = 2\cdot91037.$$

$$\log\sin x = 9\cdot7499866$$
$$\log\sin\,(a - \theta) = 8\cdot5146293$$

$$\begin{array}{c} 18\cdot2646159 \end{array}$$
$$\log\sin a = 9\cdot9375306$$

$$\begin{array}{c} 8\cdot3270853 \\ 10 \end{array}$$

$$\log\,\cdot0212366 = \overline{2}\cdot3270853$$
$$\therefore\ \sin^{-1} = \left\{\sin x\,\frac{\sin\,(a - \theta)}{\sin a}\right\} = \sin^{-1}\,\cdot0212366$$
$$= 1^\circ\,13'\ \text{or}\ 1\cdot2167.$$

$$\log\,l = \cdot6940785$$
$$\log\,1\cdot2667 = \cdot0841835$$

$$\begin{array}{c} \cdot7782620 \end{array}$$
$$\log\,\theta = 1\cdot7643683$$

$$\log\,\cdot10325 = \overline{1}\cdot0138937$$
$$\therefore\ \text{by (1)}\ \max^{m}\ \text{error in A D} = 0\cdot10325 + 2\cdot81945 - 2\cdot91037$$
$$= 0'\cdot01233$$
$$= 0''\cdot14796$$

III. To find the best position of the arc.

$$\mathrm{O\,P} = r\,\frac{\sin a - \theta)}{\sin a} = 0'\cdot 184.$$

$$\frac{r}{\sin a}\,\sin\left\{a-(\theta + \frac{\theta}{l}\times\cdot 0123)\right\} = 0'\cdot 16984.$$

Therefore $\mathrm{O}'\mathrm{P}$ lies between $0'\cdot 16984$ and $0'\cdot 184$, and it is a question what actual number to use for a first trial. The mean is rather less than $0\cdot 177$: probably this would be used for a trial, and on being found too great, either $\cdot 176$ or $\cdot 175$ in the next instance. To save space, $0\cdot 175$ will be tried at once. Those expressions which involve $\mathrm{O}'\mathrm{P}$ are placed on the left; those which do not on the right.

$2\log\cdot 175$	$=$	$\overline{2}\cdot 4860760$	$2\log r$	$=$ $1\cdot 3755928$
$2\log a$	$=$	$3\cdot 5563026$	$2\log(a-\theta)$	$=$ $\cdot 5456782$
$\log 110\cdot 25$	$=$	$2\cdot 0423786$	$\log 83\cdot 42$	$=$ $1\cdot 9212710$

$$\mathrm{O}'\,\mathrm{P}^2\,a^2 = 110\cdot 25 \qquad r^2\,(a-\theta)^2 = 83\cdot 42$$

$$\left\{\mathrm{O}'\,\mathrm{P}^2\,a^2 - r^2(a-\theta)^2\right\}^{\frac{1}{2}} = \left(110\cdot 25 - 83\cdot 42\right)^{\frac{1}{2}} = 5\cdot 18.$$

$$\left(2\,\theta a - \theta^2\right)^{\frac{1}{2}} = 59\cdot 96237.$$

$$\therefore\ \frac{\left\{\mathrm{O}'\,\mathrm{P}^2 a^2 - r^2(a-\theta)^2\right\}^{\frac{1}{2}}}{\left(2\,\theta a - \theta^2\right)^{\frac{1}{2}}} = \frac{5\cdot 18}{59\cdot 96237} = \cdot 08639.$$

Whence,

$$\frac{\theta - a}{a}\,\sin^{-1}\frac{\left\{\mathrm{O}'\,\mathrm{P}^2 a^2 - r^2(a-\theta)^2\right\}^{\frac{1}{2}}}{\mathrm{O}'\,\mathrm{P}\left(2\,\theta a - \theta^2\right)^{\frac{1}{2}}} = \frac{\theta - a}{a}\,\sin^{-1}\frac{\cdot 08639}{\cdot 175}$$

$$= \frac{\theta - a}{a}\sin^{-1}\cdot 4936571 = \frac{\theta - a}{a}\,29\cdot 581 = -0\cdot 924.$$

$$\sin^{-1}\frac{\left\{\mathrm{O}'\,\mathrm{P}^2 a^2 - r^2(a-\theta)^2\right\}^{\frac{1}{2}}}{r\left(2\,\theta a - \theta^2\right)^{\frac{1}{2}}} = \sin^{-1}\frac{\cdot 08639}{4\cdot 873} = \sin^{-1}\cdot 0177283$$

$$= 1\cdot 016.$$

$$\sin^{-1}\left(\frac{\mathrm{O}'\,\mathrm{P}}{r}\,\sin a\right) = \sin^{-}\frac{\cdot 175}{4\cdot 873}\,\sin 60 = \sin^{-1}\cdot 0311008$$

$$= 1\cdot 782.$$

Therefore by (5) $a - \theta = 1{\cdot}782 + 1{\cdot}016 - 0{\cdot}924$
$$= 1{\cdot}874.$$

The true number is $1{\cdot}8743$, so that
$$O' P = 0'{\cdot}175$$
is correct to the third place of decimals, and is as accurate as any actual work laid out would ever be.

IV. To find the maximum error in this position. It is

$$= \frac{l}{\theta} \left(a - \sin^{-1} \frac{{\cdot}175}{r} \sin a \right) - l. \quad \text{By (4}^{\text{a}})$$

$$= \frac{4{\cdot}944}{58{\cdot}1257} \, 58{\cdot}218 - 4{\cdot}944$$

$$= 0'{\cdot}007846$$

$$= 0''{\cdot}094152.$$

By (4) the maximum error in $A'' D'' = l \frac{a - \theta}{a}.$

$$= 4{\cdot}944 \frac{1{\cdot}8743}{58{\cdot}1257}$$

$$= 0'{\cdot}15942$$

$$= 1''{\cdot}91304.$$

The three errors then are—

Arc centre at gun pivot,	Maximum error	$1''{\cdot}91304$
Extreme readings correct,	ditto	$0''{\cdot}14796$
In best position,	ditto	$0''{\cdot}09415$

V. Suppose it be desired that when the gun is traversed to 40° on the arc, the actual angle shall also be precisely 40°; then

$$O' P = r \ \frac{\sin \left(40 - 40 \, \dfrac{\theta}{a} \right)}{\sin 40}$$

$$= 4{\cdot}873 \ \frac{\sin \left\{ 40 - \tfrac{2}{3} \, (58^\circ \ 7' \ 32''{\cdot}6) \right\}}{\sin 40}$$

$$= 4{\cdot}873 \ \frac{\sin 1^\circ \ 14' \ 58''{\cdot}3}{\sin 40}$$

$$= 0'{\cdot}16532.$$

Continuous Arcs.

Suppose a number of guns mounted in a circular fort as A B (*Plate* II., *Fig.* 8), the pivots $p, p, p, \ . \ . \ .$ being equally spaced along A B. Then $p \, O \, p$ is a constant angle $= A$, suppose. The number of guns that can be mounted in a fort completely circular is

$\dfrac{360}{A}$. (In what follows, for the sake of brevity, "trail left" will mean that the gun spoken of is traversed to fire as far as possible to the right, "trail right" the opposite.) Take a as the common greatest angle of traverse: then if gun No. 1 be "trail right,"

$\angle$ O p C $= \dfrac{a}{2}$. If as many guns as possible be trained parallel to

gun No. 1, then O p D $= \dfrac{a}{2} - $ A : O p E $= \dfrac{a}{2} - 2$ A ; and so on.

The arcs must be laid to read accordingly, in order that the guns brought to a common arc reading may fire at the same object. If a be an exact multiple of A, then obviously the greatest number of guns which can be trained parallel to gun No. 1, " trail right," is $\dfrac{a}{A}$; if a be not a multiple of A, this greatest number will be $\dfrac{a}{A} - 1$. Call the number of guns trained together a group. No. 1 (*Fig.* 8) will be the first gun of the first group. No. 8 will be considered the last, for No. 9 gun belongs rather to the next group, being the gun traversed "trail right," in order to advance to that next group : it is the connecting link between the two groups, and hence it is convenient to estimate it in the second group. If then a be an exact multiple of A, the number of groups in a complete circular battery will be $\dfrac{360}{A} \div \dfrac{a}{A} = \dfrac{360}{a}$. If a be 60°, the number of groups will be 6; if $a = 58°$ the number of groups will be 7, thus $\dfrac{360}{58} = 6\dfrac{12}{58}$.

As it does not affect the principle, suppose a an exact multiple of A. Suppose arc No. 1 too short; then gun No. 1, when "trail right," will fire to the right of an object the direction of which makes an angle a with Z B, the zero line of the fort. Gun No. 9, when trained parallel to gun No. 1, will also fire as much to the right of this object. In other words, the error in gun No. 1 is carried on to group 2. Similarly an error in gun No. 9 may, in addition to the former error, be carried on to group 3. In a battery of six groups an error of only half a degree in group 1 may become 3° or more in group 6.

The important question is how to mitigate this evil without reject-ing all the arcs. It has been shown that, though an arc error may be much reduced, it can never be wholly eliminated. The following table shows the deviation from the intended path of a shot due to various arc errors.

Arc Error.	Deviation corresponding for		
	Range 6000 yards.	Range 5000 yards.	Range 4000 yards.
	Feet.	Feet.	Feet.
1°	314	261	209
30'	153	127	102
15'	79	66	53
10'	52	43	35
5'	26	22	17
4'	21	$17\frac{1}{2}$	14
3'	16	13	11
2'	10	8	7
1	5	4	3
30"	$2\frac{1}{2}$	2	$1\frac{2}{3}$
15"	$1\frac{1}{4}$	1	$\frac{5}{6}$

The mean error, therefore, should not in general exceed 4'. Now, it is clear that in a battery of one group there is no difficulty. No. 1 gun would be traversed " trail right," and laid on a distant object as nearly as possible on this bearing ; the arc would then be laid so as to be exactly correct for this angle of traverse. The remaining guns being laid parallel to No. 1, the corresponding readings of their respective arcs would be treated (for the purpose of laying the arcs only) as zero, and the arcs would be laid in the best position and correct at their temporary zero. A second group being added, the difficulty begins, but it can be mitigated thus :—The No. 1 gun of a group is to be laid parallel to the No. 1 gun of the preceding group, when in the zero position of that group, as No. 9 gun in position F p, parallel to C B, in *Fig.* 8. The gun is then to be traversed, and laid on a distant object, when as nearly as possible "trail right." In these two positions the arc must read correctly, and there is no difficulty in placing it accordingly, as shown in the investigation of independent arcs. The remaining arcs of the group will be placed in the best positions, treating as a temporary zero the reading when the guns are laid parallel to No. 1 of the group. The cumulative error is thus got rid of, and the individual arc errors are reduced as much as possible, or rather as much as the method permits. It would be still better, and would reduce the individual errors to the lowest possible amounts, to treat the second, third, &c., groups, thus :—Having fixed zero line of fort, and laid arc No. 1 in its best position by previous rules, traverse No. 1 gun of first group to point of no error on the arc. Bring gun No. 1 of second group parallel to No. 1 of first group, by means of a distant object, chosen or placed. We must now have the same arc reading at pointers of both No. 1 guns. Consider this reading temporarily zero in the case of No. 1 of second group, treat the longer arm of the arc thus divided, and ascertain accordingly its best position. Now find point of no error in this longer arm as placed, traverse gun to that point, train the other guns of the group (second) parallel to their No. 1. ; place arcs of group so that all now read same as No. 1 of the group at gun pointers, and are also in best position. Thus treat group No. 3, 4. . . . . .

Example.

Let A B (*Fig.* 8) be an arc through the pivots p, p, p, . . . Let p O $p = 7\frac{1}{2}°$, $a = 60°$. Suppose arc No. 1 to be an arc of $59°$. and radius $10'$. Length of arc $= l = 10·2974$. Then the distance of proper centre of arc from pivot in best position lies between

$$10\ \frac{\sin 1°}{\sin 60°}\ \text{and}\ \frac{10}{\sin 60°}\ \sin\ \left\{\ 60° - \left(59° + \frac{59}{10·2974}\ \times ·01386\right)\right\}$$

that is, between ·20152 and ·18551. A sufficiently accurate value is, in fact, ·191. The arc would, therefore, be thus placed :—The maximum

error would be $\dfrac{10·2974}{59}\left(\ 60-\sin^{-1}\dfrac{·191}{10}\sin 60\ \right) - 10·2974 =$

$0'·0087$ or $0''·1044$, corresponding to about 3'. The reading at which there is no error at all is $= 48°$, as nearly as possible. On being traversed to $48°$, then, gun No. 1 would read the true angle, and if an object at some distance could be found or placed to lay the gun on when at $48°$ there would be no error to carry forward. No. 2 gun being laid parallel to No. 1 gun, No. 2 arc would be placed with the reading $48°$ at the gun pointer, and the best position would be ascertained just as if $48°$ were temporarily zero, and the length of the arc were the length of its longer arm : in this case $48-7\frac{1}{2} = 40\frac{1}{2}$ Suppose, for instance, the arc were actually an arc of $58° 30'$; the

portion to be considered would be an arc of $\dfrac{58\frac{1}{2}}{60}$ of $40\frac{1}{2}°$ of radius

$10'$; where $a = 40\frac{1}{2}$. The true position would then be found as before. Similarly all the arcs would be treated up to the seventh. As the eighth has no reading $48°$, the seventh must be made the No. 1 of the second group. The placing of this arc has then to be considered, and is most important, as on its correctness depends the correctness of the second group as a whole, and of all the groups to the left. We have then the reading $48°$ on the line p G, and this is to be temporarily treated as zero; the longer arm is $57°$, and the problem is to place an arc of this length in its best position. Suppose the arc to be an arc of $58°$, so that the longer arm is an arc of $\frac{57}{60}$ of $58° = 55° 6'$, or $55\cdot1$. Then $a = 57°$, $r = 10$, $l = 9\cdot6168$. The distance of proper centre of arc from pivot in best position lies between $10 \dfrac{\sin 1° 54'}{\sin 57°}$ and $-\dfrac{10}{\sin 57°} \sin \left\{ 57° - \right.$ $\left(55° 6' + \dfrac{55° 6'}{9\cdot6168} \times \cdot022744 \right) \left. \right\}$ that is, between $\cdot39533$ and $\cdot36875$. A sufficiently accurate value is $\cdot378$. The maximum error would be $\dfrac{9\cdot6168}{55.1} \left\{ 57 - \sin^{-1} \left(\dfrac{\cdot378}{10} \sin. 57 \right) \right\} - 9\cdot6168$ $= 0'\cdot0144$, or $0''\cdot1728$, corresponding to $5\frac{1}{8}'$. The reading at which there is no error is $49° 9' 20''$ from the temporary zero, or $97° 9' 20''$, as marked on the arc. If at this reading the first gun of the second group be laid on a distant object, and the other guns be brought parallel to it, the position of their $97° 9' 20''$ can be marked. They are then to be treated like the intermediate guns of No. 1 group, with the difference that they are laid from $97° 9' 20''$, as if zero, instead of from $48°$. Enough has now been given to show how the whole battery would be treated. There would be no cumulative error at all, and the individual errors would be inappreciable. The difficulty in the way is a practical one. There would almost always be great difficulty in finding the required objects to lay on. Errors creep in as soon as there is a deviation from the group zero lines in choosing objects. It is evident that as far as No. 1 gun of the battery is concerned, no object to lay on is needed, the whole question being one of measurement, calculation, and accurate workmanship. But distant objects are used to ensure the parallelism of the guns. If the means are at hand, distant objects on the required line may be dispensed with, very carefully made trammels and straight-edges being used instead; but it would appear safest to choose, if possible, or even to place objects as required.

An error of 2° in an arc of 60° is extreme, yet by careful placing of the arc such an error can apparently be reduced to one of $5\frac{1}{8}'$, so that it is probable there would seldom be any necessity to reject arcs if the above method were followed. The labour of working out the corrections appears great; in practice, however, it is not so, or need not be so. The question really is whether sufficiently careful workmanship could be obtained for laying the arcs.

M. H. G. G.

Fig. 2.

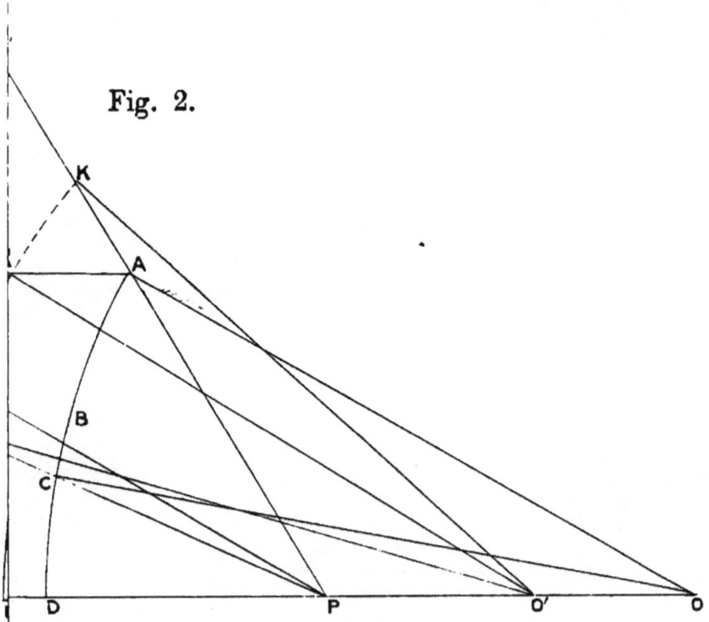

Fig. 4.    Fig. 5

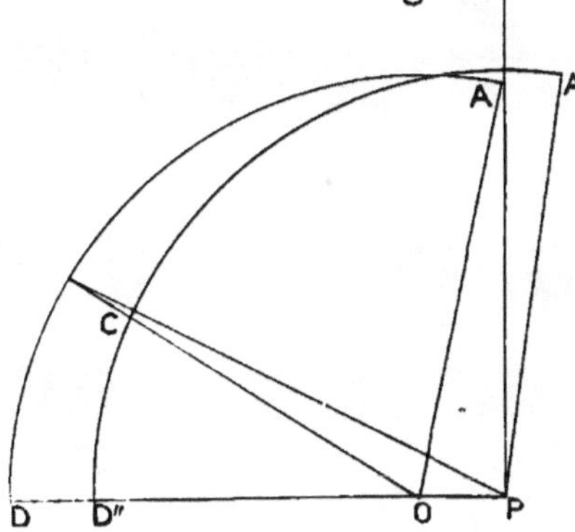

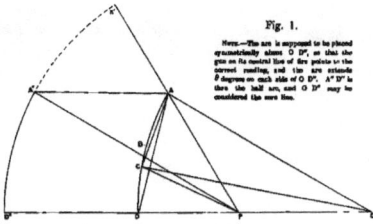

Fig. 1.

Note.—The arc is supposed to be placed symmetrically about O D°, so that the gun on its central line of fire points to the correct reading, and the arc extends θ degrees on each side of O D°. A° D° is then the half arc, and O D° may be considered the zero line.

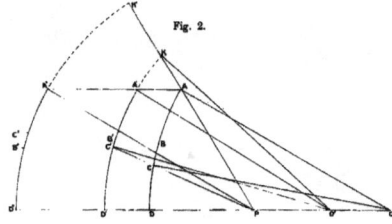

Fig. 2.

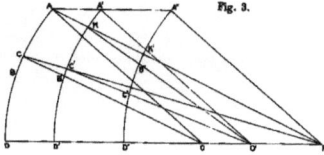

Fig. 3.

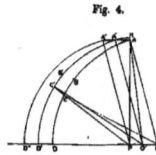

Fig. 4.

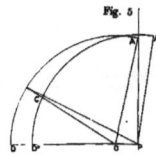

Fig. 5

Plate II.

Fig. 7.

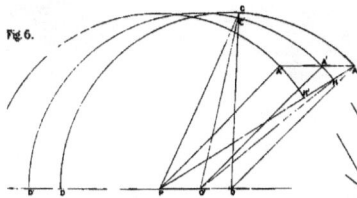

Fig. 6.

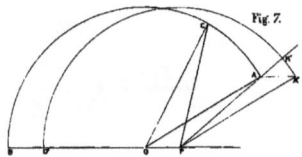

Fig. 7.

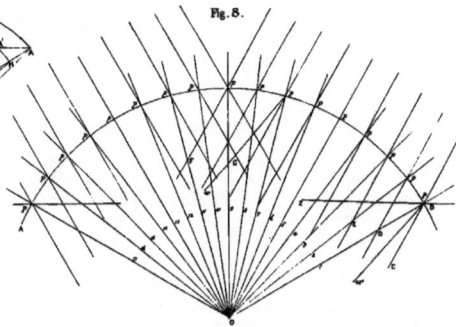

Fig. 8.

THE

CAMPAIGNS OF LORD LAKE

AGAINST THE MARÁTHÁS, 1804-6.

A course of Lectures delivered at the S.M.E., in the Spring of 1881,

BY MAJOR H. HELSHAM JONES, R.E.

I HAVE chosen the campaigns of Lord Lake against the Maráthás as the subject of a short course of lectures, partly because they are now but little known, partly because they seem very good illustrations of the way in which warfare should be carried on against Asiatics. Moreover, the Maráthás were our immediate predecessors in empire in India, and certain Maráthá states which are still independent are regarded by many as the scene of very possible operations in the future.

These campaigns were conducted against certain of the Maráthá chiefs, but in alliance with the Peshwa, whilst the Musalmán Nizám of Haidarábád (or Súbadár of the Dakhan) was an ally of the British. In order to make the subject intelligible, it is necessary to give a short account of the Maráthás, and of the way in which the territories belonging to them were distributed amongst the different chiefs at the times of which we are treating. The geography of the Indian Peninsula is one of the first things we have to consider in connection with the subject, not only as directly bearing on the place of campaign, but also, because without some acquaintance with it the distribution of territory cannot be made intelligible. As I am addressing an audience which is probably only imperfectly acquainted with Indian names and places, I shall make no apology for what those of you who have been in India may, perhaps, think rather elementary.

Every one has a general idea of the geography of India as a great triangular promontory, drained by large rivers, and fenced on the northern side by the Himalayas, but it is probably not so generally known that the ground in the peninsula rises in many places to a very considerable altitude, such as some of the peaks of the Nilgiris which rise to over 8000 ft., while an altitude of nearly 6000 ft. is reached in the Aravali range near Mount Ábú (Gúrú Sikkar 5653).

The latest authorities on its physical geography divide India into three distinct regions, namely :—

    1. The Peninsular area ;

    2. The Extra-Peninsular area ;

      and,

    3. The Indo-Gangetic plain, which separates the two first.

This Indo-Gangetic plain is of vast extent, and forms an immense expanse of flat country stretching from sea to sea. A traveller might disembark at the mouths of the Indus and might travel thence over a country to all appearance perfectly flat, until, after a journey of over 2000 miles, he again took ship at the mouths of the Ganges. In the whole of this journey he need only have reached an elevation of 900 ft. above the sea. The highest point on the water-parting of the Indus and Ganges (between Saháranpúr and Lúdiána) is 924 ft. The level of the ground at the junction of the Panjáb and the Indus is 369 ft., at a˙distance of 450 miles from the Arabian sea, whilst that at the junctions of Jamna and Ganges, about 600 miles from the Bay of Bengal, is 340 ft. only.

This great plain contains not less than 300,000 square miles, and in it lie the richest and most populous districts of India.

The regions separated by this plain are of totally different geological character, the Extra-Peninsular area being remarkable for the effects produced by great disturbances in late geological times, whilst in the Peninsular area (that with which we are at present chiefly concerned) precisely the reverse is the case; there appears to have been very little contortion or alteration of its strata since a very early period. Owing to this circumstance the drainage systems of the Peninsular area are very clearly defined and easily understood.

In *Plate* I. these drainage systems are shown in different colours. It is seen that by far the larger part of the Peninsular area is drained eastwards into the Bay of Bengal. Besides some minor ones, the principal basins are those of the Mahánadí, the Godávari, the Krishna or Kistnah, and the Kávari. To the west into the Arabian Sea we find only the Narbadda (or Narmada) and the Taptí basins, and a narrow strip of country along the western coast which is drained by a great number of small streams.

The water-partings which define these drainage systems are—

1st. The Sahyádri or Western Gháts, which extend from Cape Komorin in a direction somewhat west of north, to a point about 150 miles north-east of Bombay. From this line the drainage flows eastwards, to join the Godávari and other rivers to the south of it; westwards to form the small streams already mentioned, which flow into the Arabian Sea.

2nd. An elevation which breaks off from the Western Gháts, near Chandar (lat. 20° 25′, long. 74° 10′), and runs by Baithalwadi to Amrawati. From thence it joins the Sátpura range near Deogarh, and then passes by Chindwára (broken through by the Wain Ganga) to the Mekal Hills (22° to 22° 30′, long. 81° to 82° 30′), and then by Hazáribágh (24° 0′, long. 85° 30′), till it meets the Ganges near Rájmahál. This parting line separates the basins of the Godávari and rivers to the north of it, from those of the Taptí and Narbadda flowing west, and the Son and its confluents flowing northwards to the Ganges. The part of it south of the Taptí is called the Northern Gháts.

The 3rd of the great water-partings is the Sátpura range, which runs nearly east and west between the Narbadda and the Taptí, and separates the basins of those rivers.

4th. The escarpment of the great Vindhiyan plateau. This is often called the Vindhiyan range, but it is not, properly speaking, a range. It is the southern scarp or outcrop of the Vindhiyan or Málwa plateau which comprises Indúr, Bhopál, Bundelkhand, &c. The Kaimúr Hills are a continuation of the same scarp along the left or northern bank of the Son.

From the Vindhiyan water-parting there is a great drop into the valley of the Narbadda to the south, but on the north a gentle slope. The drainage of this slope passes to the Ganges through the Chambal, Sind, Betwa, and Ken rivers, all of which have a course nearly north at first, and gradually work round eastward to the

Jamna. Only a very small part of the plateau on the south-west is drained by the Máhí river into the gulf of Khambáyat.

5th. The Aravalí Hills, which strike nearly south-west and north-east through Rájpútána and shut in the Peninsular area to the north-west. The City of Dehli and its famous " Ridge " are at the extreme north end of this range, while the sanatarium of Mount Ábú (now the head quarters of the Rájpútána Agency) is near the southern. The peculiarity of all these main dividing ridges is, the Aravalí only being an exception, that they are merely plateaus that have escaped denudation. " Peninsular India (says Mr. Blanford) is in fact a table-land worn away by subaërial deundation, and perhaps to a minor extent on its margins by the sea ; the mountain chains are merely the dividing lines left undenuded between different drainage areas."*

The Aravalí differs from the other ranges in being entirely composed of disturbed rocks, the axis of disturbance corresponding with the direction of the chain. Of the drainage of the western slopes of these hills part is lost in the Indian Desert, part forms the Bunas and Lúní rivers which flow into the Rann of Kachh.

The whole operations of the campaigns with which we are dealing extended over a great part of the Peninsula, as well as of the Gangetic plain, for while General Lake operated for the most part in the Doáb (as the country between the Ganges and Jamna is called) or its immediate neighbourhood, the plan of the Governor-General included both the Madras and Bombay armies. The former concentrated a large force at Harihar, on the Tangabhadro (a confluent of the Krishna) in the north-west corner of Maisúr, whilst the latter operated in Gújarát. It is obvious that in countries so different as the Gangetic plain, to which the operations of Lord Lake were almost entirely confined, and the broken country of the upper basins of the Godávari and Taptí in which lay the field of General Wellesley's operations, different methods of marching and supply must be adopted, and we shall see later that this was the case. The communications in an unbridged country must of course be greatly affected by the drainage. Thus we find that, though the railway now-a-days takes a more direct line, the old road from Madras to Bombay makes a great sweep to the west, to avoid the rivers, and passes through Bangalúr, Harihar, Belgaum, Kolapúr,

---

* " Geology of India," Part I., Introduction, page v.

and Sattára, to Púna and Bombay. The campaign of 1803 opened in the beginning of August, that is to say in the middle of the rainy season, a time which both the Commander-in-Chief and Major-General Wellesley considered suitable for operations against the Máratás, because they would be unable to freely cross the river, and the incursions for which they were so famous would be greatly restricted.

Of the water-parting lines which have been enumerated the Sahyádri or Western Gháts consist to the northward of horizontal or nearly horizontal strata of basalt or similar rocks, cut into a steep scarp on the west; the summits are flat, and the highest of them (as Mahábleshwar) rise to 4500 ft. The general height of the summits is about 2000. Further south the horizontal igneous rocks are not found, and the elevation is greater; some of the peaks in the Nílgiris rise to over 8000 ft.

The Sátpuras are in their western part, as far as Asírgarh, of basaltic trap. Further east they consist partly of horizontal traps and partly of sandstone, the highest peaks, those of Pachmarhi, rise to about 4400 ft.

The Vindhiyan escarpment consists of hard red sandstone, and its summit levels are about 2000 ft. above the sea. The dip is towards the north and is very gradual. The drainage lines run in deep grooves having a general direction north. This sandstone formation is of great thickness and seems to correspond with our old red sandstone. It forms the great plateau of Málwa.

The rocks of the Aravalí belong to the transition period, and the Vindhiyan rocks are found almost horizontal on both sides of the chain. The range has a width of 20 miles. Its highest points are Jargo (4330 ft.), and Gúrú-Sikra (5050 ft.), near Mount Ábú. The heights decline towards the north.

Having now given some account of the configuration of the theatre of war, I must proceed to the political distribution of the country at the time. And here I have been fortunate in obtaining (through the kindness of the authorities at the Indian Office) a map which was sent home with the reports of the Governor-General (The Marquess Wellesley) and shows the British possessions in 1803, and those of the native princes and chiefs.*

---

* "Bengal, Fort St. George, and Bombay papers, relative to Marhatta War in 1803." Printed by order of House of Commons, 5th and 22nd June, 1804.

I need scarcely tell you that in those days the present magnificent Survey of India was not even begun, and the map has, therefore, no great pretension to geographical accuracy. Besides this, the boundaries of the native states between themselves were scarcely known to the British. From this map I have transferred the boundaries as nearly as I can to a modern map (see *Plate II.*) and it shows (nearly enough for practical purposes) the various territories of the time.

The State of Berár comprises the whole basin of the Mahánadí above the Gháts, part of the basin of the Godávari, together with the mouths of the Mahánadí, and the smaller basins between it and the Sabanríka. Sindia and Holkar divide between them the Vindhiyan plateau, whilst the former holds, in addition, a large part of the Doáb, both above and below Dehli, and the country as far up as Lúdiána.

The Peshwa's territories comprise a stretch of country extending nearly 300 miles south, and for a considerable distance north, of Bombay, and north of them we find Gújarát, the territory of the Gáikwár of Baroda. All these, the Peshwa, the Gáikwár, the Rája of Berár (sometimes called from his capital Rája of Nágpúr, and sometimes from his family name known as "The Bhonsla"), Sindia and Holkar, were Maráthás. The other great state of the time was that coloured green, the Musalmán state ruled by the Subádár of the Dakhan, commonly (but erroneously) called by Anglo-Indians "The Nizám."

The various Maráthá states are all coloured yellow, the different states being distinguished by different shades of that colour. This shows at a glance what an enormous development the Maráthá power had reached at this time, and how strong their position would have been if the various chiefs could have agreed to act together ; fortunately for the British supremacy this is just what they never could do.

Next we are struck by the dangerous military position of the Bengal Presidency ; with an undefined frontier, "marching" for 600 miles with the Maráthás of Berár, and the long narrow projecting piece of the Doáb and Rohilkhand, separated from the rest of the presidency by the independent territory of Oudh, and approached by a sort of narrow passage, which near Káhnpúr is only 30 miles wide, between the Ganges and the Jamna. The insignificant size of the Bombay Presidency at that time next calls for notice, consisting of very little beyond the island of Bombay. The narrow tract of country round the Gulf of Khambáyat had only been ceded to the Company two years before. Further, the importance which the Madras Presidency enjoyed in 1803 is brought out by this map. It presents an almost homogeneous British territory. True, a portion of Maisúr was (and still is) independent, but the power of the Maisúr State had been completely broken down on the capture of Seringapatam by General Harris (afterwards Lord Harris) in 1798. The Sultan Tippú had been killed and his territory partitioned. The small state of Travancor on the west coast is the only other exception in this direction to the prevailing red which denotes British territory. The frontier of the Madras Presidency was also far more secure than that of Bengal. For about 400 miles it runs with that of the Nizám, whose constant dread of the Marátha made him a tolerably good ally, and though for over 300 miles it joins the Maráthás of Berár, still the narrowness of this part of the territory, and the consequent nearness of the frontier to the sea base, made it much easier to defend than the corresponding frontier of Bengal.

The remaining portion of the Madras frontier between that of the Nizám and the sea to the west, is common with a Marátha state, which you will observe is marked as belonging to the Peshwa. Following out the colour you see that this extends over a very large extent of country, comprising about 700 miles of the western coast line, from 40 miles south of Goa to the Gulf of Kachh (with the small exceptions of the Island of Bombay, and the lately ceded territory in the Gulf of Khambáyat) and with a width inland of 150 miles and upwards, which increases up the valley of the Narbadda to as much as 400 miles. All this belonged to certain Marátha chiefs, who, under recent arrangements were bound to subsidise troops of the Company, and it makes a deduction from the total fighting power of a possible Marátha confederacy which was of the greatest importance.

We have now reached a point where a short notice of Marátha history, and some account of the rise and growth of the various Marátha states, and their relations with the British Government, seems essential to a clear understanding of the military position. I shall endeavour to put this before you as shortly as possible.

India, in native parlance, is separated into two grand divisions, known as Hindústán and the Dakhan. The Dakhan in its most comprehensive sense includes the whole country south of the Vind-hiyan-Kaimúr range, whilst Hindústán is the country draining to the Indus and Ganges north of that line. Neither Gújarát nor Bengal proper are considered by native authorities to belong to to either of these divisions.

Although at the time we are dealing with the Maráthás held a large part of Hindústán, their original country, called Maráshtra, lies entirely in the Dakhan. Beginning at the north-west it is approximately defined by a line starting from the western extremity of the Sátpura range, and following that range as far as the neighbour-hood of Deogarh and Chindwára. From thence the eastern boundary follows the course of the Warda (or Varada) river to Chanda, and the confluence of the Wain Ganga and Warda. The southern limit is marked by an irregular line from near Chanda, through Bídar and Kolapúr, to Goa on the west coast, while the sea forms the western boundary. In the irregular quadrilateral thus defined Maráthá is the prevailing language. Its extension to the neighbourhood of Nágpúr is said* to be due to the establish-ment of a Maráthá government at that place.

This district is broadly divided into the Konkan, and the Desh, the country above the Gháts, or Sahyádri range, which I have already described. The Konkan is the long narrow tract between the Gháts and the sea. According to native legend it was recovered in a miraculous manner from the sea. Pureshrám, a Hindú Demigod, after extirpating the oppressors of the upper country, and making it over to the Brahmans, was by them ungratefully refused the privilege of residing there. He then repaired to the western coasts and petitioned the sea for a place of residence. His request was not at once granted, whereupon he drew his bow and let fly an arrow from the top of the Gháts, at which the ocean was intimi-dated, and receding before the arrow to the point at which it fell, left dry for the hero's residence the tract now known as the Konkan†.

The Desh, or country above the Gháts, is open and though diversified is (I believe) nowhere difficult to traverse, but between it and the Konkan the Gháts (or Ghát-Mahta as it is called by the natives) is a difficult tract about 20 to 25 miles in width, full of steep, rugged, rocky hills, which are easily turned into forts, such

---

* See Elphinstone, I., p. 411, note.   † Grant Duff, I., p. 4.

as in old days were able to defy attack. These hills are intersected by deep winding valleys covered with brushwood. During the rains the full force of the south-west monsoon bursts upon the Gháts, the valleys are filled with torrents, and the most magnificent cascades are formed on the faces of the hills. These, combined with tropical vegetation, form views, the beauty of which those who have the good fortune to ascend the Gháts during the rains are not likely to forget.

The Maráthás are described by Elphinstone "as small, sturdy, well-made men, but not handsome. They are all active, laborious, hardy, and persevering. If they have none of the pride and dignity of the Rájpúts, they have none of their indolence and want of worldly wisdom. A Rájpút warrior, as long as he does not dishonour his race, seems almost indifferent to the result of any contest he is engaged in. A Marátha thinks of nothing but the result, and cares little for the means if he can attain his object. For this purpose he will strain his wits, renounce his pleasures, and hazard his person; but he has not a conception of sacrificing his life, or even his interests, for a point of honour. This difference of sentiment affects the outward appearance of the two nations; there is something noble in the carriage of even an ordinary Rájpút; and something vulgar in that of the most distinguished Marátha.

" The Rájpút is the more *worthy* antagonist; the Marátha the more *formidable* enemy; for he will not fail in boldness and enterprise when they are indispensable, and will always support them, or supply their place, by stratagem, activity, and perseverance. All this applies chiefly to the soldiery to whom worse qualities might fairly be ascribed. The mere husbandmen are sober, frugal, and industrious; and though they have a dash of the national cunning are neither turbulent nor insincere." *

Of the early history of the Maráthás little or nothing is known, until the establishment of a Musalmán dynasty in the Dakhan, called from the name assumed by the first king, the Bahmini dynasty.† This dynasty existed from 1347 to 1526, but during its

---

* Elphinstone, II., 457.

† The Musalmáns first invaded the Dakhan in A.D. 1294, under Ála-ud-Dín, nephew, and afterwards successor, of Jalál-ud-Dín, the first of the Khilji kings of Dehli. He attacked Deogíri (now Daulatabad) the capital of Rámdeo, said by Elphinstone to have been Rája of Maráshtra, and reduced him to submission. Elphinstone, II., 29.

decline five other Musalmán states had been formed. Of these states three, established at Bíjapur, or Ádil Sháhi, Ahmadnagar, or Nizám Sháhi, and Golkonda, or Kutub Sháhi, respectively, had most to do with the Maráthás. The Bíjapur house was called Ádil Sháhi because its king always bore (with other names) that of Ádil, while the Ahmadnagar house was called Nizám Sháhi, and the Golkonda, Kutub Sháhi, for like reasons.

In 1573 Maráshtra was subject to the kings of Bíjapur and Ahmadnagar, with the exceptions of a part of Khandesh held by the Sultan of Búrhánpur, the northern Konkan which belonged to Gújarát, and the possessions of the Portuguese. Bíjapúr extended from the Níra river (north of Satára) to the Tangabhadro, from Cape Bankot to Cape Ramás along the western coast (nearly 200 miles), and on the east it was divided from Ahmadnagar by a line somewhere about the course of the Bíma river.

Ahmadnagar had the greater part of Berár, parts of Khandesh, and the northern Konkan, whilst the kingdom of Golkonda extended east from the territories of the other two to the eastern coast.

Under these dynasties as well as under that of the Bahmimi kings, the Maráthás generally held the hill forts, and rank corresponding to the number of horsemen under the command of an individual (called by the Mohammedans mansúb) was given to the Maráthá chiefs. Of these, early in the 16th century one of the most important was the Maráthá family of Jadú, Deshmukh* of Sindkír, who was in the service of the Nizám Sháh of Ahmadnagar. Lukjí Jadú Rá,o held a jágír for the support of 10,000 horse.

Near Daulatabád there resided a respectable Maráthá family surnamed Bhonsla, of which one Málají Bhonsla obtained by the favour of Lukjí Jadú the command of a small body of horse in the service of Murtiza Nizám Sháh of Ahmadnagar. This Málají Bhonsla had a son Sháhjí, who in 1604, married Jíjí Bá,i, daughter of Lúkjí Jadú Rá,o. By her he had two sons, Sambají and the famous Sívají, who was born in May, 1627.

Sháhjí subsequently rose to a considerable position in the service of Malik Ambar (an Abysinnian who was minister of the Nizám Sháhi dynasty of Ahmadnagar) and when that kingdom was finally

---

* Deshmukh, (see Wellington Despatches, II., 170,) was the holder of a Revenue Office.

extinguished, and its territory portioned by Sháh Jehán of Dehli, in 1637, he entered, with Sháh Jehán's consent, the service of the king of Bíjapúr. His father Málojí had acquired, for his services to the Ahmadnagar dynasty, a large jágír, the chief place of which was Púna, and Sháhjí on entering the service of Bíjapur was confirmed in this jágír, and received in addition a large one in Maisúr.*

The rise of Sívají was very extraordinary. His father left him as a boy at Púna in the charge of a Brahman, who was the manager of the Púna jagir, Sháhjí himself with his elder son being in Maisúr. Sívají grew up among his father's horsemen, and associated much in hunting excursions with the wild inhabitants of the neighbouring Gháts. Over these men he obtained, as he grew up, great personal influence, and by the time he was sixteen he was already suspected of joining them in extensive robberies in the Konkan. In 1646 (that is to say when only 19) he obtained possession of the hill fort of Torna (20 miles south-west of Púna), and a year later he fortified another hill about three miles from Torna, and gave it the name of Rájgarh.†

About this time the Brahman died, and Sívají assumed charge of the jágír. A little later he gained possession by treachery of another strong fort called Purandhar, about 20 miles south-east of Púna, and managed to increase his power in the district round Púna without exciting the anger of the Bíjapúr government, by which Sháhjí was looked on as the responsible jagírdar.‡

Soon after this (in 1648) Sívají plundered a royal convoy in the Konkan, which led to his incurring the displeasure of the king of Bíjapúr. It was vented however, not on him but on his father Sháhjí, who was held responsible for Sívají's misdeeds, thrown into prison and informed that, if Sívají did not submit, the entrance to the prison would be walled up. As an earnest of this intention part was actually built up. Sívají thereupon offered his services to the emperor Sháh Jehán, who accepted them, appointed him a commander of 5,000, and probably used his influence for Sháhjí's release,

---

‡ Thus did Sívají obtain possession of the tract between Chakan and the Níra, and the manner in which he established himself, watching and crouching like the wily tiger of his own mountain valleys, until he had stolen into a situation from where he could at once spring upon his prey, accounts both for the difficulty found in tracing his early rise, and the astonishing rapidity with which he extended his power, when his progress had attracted notice, and longer concealment was impossible. Grant Duff, I., 136.

which soon followed. During four years Sháhjí was kept a prisoner at large at Bíjapúr, but on his being sent back to the Karnatak in 1653, Sívají was again at liberty to push on his ambitious schemes. Sívají now renewed his encroachments, procured the assassination of a Hindú Rája south of Púna and seized his territory. For two years he continued to extend his authority until Aurangzíb was sent by Sháh Jehán to the Dakhan, in 1655. Aurangzíb was engaged in war with the king of Golkonda, and Sívají fancied he might venture to attack the territories of the Moghals. Finding he had made a mistake in this, and that the successes of Aurangzíb were much more rapid than he expected, he endeavoured, when Aurangzíb proceeded to attack Bíjapúr, to make terms with him by offering assistance.* Very soon the sickness of Sháh Jehán recalled Aurangzíb to Dehli and Sívají was left exposed to the wrath of the Bíjapúr Government. An army, under a chief called Afzul Khán was sent against him. It advanced to the neighbourhood of Partábgarh, a hill fort 45 miles south-west of Púna, where Sívají was residing, and threatened to overwhelm him, but Sívají extricated himself from his difficulties with characteristic craftiness and address. He pretended to be overawed by the power and reputation of Afzul Khán, and sent a Brahman agent who persuaded Afzul Khán that Sívají only required to be assured in a personal interview of his own safety, and would then submit. An interview was arranged, and Afzul Khán, who was attired in a thin muslin robe and carried only a straight sword, was murdered by Sívají who had armed his left hand with a wágnakh† which, when pretending to embrace the Khán, he struck into his bowels. Partábgarh is situate in a country which is (or was at that day) very difficult of access, and much overgrown with wood. The murder of Afzul Khán was followed by an attack on his troops, who, taken by surprise, were easily slaughtered or dispersed, (October, 1659). During the following year, though shut up for some time in the fort of Panála (near Kolhapúr), Sívají further extended his power so much that in the beginning of 1661 the king of Bíjapúr found it necessary to take the field in person. Sívají was beaten and lost most of his possessions, but (the king being obliged in the next year to proceed to the Karnátak) he recovered them all, and about the beginning of

---

* Grant Duff, I., 161.

† A wágnakh is a sort of glove with sharp claws of steel; wág, a tiger; nakh, a claw. "Tára," a novel by Meadows Taylor, gives an interesting sketch of this period.

1663 a peace was arranged with Bíjapúr through the mediation of his father Sháhjí. Sívají at this time removed his residence from Rájgarh to a stronger fort called Raigarh, about 40 miles southwest of Púna.

At this time Sívají's territory extended along the coast from Kaliyán to Goa (about 250 miles), and included all the Konkan along that length, and the Ghát Mahta from the Bíma to the Warda, a distance of over 150 miles. The greatest breadth was between Jinjíra and Supeh, where it was under 100 miles.

In this territory he was able, owing to his predatory habits, to maintain a force wh'ch is stated at 50,000 infantry and 7,000 horse. He already possessed some ships, so that his robberies were not confined to land. Thus we see that by the age of 34 this extraordinary man had from very small beginnings actually raised himself to the position of an independent sovereign, though he as yet assumed no title.

He now felt himself strong enough to act against the Moghals, and with his horse ravaged the country near Aurangábád and Junnar. His territory was invaded and Púna occupied, but the invasion was repelled, the Moghal force retiring to Aurangábád, while Sívají with 4,000 horse set off for Surat. Though repulsed from the English and Dutch factories he plundered the native city and carried off an immense booty. This was in 1664.

Just after this Sháhjí, who had greatly extended his original possessions in the Dakhan, died, and Sívají soon after assumed the title of Rája and began to coin money. Immediately after this he was again at war with Bíjapúr, and by means of a fleet made an excursion into the territory of that state south of Goa.

In 1665, a large force was sent by Aurangzib to reduce Sívají to submission. It was under the command of Rája Jai Singh of Amber or Jaipúr, a general of great reputation. Sívají, though his forts of Singhar and Purandhar had not been taken, resolved to submit. It does not appear whether he was moved to this resolution by the hopelessness of resistance, by superstition, by the hope of indemnifying himself at the expense of Bíjapúr, or by the advantage which he expected to obtain from becoming a vassal of the emperor. Whatever may have been his motive he came to terms with Jai Singh, and agreed to give up 20 out of his 32 forts with the territory belonging to them. He was to hold the remainder as a jágír from the emperor, and his son Sambají (then 8 years old) was appointed a commander of 5,000 in the imperial service. But the most important concession which he obtained was the grant of a fourth of the revenue of certain districts belonging to Bíjapúr with the privilege of collecting it himself. This was the origin of the famous Maráthá claim for chauth, chauth meaning, in Sanscrit, the fourth part. Aurangzíb agreed to these terms* on condition that Sívají should accompany Jai Singh in his campaign against Bíjapúr with 2,000 horse and 8,000 foot, and pay a peshkash (or instalment) of 40,000 pagodas (equal to about £80,000) to the emperor.

After assisting Jai Singh in Bíjapúr, Sívají was invited by Aurangzíb to Dehli, and, having given offence by his behaviour at court, was placed under surveillance. He escaped with difficulty, and made his way south in disguise, which he did not throw off until he was safe at Raigarh, in December, 1666.

In the following year, things having gone badly with the Moghals in Bíjapúr, Sívají was able to make a most advantageous peace with the emperor. He received back most of his former possessions and in addition a jágír in Berár, which laid the foundation of Marátha power in that country. Moreover the emperor recognized his title of Rája.

The years 1668 and 1669 were spent by Sívají in internal organisation and reform, and a very interesting account of his institutions is given by Captain Grant Duff.†

Sívají's power was originally founded on his infantry, which was of two classes called Máwalis and Hetkuris, the Máwalis were natives of the Ghát Mahta, the Hetkaris of the Konkan. The arms of the infantry were a sword, shield, and match-lock. Some of the Hetkaris had fire-locks, having obtained flint-locks from the Portuguese.

Every tenth man carried a bow and arrows, for night attacks and surprises. The Hetkaris were the best marksmen, while the Máwalis excelled as swordsmen. There was a náik (or corporal) over every ten men, a hawáldár (Anglicé havildár) over every fifty, an officer called a júmladár over every hundred. The commander of a thousand was styled Ek-hazári, and there were also officers of five thousand. The chief commander of infantry was called a senápati (Anglicé Sarnobat).

---

* Grant Duff, I., 210, quotes original letter of Aurangzíb.   † Grant Duff, I., 223.

The cavalry was of two kinds, known as Bárgír and Siláhdár.* A Bárgír is a man who is supplied with a horse by the state or by some individuals, while a Siláhdár is a man who provides a horse at his own expense, like the greater part of the Bengal cavalry at the present time. Consequently a Siláhdár is considered a much more respectable person than a Bárgír. Sívají had a body of Bárgírs, mounted entirely on horses provided by the state, and called Págá. On these he placed great reliance, and with every body of ordinary Bárgír or of Siláhdár horse he mixed detachments of the Págá, to act as spies, prevent embezzlement or treachery, and to overawe the discontented.

The Maráthá weapon was the spear,† in the use of which they were very dexterous. The spearmen carried in addition a sword and a shield, in case the spear should be broken. Part of their horse carried matchlocks which they must of course have dismounted to use. Thus the Maráthás possessed, according to old European nomenclature, both lancers and dragoons.

Every 25 horsemen were under a havildár, over 125 (say a squadron) there was a jumladár, and every 5 jumlas (say 500 effective) were commanded by a súbadár. At the head of every 10 súbas was an officer called Panch-hazárí. Everyone of these officers, from the the jumladár upwards, had one or more Brahman accountants, and the " intelligence department" was largely represented by a regular establishment of news-writers, with spies and others to gain information. All plunder was the property of the state and had to be rigidly accounted for.

The Dussera (Dusahra) festival of the Hindús, which falls at the end of the monsoon, was observed by Sívají with great pomp, and was the time for a general muster and review of the troops before taking the field. At this time men, horses, arms, and equipment were inspected, and an account exacted of any plunder which had not been given up. Accounts were closed and settled, either in cash or by orders on revenue officers, never by direct orders on villages.

In regard to plunder " the only exceptions were in favour of cows (the sacred animal), cultivators, and women; " these were never to be molested, " nor were any but rich Musalmáns, or

* Siláh, arms, armour, Arabic. Bárgír, Persian.
† Grant Duff, (woodcut) III., 537.—Kit, &c., I., 226.

Hindús in their service who could pay a ransom, to be made prisoners." No soldier was permitted to carry a female follower with him in the field on pain of death.*

Sívaji's head manager, or prime minister, was a Brahman named Moro Panth,† and was styled Peshwa. The same method and strictness that characterises his military arrangements appears to have existed, theoretically at least,‡ in the fiscal and judicial departments, but the constant wars in which he was engaged can have left Sívaji but little time for the supervision of civil affairs.

When we compare all this order and system with what we know of the generality of the native states, which were administered under a sort of feudal system, the extraordinary rise and spread of Sívaji's power is to a certain extent accounted for.

I have gone into the details of Sívaji's administration at a length which the time at my disposal would not justify, were it not that his system may be taken as a type of Maráthá organization, and that by studying it in some detail we are enabled to understand the rapid rise of other Maráthá chiefs to wide dominion at a later date ; since they doubtless followed, to some extent at least, the system of their illustrious predecessor. We now revert to Sívaji's history.

Tranquility did not long reign in the Dakhan. In 1670 Aurangzíb sent an order to his lieutenants in the south to arrest Sívaji, who retaliated by seizing the strong forts of Singarh and Purandhar. The escalade of the former is described by Grant Duff, and appears a daring feat worthy to be classed with Captain Popham's surprise of Gwáliár. In October of the same year Sívaji was again at Surat and attacked the British factory, which made a successful defence. After the plundering of Surat, Sívaji ravaged Khandesh, and exercised for the first time the power of collecting chauth, which he had obtained from the emperor. This system of obtaining charters from the Emperor of Dehli, which were held (by those interested) to be valid over all India, is one of which some of our early Governor-Generals well understood how to take advantage. §

The first field action against the Moghals was fought in 1672, and gained by Moro Panth, Peshwa, who commanded the Maráthás.

---

* Grant Duff, I., 230.

† Or Moreshwar Trimmal Pingli.—Grant Duff, I., 166 and 235. First Peshwa, Shamraj Panth, Grant Duff, I., 150. ‡ Grant Duff, I., 234.

§ *E.g.*, Lord Clive when wishing to obtain the Northern Sarkárs. Grant Duff, II., 192.

I do not propose to follow the rest of Sívají's career in much detail, as it might be found tedious and would certainly take up more time than can be given to it. It must suffice to mention the different steps of his further rise, and describe the exteut of his dominions.

In June, 1674, he was crowned at Rájgarh with the ceremonies of a Moghal coronation, thus indicating that he threw off the suzerainty of the emperor. Part of this ceremony consisted in being weighed with gold, about 10 stone of gold pagodas being required.

In 1675 he for the first time sent his troops across the Narbadda into Moghal territory, and at the end of 1676 made a great expedition to the Karnatak, for the purpose of recovering his father Sháhjí's jágír. This expedition ended successfully in a compromise with his brother Venkají, who had held the jágír since the death of Sháhjí. In 1679 we find him in alliance with the regent of Bíjapúr against the Moghals, one of the conditions of the alliance being the cession to him of the sovereign rights over the jágírs of Sháhjí, thus making him the master *de jure* as he already was *de facto*. Sívají died at Raigarh on 5th April, 1680, in his fifty-third year.*

The possessions of Sívají at the time of his death† included the whole of the Konkan, except Goa, Chawal, Salsette, and Bassain, which belonged to the Portuguese; Jinjíra to the Abysinnians, and the English settlement on the Island of Bombay. He occupied the tract of Maráshtra from the Harnkassi (Gokak) river, on the south, to Indúrani, between Púna and Junnar, on the north. He held, as we have seen, large jágírs in the Dakhan, a number of outlying possessions, and at the time of his death had in his treasury a sum of money which, Grant Duff says, after a large allowance for exaggeration, cannot have been less than several millions sterling. More than all he had introduced a system of Government, a sentiment of nationality, and had set an example of zeal for the Hindú religion, which, in spite of the comparative feebleuess of his successors, held the Maráthá power together until it attained a development which made the nation for a long while supreme over the greater part of India.‡

---

* Grant Duff, I., 295.
† Grant Duff, I., 209.
‡ Elphinstone, II., 510.   Grant Duff, I., 300.

With the successors of Sívají I do not propose to trouble you in detail, but I hope that the tables* I have prepared, and a short description of the extent of the Maráthá power at particular epochs, will render the rest tolerably clear.

The immediate successors of Sívají, his sons Sambají and Rája Rám, continued for twenty years, though in a comparatively feeble manner, the personal government of their father. The first was defeated and made prisoner by Aurangzíb, who put him barbarously† to death. Rája Rám does not appear to have been ever generally regarded as the rightful rája, but as regent for his nephew Sívají, better known as Saho, or Shao, a nickname given him by Aurangzíb. After the death of Rája Rám his infant son Sívají was proclaimed, and his widow Tára Bá,í made regent. Some time later Shao was released by the Moghals, and a contest for power ensued which ended in the establishment of Shao on the musnad of Satára, mainly by the aid of Bálají Wiswanáth, who was consequently appointed Peshwa by Shao. Shao's weak character (partly due probably to his having been brought up a prisoner) led to the real power getting by degrees into the hands of the Peshwa. Shao became quite imbecile some years before his death, so that when that occurred in 1749 the then Peshwa, Báji Bálají Rá,o, had the power entirely in his own hands. 1 ought not to omit to mention that Rája Rám created a new office (in 1690) with the title of Prithi Nidhi, which took precedence of that of Peshwa, but though readers of Maráthá history will find frequent mentions of the holder of this office, it need not be taken much account of in a short sketch like the present, since the holders never appear to have attained for any length of time to the real power enjoyed by the Peshwa.

Returning to Báji Bálají, Peshwa, we find that on the death of Shao in 1749, he produced a deed from that Rája which formally transferred all the powers of government to the Peshwa, while it reserved the title and dignities of Rája to the supposed grandson‡ of Rája Rám, son of Sívají II., whose name was Rám Rája. From this time till the then representative was released by the British Government in 1818, the Rájas of Satára were, with their

---

* See Appendix I.

† Grant Duff, I., 361, eyes burnt out, then tongue cut out, then beheaded.   Rája Rám's ministry, Grant Duff, I. 370.

‡ Grant Duff and Elphinstone are of opposite opinions as to Rám Rája's legitimacy. Grant Duff, II. ,33. Elphinstone, II., 646.

families, practically prisoners in their capital. They were, however, treated with great veneration and respect, and the great object of every contending Maráthá chief was to obtain grants (sannads) from the Rája, or the dress of honour investiture with which was the symbol of the conferring of an office. The Peshwas were invariably invested with their office in this way, and until they were so, did not receive recognition from their compatriots. This transfer of power from the Rája to his Peshwa reminds one of the position of the Capets as Mayors of the palace under the Merovignian dynasty ; or of the relative positions, which till lately existed in Japan, of the Mikado and Tycoon.

Rising upon the rapid decay of the Moghal empire after the death of Aurangzíb, and held together and controlled by the single hand of the Peshwa, the Maráthá power reached its greatest development in about 1760. It is true that the collective possessions of the Marátháa at the opening of the present century were as large, if not larger, than at that time, but they were no longer ruled by one man. " At the time of which we now speak their frontier extended on the north to the Indus and the Himalaya, on the south nearly to the extremity of the peninsula; all territority that was not their own paid tribute. The whole of this power was wielded by one hand; a settlement had been made with Tára Bá,í by which the person of the Rája had been consigned to his nominal minister, and all pretensions of every description were centred in the Peshwa.*"

This great power was, however, destined to have but a short duration. In 1761 the Marátháas came in contact with the Afghans. Ahmad Shah, Abdálí, invaded India for the first time in 1759, defeated and killed Datají Sindia and occupied Dehli. This led to a great effort on the part of the Marátháas and the decisive battle occurred at Pánípat on 6th January 1761. It resulted in the total defeat of the Marátháas with enormous loss, the whole number of the slain amounting, it is said, to near 200,000. The Peshwa (Bájí Bálají Rá,o) never recovered the shock, and soon after died. Dissensions broke out after his death, and the power of the Peshwas, though the office continued for 60 years, never regained its vigour. The Marátháa nation ceased to exist as a political unit, and there arose on the decay of the central power a number of independent

---

* Elphinstone, II., 673 ; also Grant Duff, II. 126.

Maráthá chiefs who, though they played (as some of their representatives still do) an important part in the history of India, yet none of them ever reached the position of Sívají or of the early Peshwas.

The four most important chiefs were :—

    1. The Rája of Nágpúr or Berar. Sometimes called "the Bhonsla."

    2. Sindia.

    3. Holkar.*

    4. The Gáekwár.†

The Nágpúr State was the earliest of these, being founded by Parsají Bhonsla, a Siláhdár who rose to be administrator of Berár under Rája Rám in 1696. Sindia, Holkar and the Gáekwár rose later to power; the first chief of each name having served in the Maráthá armies under Báji Rá,o Ballal, Peshwa.

The Rájas of Nágpúr ceased (by the extinction of the family) in 1853, but the other three, as you are aware, are still represented by the Chiefs of Gwáliár, Indúr and Baroda, and His Highness Jaiojí Rá,o Sindia of Gwáliár holds a commission as the senior General in Her Majesty's Service.

The aggrandisement of Sindia and Holkar had been very rapid about 1750, owing to the necessity the Peshwa, Bájí Bálají Rá,o, was under of conciliating supporters after his *coup d'état,* and the two received a grant of nearly the whole of Málwa,‡ the revenue, 150 lakhs of rupees (£1,500,000), being divided between them; Sindia getting somewhat the larger share. Rugojí Bhonsla received at the same time new sannads (or grants) for Berár and Bengal. Nágpúr became the capital of Berár, Sindia and Holkar fixed their governments at Újain and Indúr respectively (places which are not more than 30 miles apart), while the Gáekwár appears to have made Ahmadábád his capital.

The most brilliant of the Sindias was Mádhojí, who succeeded to the jágírs of his father Ránojí in 1759, two years before the battle of Pánípat. War was waged between the Maráthás and the British from 1778 to 1781, the Gáekwár being an ally of the British, and Mádhojí Sindia their most prominent opponent. This war was marked by the shameful convention of Wargáon,

---

* Holkar is from Hal a plough. † Gáekwár from Gáe a cow. ‡ Grant Duff, II., 40.

concluded with Sindia by a Field Committee. The Bombay Government, being jealous of their military commander, had adopted the notable plan of sending two members of council into the field with him, the natural result being disaster; though it must be owned the commander, Colonel Egerton, appears to have been singularly incompetent. On the other hand it was marked by the brilliant surprise of the Fort of Gwáliár (on 4th August, 1780) under Captain Popham, and by a march across Central India under Colonel Goddard, (with only 5000 men) worthy of all praise, and remarkable as the first occasion of direct combination between the forces of Bengal and Bombay.*

The war was terminated by the treaty of Sálbái in May, 1781, some of the provisions of which were directed against Haidar Ali of Maisúr, who had made himself master of the Maráthá country south of the Krishna (or Kistnah), and became by his alliance with the French† an object of dread to the British.

Haidar Ali had shortly before this endeavoured to form a confederacy against the British of all the Maráthá chiefs and the Nizám.

"The Nizám," as he is called by the English, was originally the Súbadár (or Viceroy) of the Dakhan under the Moghal emperors of Dehli. The whole of the territory of the Moghals was divided into a number of provinces, each called a Súba. The way in which we have come to call the Súbadár of the Dakhan "the Nizam" is this. In 1712 a man called Mír Kammar-ud-Dín (son of Ghází-ud-Din a favourite officer of Aurangzíb) was appointed by Aurangzíb to the Súbadári of the Dakhan. This Mír Kammar-ud-Dín, received from Aurangzíb the title of Chain Kúlich Khán, and later from the emperor Farukh-Sir that of Nizám-ul-Mulkh, which means lord or chief of the country. In addition to these he assumed himself a title of Asuf Jah, and as he is named indifferently in history by any one of the former names, as well as by his title of Súbadár of the Dakhan, it is slightly perplexing at first. This Chain Kúlich Khán assumed independence on the downfall of the monarchy of Dehli, and died in 1749 at the age of 103. His

---

* Sir Eyre Coote was Commander-in-Chief in Bengal at this time. Mr Hastings Governor-General.

† Grant Duff, II., 309.

descendants have retained the succession, and he is represented at the present time by the chief of Haidarábád, whom we call the Nizám.

Nizám Ali, Súbadár of the Dakhan (son of Mír Kammar-ud-Dín), was a great rival of the Peshwa, Bájí Bálají Rá,o. Being the head of a Musalmán power nearly surrounded by Maráthá states, an alliance with him was naturally courted by the British, when anxious to curb the power of the Maráthás.

It was not long after the treaty of Salbái before Mádhojí Sindia began to push his schemes for re-establishing Maráthá supremacy in Hindústán. In 1784 he recovered the fortress of Gwáliár, which the English had made over to their ally the Rája of Gohad, and in October of the same year he was invited (ostensibly) by the Emperor, Sháh Álam* to meet him at Ágra. The invitation came in reality from Afrasiáb Khán, Amír ul Umara, who was struggling for supreme power with a rival. Almost immediately afterwards, Afrasiáb Khán was assassinated, and Sindia became the real minister. He declined the title of Amír ul Umara, but sagaciously obtained for the Peshwa that of Wakíl-i-Mutlak,† and got himself appointed deputy. The Emperor conferred on him the command of his army, and assigned to him the provinces of Ágra and Dehli, on consideration of an allowance of 65,000 rupees monthly. By this transaction the Emperor became in fact a pensioner of Sindia (as he later was of the Company), and Sindia acquired the territory stretching from Ágra to Lúdiána, which you see included in his dominions in *Plate* II.

Not long after this, Sindia had the audacity to raise a claim for chauth against the British in Bengal, and although he soon withdrew it. this led to a *rapprochement* between the British and Múdají Bhonsla Rája of Nágpúr.

Soon after the treaty of Salbái, Sindia raised a body of regular troops under M. Benoit de Boigne,‡ a Savoyard count who had served in the service of France in the famous Irish Brigade. De Boigne began by raising two battalions of 850 men, which by degrees were officered for the most part by Europeans of various nations. Thus was formed the nucleus of the force against which General Lake had to contend in 1803.

---

* Blinded by Gholám Khadir, Grant Duff, III., 30.
† Wakíl-i-Mutlak, Plenipotentiary, Vice-Regent with full powers.
‡ Grant Duff, II., 466, note.

55

In 1790 this force was further developed.* The infantry was augmented, first to two and later to three brigades; each brigade containing 8 battalions of 700 men. Each brigade had 500 horse, and each battalion five guns. Thus the force of a brigade was about 2800 infantry, 500 horse, 25 guns. Sindia's guns were cast for him by Mr Sangster, a Scotchman, who had been in the service of the Rána of Gohad. The infantry carried match-locks and bayonets, and the officers were many of them British, and very respectable by birth and education.

Later, about 1792, De Boigne's force was further augmented to 18,000 regular infantry, 6,000 irregulars,† 2,000 irregular horse, and 600 Persian cavalry. The fort of Ágra was made a depot for guns and small arms.

About this time Holkar, too, began to establish regular infantry, and raised 4 battalions under the command of a Frenchman, the Chevalier Dudrenec.

Mádhají Sindia died in 1794, and was succeeded by his great-nephew Daulat Rá,o Sindia, who was our opponent in 1803.

The power of the Maráthás in 1794, if we were to look only to the extent of their territory, to the amount of their revenues, and to the number of their troops, would be found equal or even superior to that in 1760. But the causes which excited them to conquest no longer existed, nor was there any one chief with sufficient authority to unite them.‡ A temporary union was brought about, however, by claims upon Nizám Ali, from the settlement of which all the Marátha chiefs hoped to profit. The English, under Sir John Shore's Governor-Generalship, held aloof, Nizám Ali followed the example of Sindia and Holkar, and set on foot a disciplined force of 23 battalions under a French officer, M. Raymond, and in Jan., 1795, war ensued between Nizám Ali and the Marátha confederacy. An indecisive battle took place at Kurdla (about 60 miles south-east of Ahmadnagar), but the Moghal army dispersed from a panic in the night, and Nizám Ali was forced to make terms. This led to great cessions of territory and large payments of arrears and indemnities by Nizám Ali.

It must not be supposed that British politics in India were at that day, any more than they are at the present time, wholly

* Grant Duff, III., 35.
† Najíbs and Rohillas.—Grant Duff, III., 74.   ‡ Grant Duff, III., 105.

56

independent of and distinct from European. In those days it was
France which was what our German friends call an important
"factor" in Indian politics. France still held the Mauritius, and
Pondicheri was a far more important place than at the present day,
and the French Republic had sent envoys to Seringapatám and concluded an alliance with "Citoyen" Tippú. When Lord Mornington
(afterwards and better known as Marquess Wellesley) arrived in
India, in May, 1798, his first measures had been directed to the
abatement of French influence. His views were what in the
political slang of the present day would be called "imperial," and
the change on his succeeding Sir John Shore was not unlike that
which recently occurred when Lord Lytton succeeded the Earl of
Northbrook. The first care of the new Governor-General was to
negociate with the Court of Haidarábád, and the Nizám agreed to
receive a corps of subsidized British troops numbering 6,000 men,
with a proper complement of artillery; to disband his French troops,
numbering 14,000 men; and to assign 24 lakhs of rupees a year, for
the support of the British contingent.*

This successful stroke of diplomacy was immediately followed by
a campaign against Tippú Sultán of Maisúr. Seringapatám was
taken in May, 1799, by General (afterwards Lord) Harris, the Sultan
being killed in the storm. This event consolidated British power
in the South, and enabled the British authorities to assume, towards
the Maráthás and the Nizám, a position which they had never before
been able to venture on. Meanwhile Lord Mornington had endeavoured, in 1798, to make with the Peshwa an alliance similar to
that with the Nizám, but was unsuccessful. Nor did his efforts
meet with any better success at the Court of Nágpúr.

The French invasion of Egypt which took place in 1798, had
caused the home authorities, in alarm for their Indian possessions,
to approve of the war against Tippú as an ally of the French
Republic. In 1800, General Baird, who had borne a leading part
in the capture of Seringapatám, was sent to Egypt with a force of
4,000 Europeans and 5,000 Sepoys to co-operate with General Sir
John Hutchinson (Sir R. Abercromby's successor) against the
French. The report of his approach aided Sir J. Hutchinson in
concluding an arrangement for the capitulation of the French army
under General Hoche.

---

* Marshman, II., 78; or, Grant Duff, III., 173.

Although the Peshwa Báji Rá,o Rugonáth refused in 1798 to come to terms with the Governor General, it was not long before he saw reason to change his views. In March, 1800, died Nána Farnavís* who had long been the moving spirit in the Marátbá government, and had supported the Peshwa's authority against the growing tyranny of Sindia. The Peshwa was for a time relieved by the rise of Jaswant Rá,o Holkar which led to a war in Málwa, between Holkar and Sindia, in which the rival capitals of Újain and Indúr were sacked in their turn. Holkar in 1802 moved on Púna, intending either to capture the Peshwa and make use of his authority, or perhaps to avenge on Báji Rá,o the barbarous murder of his father Witojí. On 25th October, 1802, a great battle, in which no less than 84,000 men are said to have been engaged, was fought under the walls of Púna† and resulted in the total defeat of Sindia, with the loss of all his baggage, stores and ammunition.

The Peshwa (who was greatly wanting in personal courage) fled early in the day, and sent a message to Colonel Close, the Governor-General's Agent, agreeing to all the terms he had previously refused, and binding himself to subsidize 6 battalions of Sepoys, and to cede revenue to the amount of 25 lakhs of rupees for their support. He not long after took refuge at Bassain where, on the 31st December 1802‡, was concluded the treaty of Bassain by which the Peshwa sacrificed his independence in return for the protection of the British.

This treaty is one of the most important ever concluded in India. It declared itself to be "for the purpose of general defensive alliance and reciprocal protection of the territories of the Peshwa and the Company." A subsidiary force of not less than 6,000 regular infantry, with artillery and European artillerymen, was to be maintained in the Peshwa's dominions. The Peshwa undertook not to have in his service any European of a nation hostile to the English, a provision aimed directly against the French. Districts yielding a revenue of 26 lakhs of rupees were ceded for the support of the troops the Peshwa; relinquished his claims on Surat, and agreed to submit to British arbitration his difference with the Nizám and the Gáekwár. Further, he was neither to engage in hostilities, nor even to enter into any negotiations, with any other power without

---

* Grant Duff, III., 167.　　† Grant Duff, III., 206.　　‡ Grant Duff, III., 225.

58

the concurrence of the British Government. Báji Rá,o had no sooner concluded the treaty than he began to intrigue with Sindia and the Bhonsla to render it nugatory. No efforts of his were needed, however, to render both of these chiefs intensely hostile to the treaty. They could not fail to perceive that it struck at the very root of Maráthá power, and they soon formed a league to oppose it. The Rája of Nágpúr did all he could to induce Holkar to lay aside his hostility to Sindia and join the league, but Holkar with characteristic perfidy, though he pretended to do so and obtained important cessions as the price of his consent, not only left the confederates without his support, but also availed himself of the embarrassments of his rival to plunder Sindia's territory.

The Governor-General lost no time in fullfilling his engagement to replace the Peshwa on his masnad at Púna. How this was done I will endeavour to shew in my next lecture.

CAMPAIGN AGAINST SINDIA AND THE RÁJA OF NÁGPÚR.

Before proceeding to describe the measures taken by the Governor General to fulfil his engagement with the Peshwa, let us briefly examine the force which could be arrayed on either side.

According to a statement for which I am indebted to Colonel T. K. Wilson, C.B., Military Secretary at the India Office, the regular forces of the three Presidencies on 30th April, 1803, were as follows :—

	NATIVE TROOPS.			EUROPEAN TROOPS.		KING'S TROOPS.		Remarks.
	Cavalry. Regts.	Infantry. Batins.	Pioneers. Batins.	Artillery. Batns.	Infantry. Batns.	Cavalry. Regts.	Infantry. Batns.	
Bengal... ...	6	40	—	3	1	3	3	
Madras ...	7	38	2	2	1	3	7	
Bombay ...	—	17	—	1	1	—	6*	*Perhaps more. These were in Gújarát.
Totals	13	95	2	6	3	6	16	

In addition to these there were a few battalions of garrison troops and irregulars.

The strength of the native cavalry regiments was about 450 sabres, that of the Bengal battalions of native infantry 800 bayonets, while those of the other two presidencies averaged rather more. The Bengal Artillery battalions had 7 companies each. There do not appear to have been any field batteries regularly organised, and only an "experimental" troop of Horse Artillery in Bengal, commanded by Capt. Clement Brown.

The King's Cavalry Regiments (all Light Dragoons), averaged something under 500 sabres, and the Infantry battalions somewhat under 800 men.

The Native Infantry regiments had each two battalions, but they were worked by battalions, not by regiments.

Thus the regular forces of the three Presidencies made up about;

British Cavalry,   6 × 480   = 2,880.
„   Infantry, 16 × 800 + 3 × 700 = 14,500.
Native Cavalry, 13 × 450   = 5,850.
„   Infantry, 97 × 840   = 81,480.

or a total of 104,710 cavalry and infantry, with 2,400 artillerymen.

Of this total about 60,000 were made available for field service after deducting garrisons, &c.

It is not possible to ascertain with any approach to accuracy what the forces of the confederates were. A tabular statement is given by Major Thorn, which he says was considered accurate, of Sindia's organised force under the French officers, which shows 72 battalions, numbering 39,000 men, with 4,600 irregulars attached to the battalions, apparently as skirmishers, and 464 guns. The field guns, as was ascertained when most of them were captured by the British, were not greatly inferior to our own. In one of Major-General Wellesley's letters, he says he found them good, and was able to make use of them, which he could never do with Tippu's.

SINDIA'S DISCIPLINED FORCE.

From Thorn, p. 78, "Table drawn up on accurate information, particularly that given by Mr. Stuart, a British Officer who quitted Sindia soon after the commencement of hostilities."

Description.	Stations.	No. of Batns.	No. of Men.		Total.	No. of Guns.	Remarks.
			Regr. Infy.	Ali-gools.			
1st Brigade— M. Louis Bourquin	Debli.	8	6000	1000	7000	50	Aligools were irregulars armed with match locks, sword & shield.
2nd Brigade— M. Hessing	Sekandra.	7	4000	1600	5600	50	
3rd Brigade— M. Pohlam	Dakhan with Sindia.	8	5000	1000	6000	80	1st and 2nd Brigades were in battle of Dehli, 3rd at Assye, 4th in battle of Agra.
4th Brigade— M. Dudernaigue	Do.	7	4000	1000	5000	70	
5th Brigade— { Aligarh, 2 Dehli, 2 Agra, 3	with Sindia.	7	4000	not known	4000	—	
Corps under M. Dupont	with Sindia.	4	2000	Do.	2000	ab't 20	M. Dupont's Corps at Assye, also the Begum's.
Corps under Major Brownrigg	Do.	5	2250	Do.	2250	30	
Begum Sumroo's force	Do.	4	2400	Do.	2400	20	
Late Filozo's Brigade, now commanded by Jean Baptiste	Újain.	6	3000	Do.	3000	60	
Ambaji Inglia's Brigade	with Sindia.	saidto be 16	6400	Do.	6400	84	
		72	39,050	4600	43,650	464	

We must now go back a little in order to complete our view of events prior to the opening of the campaign in 1803.

In 1802, in consequence of the disturbances in the Maráthá territory, and with a view to the eventual establishment of a subsidiary force at Púna, a considerable portion of the Army of the Madras Presidency had been collected, by order of the second Lord Clive, Governor of Madras, at Harihar, on the Tangabhadro (Tumbudra), and a return of 29th November, 1802, shows this force to have been just over 20,000 men with 70 guns. Harihar is on the north-west frontier of Maisúr, and on the old main road from Madras to Púna, which, as I have already been pointed out, sweeps round by the west to avoid the great rivers. At the same time that Lord Clive took this step, in anticipation of the Governor-General's approval, the Governor of Bombay, Mr. Duncan, prepared his force to take the field, and the subsidiary force at Haidarábad was, at the request of Lieut.-Col. Close, Resident at Púna, also held in readiness for field operations.

When therefore, at the beginning of 1803, the necessity for moving a force on Púna to carry out the engagements of the Treaty of Bassain arose, the actual dispositions was perfectly suited to the object in view.

In February, the Governor-General directed Lord Clive to send an advanced detachment from Harihar to Míraj, or any other stations where the Peshwa could join it, and Lord Clive requested Lieut.-General Sir J. Stuart (the Commander in Chief) to send not less than 7,000 men forward under the command of Major-General the Hon. A. Wellesley, who was then administering the Government of Maisúr. Sir J. Stuart placed an advanced division of 10,000 men under Major-General Wellesley's command, and on 9th March General Wellesley left Harihar, and reached Míraj on 3rd or 4th April. When in camp on 19th April, 40 miles from Púna, he learned that Holkar's General, Amrit Rá,o, who was in possession of Púna, intended to burn the city on the approach of the British. He therefore marched with his cavalry in the night, and arriving early on the 20th at Púna, saved the city, Amrit Rá,o marching off precipitately.

Major-General Wellesley, after restoring the Peshwa to his seat at Púna, marched again on 4th June, and on 15th reached Ágar, a short distance from Ahmadnagar, then a fortress belonging to Sindia.

General Stuart had shortly before moved into the country between the Krishna and Tangabhadro, and encamped at Múdgal. The force remaining with General Stuart was somewhat under 8,000 men.

Before detailing the disposition of the other parts of the British force at the opening of the campaign of 1803, it will be advisable to describe the plan of operations framed by the Commander-in-Chief, in communication with the Governor-General.*

In those days the actual Head Quarters of the Bengal Army were at Kánhpúr,† and there the Commander-in-Chief was residing in the hot weather of 1803, the Governor-General being at Calcutta. An active correspondence was carried on between them, and on the

---

* I am indebted to Colonel Allen Johnson, C.B., Military Secretary to the Government of India, for a copy of General Lake's plan of campaign, which is in the records at Calcutta.

† Calcutta was nominally Army Head Quarters.

28th June the Governor-General wrote to General Lake, and described the object of operations in the event of war with Sindia,* as being four in number, viz. :

1st. To seize all his possessions between the Ganges and Jamna.

2nd. To take the person of the Moghal Sháh Álam under our protection.

3rd. To form alliances with the Rájputs, and other inferior states beyond the Jamna, for the purpose of excluding Sindia from the northern districts of Hindustan.

4th. To occupy Bundelkhand, and thus strengthen the frontier of the province of Banáras against Sindia or the Rája of Berár.

At the same time, the 27th June, the Governor-General wrote to Major-General Wellesley directing him to obtain a final answer as to peace or war from Sindia and the Rája of Berár, and informed him of the arrangements which should be made with Sindia, in the event of the war not leading to the entire reduction of his power. In addition to the objects to be pursued in Northern India, as just mentioned, these included the cession of Bharuch, then a seaport of Sindia's, and all his maritime possessions, his rights in Gújarát, and all his possessions south of the Narbadda. The last mentioned were to be divided between the Peshwa and the Nizám, some part to be exchanged with the Peshwa for his territory in Bundelkhand.

From the Rája of Berár was to be obtained the cession of Katák, either absolutely or on payment, in order to give the British the whole coast of the Bay of Bengal. This, together with the seizure of Gujarát, would place the whole of the littoral provinces in British hands, and shut the door to the much dreaded intercourse with the French.

Major-General Wellesley had full powers to treat for peace, of course with a view to the fact that both Sindia and the Bhonsla were in the Dakhan, and would probably be opposed to him in person. In the event of Sir J. Stuart taking the field in person, he was to assume the powers entrusted to General Wellesley.

General Lake was likewise invested with full political powers, and with reference to military details, the Governor-General, well un-

* *Authorities:—*

1. Governor-General to Commander-in-Chief, Bengal Papers, 28th June, 1803, p. 154.
2. Commander-in-Chief to Governor-General, (about 8th) July, MSS.
3. Governor-General's remarks, 18th July, MSS.
4. Governor-General's additional notes, 23rd July, MSS.
5. Commander-in-Chief in reply to additional notes *about* 30th July, MSS., (before 7th August, when he took the field).

derstanding the principle that every man should do his own work, explicitly stated that he purposely avoided interference in all questions as to the strength of the main army or the different constituent parts, while he promised to His Excellency the most effectual support.*

Acting upon these general instructions, the Commander-in-Chief made his plan for attacking in the first place "the French State" in the Doáb. I have already mentioned De Boigne as having formed a large disciplined force for Sindia. Count de Boigne retired to Europe in 1796, and was succeeded by M. Perron, a Frenchman who, assisted by a number of his compatriots, exercised an authority at Dehli which, though really in subordination to Siudia, appeared almost independent.

In the first instance the Governor-General had been inclined to open the campaign by attacking Ágra, and had feared that M. Perron would abandon the Doáb and, retiring across the Jamna, carry on a war of posts. Moreover he was greatly apprehensive that the Maráthás might follow their old game and enter Hindustan with a mass of marauding horsemen, and, with a view to preventing this, was somewhat in favour of an early occupation of Gwáliár.

General Lake pointed out that it would be impossible for M. Perron to abandon the Doáb, because if he did so he would lose his principal magazines, and the means of paying his army, and further that his retreat would prove his inferiority, and lead to the defection of his Sikh and other allies. Also that during the rains it was difficult, if not impossible, for Perron or the Maráthás to cross the Jamna, and further that to attack Gwáliár would compel Ambají Inglia and his brother Kandrají, who held it and other forts in that country, to take an active part against the British; while it was not impossible that if left to themselves they would remain quiet, owing to their being on ill terms with Sindia and his minister Jádu Rá,o.

Seeing the force of the Commander-in-Chief's reasoning, the Governor-General wrote on the 18th July, "I am now convinced that the primary object of the campaign ought to be the defeat of Perron's regular corps," and the Commander-in-Chief, assured of the confidence and support of Lord Wellesley, lost no time in proceeding to carry his plans into execution.

---

* Bengal Papers, 161.

To carry out the extensive programme of the Governor-General, troops were assembled, besides the army of the Commander-in-Chief at Kánhpúr, and that of Sir J. Stuart at Harihar: [1]

 a. At Allahabad under Lieut.-Colonel Powell, to operate in Bundelkhand, about 3500 men. [2]

 b. At Mirzapúr, a corps of observation under Major-General Deare, about 2000 men. [3]

 c. At Fort William under Lieut.-Col. Harcourt, for the capture of Katák, about 5,000 men and 8 guns. [4]

 d. At Baroda under Lieut.-Col. Woodington, for the seizure of Gújarát, about 4200 men. [5]

General Lake's arrangements were as follows :

The main army was assembled at Kánhpúr. It consisted of four brigades of infantry, and three of cavalry (see order of battle*), with 71 guns. It was to move under the personal command of His Excellency. All the infantry brigades had three battalions, the first and second having half a battalion more. The only European infantry regiment was the King's 76th. The first and second cavalry brigades had one European and two native regiments ; the third only one of each. The King's regiments were the 8th Light Dragoons (now Hussars) and the 27th and 29th Light Dragoons. Each battalion had two six-pounders attached to it, and each cavalry regiment two galloper guns, as they were called. They appear to have been mostly three-pounders ; besides these there were three or four pieces of artillery, (12-pounders, 6-pounders, and 5-½-inch howitzers) attached to each brigade of infantry.

The second infantry brigade, and the 6th Native Cavalry were not at Kánhpúr, however : they were cantoned at Anúpshahar on the Ganges to watch the frontier, but, as no invasion was apprehended during the rains, were to be drawn towards the army on its advance. The 8th Light Dragoons were not yet ready to march, having recently arrived from the Cape, and being busy with remounts at Kánhpúr.

General Lake marched from Kánhpúr on 7th August, and on the following day, Major-General Wellesley opened the campaign in the Dakhan by attacking Ahmadnagar ; capturing the town on that day, and obtaining possession of the fort by capitulation on 12th.

---

[1] Bengal Papers, p. 307.   [2] Bengal Papers, p. 238.   [3] Idem, p, 238.   [4] See Thorn, p. 72, Bengal Papers, p. 244.   [5] Thorn, p. 71.
* *Plate* IV.

It is not my intention to follow the campaign of General Wellesley in detail, but only to give its chief features as they acted upon the general combined plan.

General Lake crossed the frontier near the town of Koel on 29th August, and immediately attacked a large body of Maráthá Horse, which he found drawn up near the fort of Aligrah, and numbering, it was supposed, nearly 15,000 of all sorts. The fort of Aligrah is 3½ miles north of Koel, and has given its name to the present civil station (formerly a cantoument) and station of the East Indian Railway. General Lake determined to attack with his cavalry, and to turn the enemy's left. Their front was covered by a swamp, and their right supported by the fort. General Lake, as was his wont, led the attack in person, and the imposing aspect of the British cavalry was such that the enemy did not wait for the collision but abandoned the field. The moral effect of this affair seems to have been very great, though the Commander-in-Chief did not succeed in bringing on a general action.

The next thing to be done was to capture the fort, and this appeared a formidable undertaking. The fort is of a rectangular plan, and had at that time circular bastions.* The rampart was covered by a *fausse-brai* with a wide terreplein, and was surrounded by a ditch over 100 feet wide, and with 10 feet of water in it. It was armed with 99 guns of various calibres, and 180 wall-pieces, and was well supplied with ammunition.

It is situated on a perfectly open and level plain which at that time of year was, in those days, so much inundated that regular siege operations could scarcely have been carried on. The General therefore determined on a *coup de main*, a determination in which he was, no doubt, influenced by an offer from Mr. Lucan (who had just deserted from the enemy) to point out the way into the fortress.

It was decided to make an attempt at 4.30 a.m. on the 4th September, and a force consisting of 4 companies of the 76th, 1½ battalions of Native Infantry, with another battalion of N.I. in support, was told off for the duty. Lieut.-Col. the Hon. W. Monson, of the 76th Regiment was in command. To cover the attack, two batteries of four 18-pounders each were placed in position during the night.†

---

* It has since been modified ; see plan in Thorn.
† One of these batteries was at General Perron's house (which is still standing), the other at a villiage to the east of it.

The assault was delivered at the time fixed and, after a severe struggle which lasted nearly an hour, the fort was captured with a loss of 6 European and 6 Native Officers, and 43 men killed, and 180 of all ranks wounded. The entrance was forced through a winding passage, about 500 yards long, commanded for the most part by musketry, and delay was caused by the necessity of bringing up first a 6-pounder, and then a 12-pounder, to blow open one of the gates. This gate resisted the attempt, but Major McLeod of the 76th forced his way in through the wicket, and led the men on the ramparts. The enemy's loss was great, at least 2,000 killed, many of whom were drowned in attempting to escape and others, refusing to surrender, were cut up by the cavalry outside. Gen. Wellesley said, " I think that Gen. Lake's capture of Aligarh, is one of the most extraordinary feats that I have heard of in this country."*

While these events were passing before Aligarh, the British line of communications had been attacked on 2nd Sept., at Shikohábád, by a large body of Maráthá horse under M. Fleury.

The attack on 2nd was beaten off but was renewed on 4th with more success, the garrison being forced to retire under a convention. A brigade of cavalry detached from Aligarh arrived too late to do more than drive the enemy back across the Jamua.

On 7th September General Lake renewed his march, leaving a battalion of N.I. to garrison Aligarh, which now formed a valuable link in his line of communications, and a pivot for further operations. His troops seem, however, to have carried with them an enormous amount of supplies, and to have been to a great extent independent. I will revert to this subject by-and-bye.

On the 11th September the army crossed the Hindan River, and had, after a march of 78 miles, scarcely settled into camp about noon, near the village of Gejuh† (about a mile beyond the river), when the enemy appeared in force. General Lake immediately proceeded with the cavalry brigade‡ to reconnoitre. He found the enemy (16 battalions of regular infantry, 6,000 cavalry, and a large train of artillery under M. Louis Bourquen) strongly posted between two villages,§ with his flanks each covered by a swamp. The front was intrenched and garnished with artillery,.

---

* Wellington Despatches, I., 416.   † Or Ghejapúr.
‡ Only 3 Regiments present : 27th Dragoons, 2nd and 3rd Native Cavalry.
§ Probably Suddurpúr and Agahpúr.

and was concealed by grass jungle. Orders were instantly sent for the infantry and artillery to come up, and meanwhile the cavalry remained in front of the enemy, suffering considerable loss in men and horses.

In this battle General Lake did not attempt any extended manœuvring, but the details of it are interesting, as shewing the formations then used.

The army still followed the tactics of Frederick. It encamped in order of battle, and preserved the same general formation on the march. *Plate* IV. shows "the order of *battle, march* and *encampment* of the army*," and, allowing for detachments, also represents the actual order of battle on 11th September, except that the post of honour on the right was given to the King's 76th Regt.

The line fell-in in front of the camp (which was left standing), and each battalion moved to the front in column of grand divisions, (which were much the same as what we now call double companies). In this order, the force, consisting of eight battalions only, advanced about two miles until it came up with the cavalry. The General (who in the mean time had had his horse shot under him) determined to retire the cavalry with a view to drawing the enemy from his strong intrenched position.

When, therefore, the infantry were near enough he ordered the cavalry to retire, which it did in perfect order until the infantry line was reached. It then opened out from the centre and cleared the front of the infantry. The feigned retreat had produced the desired effect. The enemy advancing from his position, with his artillery, amidst loud shouts and cries, was met by the British infantry formed on one line. The cavalry formed up in second line only about 40 yards in rear of the right wing and detached a party to the right with two " galloper " guns, to hold in check a large body of Sikh cavalry which was massed on the enemy's left. The British left was covered by the 1-2nd Native Infantry with four guns. The whole force then moved on (the Commander-in-Chief at the head of the 76th Regiment) under a heavy fire of artillery, the infantry with shouldered arms until their line was within a hundred paces of the enemy. Then the infantry fired a volley and charged with the bayonet, and with such impetuosity that the enemy gave way and fled. The line was then halted and broken into columns of companies, the cavalry with its guns passed through the intervals and took up the pursuit to the front and right, and con-

68

tinued it as far as the passage over the Jamna. General Lake with the infantry pursued the enemy towards the left into the ravines near the river, capturing all their artillery and stores.

The losses in this battle were considerable, amounting to 461 killed and wounded, or 10 per cent. of the force engaged. Of this the 76th alone lost 137. The enemy's loss was estimated at not less than 3,000. His army was dispersed. The number of guns taken was 68.

At the present time it would be probably objected to General Lake's arrangements that he ought not to have made a frontal attack. But there seems to have been good reasons against the turning movement which has been so often decisive in actions against Asiatics. In the first place, the force present was very small, only 4,800 men. Then the camp with all its encumbrances had been left standing, and the enemy's flanks were well secured. Any turning movement would therefore have had to make a considerable circuit, and could not have escaped the notice of the enemy. The hostile army was 19,000 strong, and the Commander-in-Chief could not have divided his force without exposing the part left to perform the duty of "retaining" the enemy to almost certain destruction, which would have involved also the loss of his camp. The actual course adopted shows that the troops must have been very well trained, and of high morale, and that the General must have possessed their confidence in a very complete degree. The scouting duties seem however to have been imperfectly performed by the cavalry, as we are told that the grand guard and piquets had to turn out on the unexpected appearance of the enemy, and this although intelligence had been received of his having left Dehli to attack the British.

After the battle the camp was moved 3 miles nearer to Dehli, and formed east of the village of Chalera.* On the 12th, the army marched to Patparganj, and on the 14th crossed the Jamna and entered Dehli. On the same day M. Louis Bourquin† and four other French officers surrendered to General Lake.

The power of the French State, as it had been called by the Governor General, and now completely broken, its army beaten and dispersed and its chief officers in British hands. The Emperor, Sháh Álbm gladly accepted British protection, and a British resident was to be appointed.

---

* See Note on position of the battle.   † Variously spelt, Bourquin, Bourquen, Bourquein, Bourquien.

General Lake remained 10 days at Dehli, after which he moved on Ágra. Before proceeding with the description of the campaign it may be well to glance at the manner in which an Indian army marched in those days. Without some knowledge of that sort it is impossible to appreciate the difficulties which a commander had to contend with.

Major Thorn, in his memoir, gives a vivid sketch of the camp. He says that no regular supplies could be reckoned on, especially when operating against the Maráthás, who were in the habit of devastating the country as they retired. All necessaries had to be supplied before hand, or obtained from followers whose desire of gain attached them to the army.

The chief purveyors of grain were the Birinjáris,* a peculiar class of Hindús. The army was accompanied by a number of these people, who had from eighty to a hundred thousand bullocks laden with grain. The men were armed with matchlocks, spears, scimatars, and shields, and were in the habit, when their stock was exhausted, of setting out to procure fresh supplies either by purchase or by plunder.

Of followers, Major Thorn states, there would be about ten to every fighting man. This, since General Lake's force numbered when all united about 10,000 men, gives a hundred thousand followers. Of elephants there were several hundreds, and some thousands of camels. Tent lascars were present in large numbers. Palanquins and doolies for the sick and wounded required a great number of bearers. Horses, as is still the case, required most of them two attendants each, a saís (or groom) and a grass cutter to collect forage. The officers in those days received no rations, and each had to provide his own live and dead stock, including goats to supply them with milk for their tea.

Their servants are reckoned at 10 for a subaltern, 20 for a captain and 30 for a field officer. Besides what may be termed the legitimate followers, there were a multitude of women and other adventurers.

The army encamped in the same order in which it marched, *Plate* IV., the infantry and cavalry forming the outside, and thus protecting all within the enclosure. As soon as the camp was formed long streets of shops might be seen springing up. Here

---

Birinjárí, a grain merchant.

were to be found shroffs or money-changers, confectioners, European merchants selling wines, liquors, or groceries ; traders in cloths, muslins and shawls ; gold and silver smiths were there, as well as quacks, jugglers, and dancing girls.

"The march had the appearance of a moving citadel in the form of an oblong, the ramparts defended by glittering swords and bayonets." On one side marched the infantry on the other the cavalry, in parallel lines preserving as nearly as possible their encamping distance. The front was covered by the advanced guard, composed of all the picquets coming on duty, the rear by all the piquets coming off duty forming a rear guard. The parks and artillery moved inside and along the road and next to the infantry, which moved at a short distance from it. The remainder of the space was occupied by the baggage cattle and followers of the camp.

Notwithstanding the immense size of this moving mass, nothing, says Major Thorn, could exceed the regularity of the troops in preserving their distances. The Commander-in-Chief was careful to impress on officers and men the necessity of preventing any undue lengthening out of the line of march, and that they were on no account to be provoked to leave their ranks and thus give the numerous cavalry of the Márathás, which would hover round, an opening to break into the square.

When the difficulties of conducting such a march as this are considered, we shall be ready to give due credit to a general who, in spite of them, could move his army 15, 16, and 18 miles in the day.

It is obvious that such a method of marching could be adopted only in a very open country, such as the great Gangetic plain, and in a country which was not obstructed by cultivation ; and doubtless in 1803 the Doáb was far less cultivated than it has now become under the settled government it has so long enjoyed.

Such a "moving citadel" was impossible in the Dakhan, and a different formation had to be adopted by Major-General Wellesley. It is thus described in the journal of Sir Jasper Nicolls : "Marched by the left in the following order which is the usual one. A body of Maisúr Horse, about four hundred, leads the column of march ; this, at some distance, is followed by the cavalry ; the new piquets of infantry march in their rear, then the line of infantry, followed by the park, store, and provision carts ; the guns of the allies close the line of carriages, the ammunition and park bullocks follow them, and the rear guard, consisting of the old piquets ; a squadron of cavalry, which moves on the reverse flank, and another body of 400 Mysoreans close the line. Detachments of pioneers attend the leading divisions of the cavalry, advanced guard, the line, and the park. Guides are sent every morning before the assembly beating, to the heads of the cavalry advanced and rear guard. The baggage is ordered to be kept on the reverse flank entirely, and in a great measure it is so. The horsemen, etc., of the allies march on either flank, as is most agreeable to their leaders. The Brigadier of Cavalry is ordered to halt wherever he may exceed the distance of three quarters of a mile in front of the infantry; the long roll for a halt is beat by any corps which may by any accident be so long stopped as to occasion a break of one hundred yards; this is to be repeated from front to rear by every corps; and when ready to move again, the taps are passed, as before, along the line, which proceeds."*

Whilst the Commander-in-Chief with the Bengal Army is enjoying a few days of hardly earned repose at Dehli, let us glance at the proceedings of the subsidiary forces, and of the Madras force under Major-General Wellesley. Into the details of those operations I do not propose to enter.

We left General Wellesley on 15th June, at Ágar, threatening Sindia's fortress of Ahmadnagar. Colonel Collins† was carrying on negotiations with Sindia who was in camp at Chikli near Burhánpúr on the Taptí, where he was joined by the Rája of Berár on the 4th June. The negociations led to no result. On the 8th August, Major-General Wellesley took the town of Ahmadnagar, and the capitulation of the fort followed on the 12th. Whilst engaged in establishing authority in the district he detached Colonel Stevenson, with the Nizám's subsidiary force and native troops, towards Aurangábád. That place was occupied on 29th August. On 24th August, Sindia and the Rája entered the territories of the Nizám by the Ajanta Ghát (one of the openings in the Northern Ghás) with a view to marching on Haidarábád, but were compelled by the manœuvres of the Major-General to withdraw. At the Ajanta Ghát they were joined by a detachment of 16 battalions of regular infantry, and a large train of artillery, under M.M. Pohlman and Dupont, and then proceeded to take up a position

---

* Journal of Sir Jasper Nicolls, K.C.B., quoted in Wellington Despatches, I., 435,
† Resident with the Peshwa.

72

between Bokerdun and Jaffirábád. On 21st Sept., Major-General
Wellesley was joined by Colonel Stevenson's force at Budnapúr,
and he decided to attack the enemy on the morning of the 24th.
On the 22nd* the force was again divided, and Colonel Stevenson
marched by a western, the Major-General by an eastern, road through
the hills.

On the 23rd, Major-General Wellesley, after marching 14 miles
to Naulnair, learned that the enemy were only 6 miles off (instead
of 15 or 16, as his information had led him to believe) and near the
village of Assaye. He determined to attack without waiting for the
other division. The force at his disposal consisted of two battalions
of King's Troops (the 74th and 78th Foot) and parts of 6 battalions
of Native infantry, the 19th Light Dragoons, and 3 Regiments of
Native Cavalry. It numbered in all about 8,000 men and only 17
guns, with some Maisúr cavalry and cavalry of the Peshwa in
addition. On the other side were, besides upwards of 10,000 regular
troops from Dehli, a large mass of Maráthá cavalry and infantry,
belonging both to Sindia and the Rája of Berár. The whole numbered 50,000 men, strongly posted and having upwards of 100 guns.

In the battle which ensued the British, in spite of severe loss,†
were successful. The army of the confederate Rájas was driven off,
a large number killed and wounded, and of their artillery 98 guns
were taken. The British per centage of loss was nearly 20.

This occurred on the day before General Lake marched from
Dehli.

In Gujarát, Lieut.-Colonel Woodington marched on 21st August
from Baroda with about 1,000 men.‡ On the 29th (the same day
on which General Lake crossed the frontier near Koel) he took
Bharuch, at the mouth of the Narbadda, by storm, with
trifling loss. On the 17th September the almost inaccessible fort
of Powangarh (20 miles north-west of Baroda) capitulated to Col.
Woodington, after a breach had been formed in the walls. These
successes made the British masters of the whole of Gújarát.

A little later, Katák and Bundelkhand were occupied. The main
force intended to occupy Katák§ was assembled at Ganjam, and

---

* Wellington Despatches, I., 400. Atlas of India, Sheets 38 and 55.
† 1566 killed and wounded, or nearly 20 per cent. of force engaged. See Returns Bengal
Papers, 281. Thorn, p. 280.
‡ The King's 86th contributed 500 men. See Bengal Papers, p. 274.
§ Thorn, ch. vii., 253-265.

smaller detachments were employed, one of them to seize Bálásúr, and another to move from Jálásúr to unite with this. Colonel Harcourt, commanding the main force, occupied Jagannath on 18th September. On the 14th October he took the Fort of Bárabatti, near the town of Katák, and this success was followed by the submission of the whole province. The resistance met with had not been serious, and the difficulties of the undertaking were such as were caused by the nature of the country, which is the delta of the Máhánadi, rather than by the numbers or valour of the enemy. After completing the settlement the Katák force prepared to enter the state of Berár, but the conclusion of peace rendered this movement unnecessary.

The operations in Bundelkhand were not less successful. By the treaty of Bassain, the Peshwa made over this province to the British in lieu of payment of subsidies. The possession of Bundelkhand was of great value to the Company as it lay along the flank of territories ceded by Oudh in 1801, and whilst it remained in Maráthá hands they were exposed to irruptions.

Lieut.-Colonel Powell marched from Allahábád on 6th September. A chief named Shamshír Bahádhar resisted the transfer of the province, but was easily defeated by Col. Powell, on 10th October, west of the Ken River near Kapsah. Shamshír Bahádhar then offered to submit, but he protracted negociations for so long that Colonel Powell at last resumed operations, and, on 4th December, captured Kálpí.

We now revert to the proceedings of the Commander-in-Chief. Arrived at Dehli on 14th, he was received on 16th September in darbar by the Emperor Sháh Álam. The emperor was old and blind (his eyes having been put out by the infamous Gholám Kádir in 1788), and so low had the once powerful Moghals fallen that their representative, though still inhabiting his magnificent palace, was found reduced to poverty, and seated under a tattered canopy. This was not the first time that Sháh Álam had been in the power of the English. He had in his earlier days resided at Allahábád under British protection, but had quitted it in 1771 to take up his residence in the imperial city. At Dehli he had undergone many misfortunes during the subsequent thirty years, being sometimes in the

power of the Maráthás, and sometimes in that of rebellious subjects
like Gholám Kádir. He lived three years after the time of which
we are now speaking, dying in December, 1806. His son and successor, Akbar, was father of Muhammad Bahádur Sháh.*

General Lake marched on 24th September for Ágra, leaving
Lieut.-Colonel Ochterlony at Dehli as Resident, supported by 1½
battalions of N.I., and some irregular troops. The character of the
country traversed in this march differs considerably from that of
the Doáb, or country between the Ganges and Jamna, through which
he had marched on Dehli. In my first lecture, I mentioned the
Indo-Gangetic plain, of which the Doáb is a part. In the Doáb the
plain appears interminable. Except where some village of very
ancient date has made for itself a trifling mound out of the accumulated mud bricks of ages (brought from the plain below), there is
nothing to break the universal flat which extends as far as the eye can
reach. But at Dehli we are in sight of hills. The famous ridge
held by the British in 1854, is the extremity of the Aravali Hills,
which I described in my first lecture as running south-west
and north-east through Rájputána. In marching from Dehli
to Ágra on the left bank of the Jamna the outlying spurs of these
hills are always within sight, and afford a most agreeable variety
in the views. The nature of this country, so close on the flank
of his march, must have led to additional precautions on the part
of the general, and must certainly, in some places, have rendered
absolutely necessary a departure from the order of march which
I have described.

Passing, on the 2nd October, within 20 miles of Díg, which was
to become famous in the campaign against Holkar, the army arrived
before Ágra without opposition on the 4th, and encamped near the
village of Sháhganj.†

Ágra is still partially a walled city, and in 1803 the walls were,
no doubt, intact. The fort of Akbar, situated on the banks of the
Jamna, commands the town. It has lofty walls and flanking
towers, with a deep ditch and a *fausse brai*. It lies to the south-
west of the city, and the city walls abutted on the fort on two sides,
where the Rájputána Railway Station now stands. To the south
and south-west of the fort are a number of ravines running to the

---

* The 17th and last of the Moghal Emperors, who died at Rangoon, 7th November, 1862.
† Apparently on the site of present cantonments.

Jamna. About 250 yards from the fort, and to the north-west of it, and therefore inside the city, stands the Jamma Masjid, or Great Mosque, on an elevated site.

When General Lake arrived he found the city and the fort occupied by the enemy, and a camp of regular troops with a large number of guns on the glacis. This movable force rendered it impossible for the Commander-in-Chief to open the siege of the fort, and therefore, after investing the place as far as possible with his cavalry on the 7th, he decided to make an attack on the 10th October upon the town and the force outside. For this purpose Brigadier-General Clarke, with the 2nd Brigade, was directed to attack the town, whilst three Native Infantry battalions, under Lieut.-Colonel McCulloch of the 14th Native Infantry, were sent to occupy the ravines. This attack was subsequently supported by another battalion of Native Infantry (the 2-2nd Native Infantry). Both attacks succeeded. The city was, after a sharp struggle, cleared of the enemy and the ravines were occupied. The enemy were pursued upon the glacis, where 26 fine brass field-guns were captured, in spite of a fire of musketry and grape from the fort. The losses were 229 of all ranks killed and wounded; probably about 5 per cent. of the force engaged.

On the 12th, the remainder of the enemy's troops outside the fort agreed to desert, and on 13th (to the number of 2500) marched into the British camp. The ground being thus cleared, the Commander-in-Chief lost no time in making approaches through the ravines, and erected a breaching battery of eight 18-pounders, and four howitzers, 350 yards from the fort.* On the morning of 17th October, fire was opened on the south-western bastion, and a breach would soon have been made had not the garrison capitulated the same night. It numbered nearly 5,000 men. In the fort were found 164 guns of different natures, a large quantity of ammunition, and over a quarter of a million of money. One of the guns was a very remarkable piece. It was almost cylindrical in shape,† 14ft. 2ins. long, with a calibre of 23 inches. The bore was 8ft. 8ins. in length, and had a powder chamber 4ft. 4ins. long, and only 10 inches in

---

* In throwing up this battery, volunteers from 8th, 27th, and 29th Dragoons were employed. There were also an enfilading battery of four 12-pounders on the left, and a two-gun battery (12-pounder) at the bank of the river to the right.

† Stubbs, I., p. 219 and 243; Thorn, 188.

diameter. The gun was calculated to weigh 54 tons, and throw an iron shot of 1500 lbs. A marble shot (which it was probably intended to use) would weigh 567 lbs. only.

The capture of Ágra secured the conquest of the territory in the Doáb. The British now held Aligarh, Dehli, Mathra, and with Ágra in their hands, not only were their communications with Dehli protected, but also an important base was gained for further operations against Central India. All this had been accomplished in 50 days*.

During the operations against Ágra, a considerable force of the enemy (including 15 regular battalions which had been sent by Sindia from the Dakhan, and two which had escaped from Dehli) had been encamped at a distance of about 30 miles from the place to the westward, somewhere near Bhartpúr. Although this force had not made any attempt to disturb the siege operations, yet, as it possessed a formidable artillery, and was believed to be threatening Dehli, the Commander-in-Chief determined to break it up. Having determined on this, General Lake acted with his usual vigour. He left Ágra on 27th October. His infantry had been reduced by detachments left at Aligarh, Dehli, Mathra, and Ágra to 8† battalions, but the three cavalry brigades were still complete. On the 27th he marched 16 miles to Karauli kí Sarai.‡ There he was detained by a very heavy fall of rain, very unusual at that season, on the 29th. On the 30th, he marched 12 miles, passing Fatehpúr Síkrí. During this day a cannonade was heard, which proved to be the bombardment of Khatúmbar by the Maráthás. On the 30th, the Commander-in-Chief left his baggage and heavy guns under the protection of two battalions of Native Infantry,§ and marched 16 miles, to Sinfini. Next day, after a march of 20 miles to Museri near Khatúmbar, the Commander-in-Chief found himself close to the camping ground quitted that morning by the enemy. This information determined General Lake to make an effort to overtake them the same night, and accordingly he marched with the whole of his cavalry at 11 p.m., having given orders that the infantry should march at 3 a.m. After a night march of 23 miles, he found

---

* Crossed frontier at Koel, 29th August. Fall of Ágra, 17th October.

† 2-12th, 1-15th, 2-15th, 2-16th, N.I.; H.M's. 76th; 2-8th, 2-9th, and 1-12th N.I.

‡ Thorn, 212; Bengal Papers, 251. § 1-2nd, 2-2nd, or 1-14th, of 4th Brigade; see Thorn, 212.

himself, at sunrise (5 a.m.), on the 1st November, in presence of the enemy. They numbered about 14,000 men and 72 guns.

The battle field of Laswári lies on the north bank of the Ruperat, Badi or Báráki, Nullah, which comes from the hills south and west of the town of Alwar, and flows eastward. The banks of the Nullah are very steep and difficult of access. On the north bank, and close to it, is the village of Naswári,* and about 2,000 yards west by north the village of Málpúr.† Just above the village of Laswári is a dam across the Nullah from which a canal is carried to Govindgarh, a small town to the eastward. When General Lake arrived near the passage of the Nullah, he saw the enemy in confusion about Málpúr, and judged that they were retreating. He therefore decided to attack immediately with the cavalry alone. But the enemy was not really retreating. He had cut the bank of the canal and flooded the road, and his movements were covered by the dust raised by his cavalry, so that by the time the British force had overcome the difficulties of the crossing, he had had time to complete his formation. His position was then seen to be a formidable one. Its right rested on Laswári and the Nullah, and left on Málpúr, whilst the front was concealed by high grass, and covered by a powerful artillery. Nevertheless the attack was delivered. The 1st Brigade (8th Light Dragoons, 1st and 3rd Native Cavalry) passed along the whole front of the position, and attacked Málpúr, where it penetrated the enemy's line, and captured some guns which, however it had no means of carrying away. On the enemy's right, the 3rd Brigade (29th Dragoons, and 4th N.C.) charged three times through their line, but with no more lasting effect than the first. Then the Commander-in-Chief, finding nothing could be effected, withdrew the cavalry from the attack, and formed them up between Sáhajpúr and Singráka, to await the arrival of the infantry.

He had not very long to wait. The infantry marched at 3 a.m. It had to cover 24 miles under a sun which, on 1st November, is still hot, but about 11 o'clock it appeared upon the field. General Lake gave the men a short time for repose and refreshment, during which the enemy proposed on terms to surrender their artillery. Nothing came of this negociation, however, and after the cavalry attack had ceased, the enemy had taken advantage of the pause to

---

* Or Laswári in the despatch.   † General Lake called this village Laswári, and hence the name by which the battle is known. L and N are interchangeable; Laswári or Naswárí.

change his ground. His position now faced east, with the village of Málpúr behind the left and left centre, and the right extending towards the Nullah (DDD in *Plate* VII.), but not reaching it by a considerable distance (probably 3 or 4 hundred yards). A second line was formed, parallel to the first and in rear of the village.

The Commander-in-Chief's plan was to force his way between the enemy's right and the Nullah, and then assault the village of Málpúr. For this purpose, the right wing of the infantry,* 76th Regt., 2-12th N.1., 1-15th and 2-15th and part of 16th N.I. was formed in column under Major-General Ware. It was followed by the left wing,† also in column, under Maj.-Gen. the Hon. Fredk. St. John. Of the cavalry, the 3rd brigade (29th Light Dragoons and 4th N.C.) was to support the infantry; the 2nd Brigade was sent to threaten the enemy's left and cut off his retreat, whilst the 1st Brigade formed the only reserve of the army. The "galloper" guns belonging to the cavalry, with as many other field-pieces as could be brought up, were formed into four batteries for the occasion. Three of these were distributed along the front, and the other moved with the infantry to take up an enfilading position near the Nullah. (See *Plate* VII.)

The leading column, which had to march nearly a mile to gain the enemy's flank, escaped notice at first in the high grass and inequalities of the ground near the Nullah, while the 29th Light Dragoons appear to have marched in the hollow below the bank. As soon as the enemy perceived the column he opened a heavy fire of artillery on it, and at the same time threw back his right, pivotting on the village of Málpúr, to frustrate the attack. The Commander-in-Chief, who, as usual, was in the thickest of the fight, thereupon determined not to await the deployment of the whole column, but as soon as the 76th had formed led it, with as many of the Native Infantry as had closed to the front, direct to the attack. The artillery came into action at the intended point, and the 29th Light Dragoons were in the low ground to the left of the head of the column, and unfortunately so placed that the enemy's shot which went over the artillery fell into their ranks.

As soon as the 76th (" this handful of heroes," as the General calls them in his despatch)‡ came within canister range of the enemy,

---

* Thorn, p. 220.   † 2-8th, 2-9th and 1-12th.   ‡ Despatch is in Bengal Papers, p. 288.

a terrible fire was opened upon the regiment, which checked its advance. At the same moment, a body of the enemy's horse attempted to charge, but was repulsed by the regiment. It however rallied, and maintained so threatening an attitude that the 29th Dragoons were ordered to charge it. The Dragoons had to come out by files from the ravine, and formed up on the left of the 76th, amidst cheers from their ranks. They immediately charged, and passed through both lines of the enemy in a manner which earned for them the warmest acknowledgments of the General. He followed with his infantry, the native battalions of the leading column having now formed up, and led them to the attack of the enemy's second line. An obstinate struggle ensued, Major-General Ware was killed, his head being carried off by a round shot, and the enemy continued to resist until all his guns had been captured. Even then their left wing attempted to retreat in good order, but the 27th Light Dragoons and 6th Native Cavalry, under Lieut.-Col. Vandeleur, broke their column, and after killing many, forced the rest to surrender. By four o'clock the battle was over, and the enemy's force had been, for practical purposes, annihilated. The 17 regular battalions had been destroyed. 2,000 prisoners were taken. 7,000 men are said to have remained on the field. The whole of the artillery, 72 pieces; the camp equipage, stores, elephants, camels, 1600 bullocks, and a great many colours, became the prize of the victors. The British loss was 172 killed, and 652 wounded, total 822 out of a force of about 8,000 men; or upwards of 10 per cent.

By this victory the work of the Commander-in-Chief's army was completed; Sindia's trained and organised force being entirely destroyed, and the territories assigned to him by the Emperor conquered.

The army halted at Laswári until 8th November, when it resumed its march, and moved leisurely to Pahesar, 13 miles west of Bhartpúr, and there halted from 14th to 26th November. Whilst there, treaties were concluded with the Rája of Mácheri or Alwar, with the Rájas of Jaipúr and Johdpúr, and with the Begum Sumrú. The Rája of Bhartpúr, from whom the British arms were destined in the following year to receive so severe a check, had already concluded a treaty in September, while the army was on the march from Dehli to Ágra.

On 27th November, a move was made to Halena on the Bánganga, and after some marching and countermarching along the Bánganga (or Utangan) River, the reasons for which are not now apparent, the army arrived at Biána on the Gumbhír. This choice of a winter camp was due to the necessity for watching Holkar.

Whilst there the Commander-in-Chief became aware that Sindia and the Rája of Berár had signed peace in the Dakhan; but before proceeding to describe briefly the operations of Major-General Wellesley, which combined with General Lake's successes to produce that result, it will be well to complete our review of the subsidiary operations in Northern India.

Nothing further of any importance occurred in Katák, the complete occupation of which province has already been described. But in Bundelkhand we left Col. Powell at Kálpí, which he had just captured (4th Dec.). Shortly after that, Shamshír Bahádhar submitted, and his submission was soon followed by overtures from the Subadhár of Jhánsí (who was ancestor of the Rani who fell gallantly fighting against us at Gwáliár* in June '58). Still more important was the defection from Sindia of Ambaji Rá,o Inglia, leading as it did to the capture of Gwáliár. Ambaji Inglia exercised the authority of Sindia over a considerable territory, which included Gwáliár and Gohad. He agreed to deliver the fortress of Gwáliár and territory north of it to the British,† and, accordingly, Lieut.-Col. White was detached by Gen. Lake, on the 21st December, with a force of Native Infantry to occupy the place. But when the colonel arrived, the Killadár (or Governor) refused to surrender. The Commander-in-Chief then reinforced Lieut.-Col. White, bringing his strength up to‡ about four-and-a-half battalions of Native Infantry, and the flank companies of the 76th Regt., together with a company of artillery, and some heavy guns.

The fortress of Gwáliár (I have here a very beautiful plan made by Captain C. Strahan in 1876) is a place of great natural strength. A narrow rock, $1\frac{3}{4}$ miles long and nowhere more than 600 yards wide, rises abruptly above the plain to a height of over 300 feet. The top is nearly level and the sides are in many places formed in natural precipices towards the top, with a long slope below. These natural escarpments have been improved, so that a great part is absolutely

---

* Malleson, History of Indian Mutiny, I., 181..

† In this Ambají was acting a treacherous part, as he was a servant of Sindia.

‡ 1/14 N.I., 2/9 N.I., 2/11 N.I., 2/18 N.I. Det. of 16 N.I. Flank Companies 76th Regt.

inaccessible. A rough wall of dry stone-work follows the contour of the hill, which has a total perimeter of nearly five miles. On the north-west is a curious valley which runs up into the hill, and contains an ample supply of water in wells. Inside the fort are several Jain temples, and on the eastern face a very curious old Hindu palace, which served the Moghal emperors as a state prison. All round the rock are caves in which are figures, many of them of a gigantic size, cut out of the solid rock. The fortress first fell into our hands in 1779, when it was surprised in a very gallant manner by Major Popham, who escaladed the western face during the night.

Colonel White opened a regular attack. He established batteries and breached the walls, close to the place which Popham escaladed, notwithstanding their great elevation above the level of the batteries, and was about to storm on the 4th February, 1804, when the garrison surrendered.*

The possession of this fortress was of great importance, not only on account of its actual strength and its position covering Ágra, but also on account of the reputation for impregnability which it had with the natives.

The long line of frontier which had before been so much exposed (see Plate II.) was now secured. . With Gwáliár and Bundelkhand occupied by British troops, the passes through Rewa held by Major-General Deare's force (whose Head Quarters were at Chunár), the line from the Son River to Pachít by Lieut.-Colonel Broughton, and from Pachít to the sea by Colonel Fenwick (who had his Head Quarters at Midnapúr), there was no longer any ground to fear an irruption of the Maráthás.

Indeed Colonel Broughton was able to take the offensive. In December he marched into Berár and on the 3rd January, 1804, obtained possession of Sambhalpúr on the Mahánadí.

We now revert to the Dakhan, where we left General Wellesley on the field of Assaye. Though successful in that battle he was not able to follow it up by a vigourous pursuit because his cavalry† had been used in the action. Consequently the army of the confederate Rájas, though beaten and driven off the field, soon recovered

---

* A copy of the original survey of 1779 is in the Qr.-Mr. General's office at Gwáliár. The site of Popham's escalade and of White's breach are marked on Captain Strahan's plan.

† Wellington Despatches, 445,

consistency enough to be again formidable, although it had abandoned a great many guns in its flight.

During the months of October and November, some very extraordinary marches were made by General Wellesley,* but unfortunately he does not give the names of the places at which he encamped, most of his letters and despatches are dated merely "Camp" and day of the month, and therefore it is not possible to lay down his route on the map. Moreover he formed no exception to the general rule that Englishmen show a supreme contempt for the spelling of native names; and consequently only a part of the few names given can be identified.

[It may not be out of place to give you a practical hint as to names in India. It is this, *never put a name into a man's mouth.* Politeness, sometimes laziness, inattention or inability to understand your pronunciation, all are in favour of his acquiescing. The only safe way is to get the word spelt for you by some head-man of the village, and to transliterate it carefully. It can then always be identified with certainty.]

That these marches were extraordinary there can be no doubt. General Wellesley, who never exaggerated, writes on 26th October to Major Shawe as follows :—

"Since the battle of Assaye, I have been like a man who fights with one hand, and defends himself with the other. With Colonel Stevenson's Corps I have acted offensively, and have taken Asserghur; and with my own, I have covered his operations, and defended the territories of the Nizám and the Peshwa. In doing this, I have made some terrible marches'.'† Again he writes in a private letter, to his brother Henry Wellesley, on 24th January, 1804.

"Marches, such as I have made in this war, were never known or thought of before. In the last 8 days of the month of October, I marched above 120 miles and passed through two gháts with heavy guns; and in the few days previous to the battle of Argaum I never moved less than between 17 and 20 miles, and I marched 26 miles on the day on which it was fought."‡

The object of these long and continued marches was to keep Sindia and the Rája of Berár from entering the dominions of the Nizám, or advancing on the Peshwa's capital of Púna. General

---

* Wellington Despatches, I., 408 and 410.   † Wellington Despatches, I., 473.
‡ Wellington Despatches, II., 75., or Owen 338.

Wellesley was not able to move after the battle of Assaye until 8th October, because he could not provide for the security of his wounded. Having then placed them in the Fort of Ajanta, he moved southward to anticipate the confederates who had gone west along the Taptí, and seemed to aim at Púna through the Kásabári Ghát or pass. At the same time he sent Colonel Stevenson with his division and some siege guns to Burhánpúr. He gives as his reasons why this detachment could be safely made, that two out of the three campos (or regular brigades) opposed to him at Assaye had been destroyed.* Colonel Stevenson occupied Burhánpúr on 16th October, and on 21st opened his batteries against Assírgarh which surrendered. Meanwhile Major-General Wellesley had returned northwards as far as Fardapúr, but on the 25th October he again moved southwards to "turn" the Rája of Berár, who had left Sindia on the Taptí, and gone south to plunder.†

Having succeeded in this the Major-General again moved northward, and on 11th November, while in camp at Jaum, received an emissary from Sindia, with propositions for peace. At that time Sindia had only lately heard of the capture of Dehli by the Commander-in-Chief.‡

On the 23rd the negociations were formulated into an agreement for an armistice, one of the conditions of which was that Sindia should withdraw his army to a point 40 miles east of Ellichpúr.

Meanwhile Colonel Stevenson had been preparing for the siege of Gáwilgarh, a strong place belonging to the Rája of Berár, and on the 24th November the Major-General descended the Gháts by the Rajúra pass§ to co-operate with him.|| On the 29th the whole force concentrated at Pathalda, in the valley of the Taptí, and found the Rája of Berár in force at Argaum. Sindia had not fulfilled the conditions of the armistice by withdrawing eastward, and a large force of his cavalry was with the Rája of Berár.

The British troops had made a long and fatiguing march to their camping ground at Pathalda, but nevertheless the General, finding the enemy in sight at a distance of about six miles, determined to attack. He, therefore, marched in the afternoon in one column, the cavalry leading, and then formed to the right the infantry in front line, the cavalry in rear and supporting the right. In this

---

* Wellington Despatches, 432 and 434.   † Wellington Despatches, 475.   ‡ Wellington Despatches, I., 497.   § Where is this? || Questionable strategy; see Wellington Despatches, I., 533—" It is a curious circumstance," &c., also II., 74.

order the enemy's line, which extended for five miles, was attacked and put to flight, with a loss of 46 killed and 293 wounded. Sixty-eight pieces of artillery, with all the enemy's ammunition, were taken; and the cavalry continued the pursuit by moonlight. In this action success was endangered by the panic of three Native Infantry battalions, which had behaved well at Assai, but fortunately the General himself happened to be close at hand and restored the fight.

General Wellesley's next operation was the siege of Gáwilgarh, for which Colonel Stevenson had been some time equipping his corps at Assírgarh. On 6th December he was at Ellichpúr, and, after arranging there for the comfort of the men wounded at Argaum, he marched on the 7th.

The fort stands just within the southern skirt of the hills which divide the Púrna from the upper Taptí, 14 miles north-west of Ellichpúr, and at an elevation of 3,600 feet above the sea.

It has three approaches, one of which, to the south, is long and steep and only for foot people; one to the north-west passes round the western side of the fort, and is exposed to its fire; whilst only the third, on the north, is suitable for a siege attack, the ground on that side being level with the fort.

To reach this last, a circuit of 30 miles had to be made from Ellichpúr, through the hills, over a country devoid of roads except such as the troops could make for themselves. The duty of opening siege works was assigned to Colonel Stevenson's division, whilst the General covered the siege to the south, his camp being at Deogáon. When once the natural difficulties had been overcome the garrison speedily gave way. Colonel Stevenson opened his batteries on the 12th December, and on the 14th the fort was stormed with little loss.

The road to the capital of Berár, which is just 100 miles east of Ellichpur, now lay open to General Wellesley. The Rája saw the necessity of submission. He opened, with General Wellesley, negociations for peace on the 16th December, and a treaty was concluded on the following day. He ceded to the British all his territory west of the river Warda, and south of Narnalla and Gáwilgarh. He also ceded the province of Katák and district of Bálásúr, and undertook to have no Frenchmen in his service, or subjects of any other power hostile to the British Government.

At the same time General Wellesley gave notice to Sindia that the suspension of hostilities would be terminated on the 27th December, if he did not make peace at once. The result was that Sindia followed the example of the Bhonsla, and a treaty of peace was signed at Surji Anjangáon (a village 15 miles west by south of Ellichpúr), on 30th December, 1803.

By this treaty, Sindia ceded to the Company all his territory in in the Doáb, including Dehli and Ágra, and the fort of Aligarh, as well as all other territory north of Jodhpúr and Gohad, except some family estates; the fort and territory of Bharuch; the fort and territory of Ahmadnagar; and all his territory south of the Ajanti hills about Jaulnapúr and Gundapúr. He made engagements as to the employment of Frenchmen or other foreigners similar to those exacted from the Bhonsla. Both chiefs abandoned *all claims* on the territories of the Company and the Nizám, thus putting an end to chauth. Out of the ceded territories the country westward of the Warda river, and south of the hills between Púrna and Tapti, was given to the Súbadár of the Dakhan. So was the country about Aurangábád, between the Ajanti Hills and the upper Godávarí. Ahmadnagar and its territory was given to the Peshwa.

Thus the campaign against the allied Rájas really ended with the year 1803, though of course in those days the news of the treaties concluded in the valley of the Púrna could not have reached the head quarters of the Bengal army at Biána until the middle of January at the earliest. Still, with the exception of the operations of Colonel White at Gwáliár, no actual hostilities were carried on after the conclusion of peace in the Dakhan.

One of the most admirable features of this campaign is the skill and forethought with which operations covering so large an extent of country were, in those days when communications were so inferior to what they now are, combined into an almost simultaneous attack on all sides upon the confederate chiefs. It has been objected, especially by foreign critics,* that the plan of campaign directed against an enemy in a central position, would have brought ruin upon the British if they had had to deal with chiefs of experience. But abstract criticism, not based on the actual facts of each case, is of little value. Not to mention the difficulty which Sindia and the Bhonsla would have had in massing all their heterogeneous troops, and moving them rapidly over the enormous

---

* Brialmont quoting M. Petit de Baroncourt. Gleig's Brialmont, I., 97.

distances which would have had to be covered; if, for instance, their plan had been to overwhelm General Lake in the Doab, while "retaining" General Wellesley's force in the Dakhan; the Governor-General could safely reckon that the Bhonsla would not consent to leave his territories in the Dakhan exposed to attack, in order to join in any strategical movement in the Doáb.

The chronological table which I have prepared, shows the sequence of events, and the admirable way in which the operations of so many distinct and widely separated forces were combined to the common end.*

Campaign against Holkar.

We now come to the campaign against Jaswant Rá,o Holkar; which may be almost said to have begun as the other terminated, though it was not actively prosecuted at first. Holkar's movements all through the campaign of 1803 were the cause of anxiety to the British, and it is indeed surprising that he did not cast in his lot with his brother chieftains, in a *combined* struggle against British supremacy.

Just before the end of the war with Sindia he marched north and threatened the territories of Jaipúr. Checked by General Lake's movement in that direction, after the battle of Laswári, he returned southwards and plundered Muhesar, a wealthy city on the Narbadda. It is said that he obtained in this way as much as a crore of rupees, or one million sterling. Holkar had, as you may remember, defeated Sindia under the walls of Púna in 1802 (25th October), and now that his army had been augmented by large numbers both of horse and foot, which had been disbanded by Sindia after his defeats, and which the plunder of Muhesar enabled him to "entertain" (as it is called in India), he deemed himself singly a match for the English. The Governor-General was desirous of avoiding war, and so late as the 10th February 1804, sent assurances to Holkar, that so long as he refrained from attacking the territorities of his Company or its allies he would not be molested. On the

* Appendix II.

29th January the Commander-in-Chief, in conformity with these assurances, had invited Holkar to send wakíls (agents) to his camp for the purpose of accommodation, and to withdraw his army from the threatening position it occupied; but though Holkar responded with fair words it was discovered that he was at the same time trying to excite revolts in the British provinces, and also to detach the Rajor of Mácheri (Alwar) from his alliance* with the British. Besides this he vented his spleen by the barbarous murder of three British subjects who were officers in his service. Holkar appears at this time to have been encamped somewhere near Tonk, and on 14th February General Lake advanced to Hindan to cover the roads leading into the British territories from that direction. On 16th March two wakíls arrived from Holkar in General Lake's camp, and on the 18th propounded Holkar's claims. These comprised demands for chauth, for certain cessions of territory in the Doáb and Bundelkhand, and for a guarantee of the territories actually in his possession. Further, he desired that a treaty should be concluded with him on the same terms as that with Sindia. †

Holkar was informed that these demands could not be entertained, but nogociations were not broken off, the Commander-in-Chief still trying to induce him to come to reasonable terms.

Holkar in the mean time intrigued with Sindia, endeavouring to induce him to join in a league against the British. But Holkar's conduct during the late campaign had not been calculated to encourage Sindia to join him, and Sindia had no doubt learned that even their combined efforts were not likely to meet with success. At the same time he was not sorry to see Holkar attacking the British. Any successes he might obtain could not but be gratifying to Sindia, who had just been beaten by them, whilst on the other hand as Holkar was his rival he would be equally pleased to see him worsted.

Some time in February Holkar also addressed General Wellesley by letter, making the same demands as he did on the Commander-in-Chief and accompanying them with threats.

At the end of March he moved into Ajmír, then belonging to Sindia, where in the first days of April he levied contributions. From thence depredations were also committed on Jaipúr territory. About this time General Lake wrote to the Governor-General,

---

* Notes on the War in India, Vol. II., 4.   † Thorn, 332.

"If Holkar should break into Hindústán, he will be joined by the Rohillas. I never was so plagued as I am with this devil. We are obliged to remain in the field at an enormous cost. If we retire he will come down upon Jaipúr, and exact a crore from the Rája, and thus pay his army and render it more formidable than ever. If I advance and leave an opening, he will give me the slip, and get into our territories with his horse and burn and destroy."*

The Governor-General now became convinced that there was no hope of maintaining peace with Holkar. On the 16th April he wrote both to General Lake and Major-General Wellesley to take action against him.

He desired His Excellency to adopt measures to undertake active operations in the manner he might deem most advisable, without awaiting further orders. † He on the same day ordered Major General Wellesley to co-operate with the Commander-in-Chief, and desired the Resident with Sindia to prepare that chieftain to act in concert with the British forces both in Hindústán and the Dakhan. The orders for Major-General Wellesley were sent through the Resident at Haidarábád, and were received by Major-General Wellesley on 7th May at Bombay. He had written a fortnight before to General Lake‡ giving the Commander-in-Chief accounts of the strength and position of the troops in the Dakhan, in case the necessity of attacking Holkar should arise.

The force in the Dakhan was 1 Regiment of European and 5 of Native Cavalry, 3 Battalions of European and 16 of Native Infantry, besides Artillery and Pioneers. In Gújarát (under Col. Murray) were:—The King's 65th and 86th Regiments, and six Battalions of Native Infantry (one 1600 strong), and two more Native Infantry Battalions just joining.

The bulk of this Gújarát force was in camp about 70 miles north of Baroda. Holkar's possessions in the Dakhan comprised only the district of Amber, north of the Godávari, half of another which he shared with Sindia, Sieugaum§ south of that river, the strong fort of Chandúr on the Northern Gháts and a few districts in Khandesh. General Wellesley said that he should have had no doubt of being able to obtain early possession of all of these, were it not for the state of the country through which the troops must march. Owing

---

* Marshman, II., 167.   † Wellington Despatches, II., 231.   ‡ Wellington Despatches, 213.
(23rd April).   § (?) Name.

to the disturbances of previous years great scarcity prevailed in the Dakhan, which had become actual famine. Even at Púna the horses of the dragoons were being fed on rice, the only grain obtainable, and General Wellesley very much doubted his ability to move from Púna until a late period of the rains, when new grass and new crops would have appeared. Beyond Chandúr the country was, he said, a desert as far as the Taptí, having been the scene of the depredation of Sindia and Holkar for some years.

General Wellesley proceeded to give the Commander-in-Chief his views on the plan of campaign, and it is curious to observe, as an indication of the then state of geographical knowledge of India, that so accurate a man should believe that the distance from Púna to Indúr (the enemy's capital) was six hundred miles.*

He goes on to state that even if it were possible to reach and capture Chandúr immediately, it would not be proper to move the British troops out of the Dakhan, as an army of freebooters would immediately take advantage of their absence to ravage the country.

His suggestions were:—1st, That Sindia's army, strengthened by the subsidiary force attached to him, should be placed in a forward position northward of Újain; 2nd, That the Corps in Gújarát under Col. Murray should be moved forward re-inforced by the Gáekwár's cavalry, and he concluded:—

"These two armies upon Holkar's rear, while your Excellency would push him in front, must destroy him in a short space of time." But if the operations are not to be active, till I can arrive in Hindústán to take part in them, and if it should be decided that the British troops are to quit the Dakhan, it would be best to delay the commencement of the war, if that should be possible, at least till the month of August.

This letter would probably reach General Lake about the 10th May, or a few days later than the Governor-General's orders, and would show the Commander-in-Chief that he could hope for no very active co-operation on the side of the Dakhan.

Immediately on receipt of the Governor-General's instructions, Major-General Wellesley sent orders to Col. Murray, † thus; He assumed that General Lake's operations would be directed to defeat Holkar in the field, or if he should avoid an action, to press upon him so closely as to oblige his troops to disperse. This operation could be materially aided from Gújarát.

For this purpose Col. Murray, after providing for the defence of Gújarát, was to move forward with the two King's regiments and four battalions of N. I., and to post himself in such a manner as to stop and embarrass Holkar in his flight before the Commander-in-Chief as much as possible, and endeavour to bring him to action. General Wellesley assumed that Holkar would not retire towards Gújarát for fear of entangling himself amongst rivers which would become impassable in June, but rather fall back towards Újain. If he should do so Colonel Murray was to join Sindia's army with all speed.

Major General Wellesley suggests as points on which to march in the first instance, either by Lúnawára on Dongapúr to cover Gújarát, or by Dohad or Rutlám to be nearer Újain. He adds that Col. Murray's local knowledge may suggest some central point in the Banswáda district. * Further he informed Colonel Murray that he would suggest to the Resident with Sindia, that the troops of that chief should take possession of Indúr without loss of time.

At the time the Governor-General's orders reached him General Lake was in camp at Snolia, a village about 25 miles N.E. of Tonk.

A few days before (on 18th April) General Lake had detached from his camp near Dosa a force of 3 battalions of N. I., † towards the city of Jaipúr to protect that place, as it was threatened by Holkar who had returned from Ájmír. This detachment was commanded by Lieut.-Colonel Hon. W. Monson, and it arrived near Jaipúr on 21st April. The consequence of this movement was that Holkar, who had previously sent his guns, and apparently his infantry also, away towards Málwa, began to retire rapidly south-wards. General Lake advanced on 27th April and, moving slowly, was on 8th May at Nawái about 15 miles N.E. of Tonk. During this advance the Commander-in-Chief was preceded by Colonel Monson's detachment, whilst Holkar was watched by parties of irregular horse under European officers. In a few days Holkar had fled as far as Kotah, 120 miles South of Jaipúr.

The general situation, then, about the end of the first week in May was this; Holkar at Kotah, much harrassed by a hasty retreat

---

* Notes on the War in India, etc., Vol. III. 22.   † 2/2nd, 1/12th and 2/12th N. I.

through a line of country which afforded a scanty subsistence to his people, because it had been desolated by his own former outrages.* The Commander-in-Chief at Nawái, 15 miles N.E. of Tonk, with what remained of his army after losses and detachments. Lieut.- Colonel Monson a march or so in front of the Commander-in-Chief, probably on the Banás near Tonk. Colonel Murray somewhere north and east of Baroda, on the Máhí river, preparing to advance to about Bauswáda.

Sindia's army and the subsidiary force were not yet ready to move, Sindia had indeed agreed to act as desired, but of this General Lake could not yet have been informed.†

General Lake's force must have been much in need of some repose, and it is not surprising that he desired, equally with General Wellesley, to postpone further active operations until after the rains. The hot winds in that country are extremely severe, and his troops were no doubt already beginning to feel their effects.

From Nawái, His Excellency, on 10th May, detached Lieut.-Col. Don with three Battalions of N. Infantry,‡ some artillery and cavalry, to capture the Fort of Rampura which lies twenty three miles S.E. of Tonk. Lieut.-Col. Don stormed the place on 16th May. Whilst the storm was going on a battalion of the enemy from Tonk was posted outside the fort on the glacis, and took part in the defence. Some military stores and a small quantity of grain were found in the place, which General Lake in his report to the Governor-General, calls an important fortress. He adds that the capture of the Fort "puts us in possession of the whole of the territories of Jaswant Rá,o Holkar on this side of India."§

Holkar now hastily recrossed the Chambal, and his rapid retreat, together with the distance he had placed between himself and the Commander-in-Chief, led General Lake to believe it highly improbable that any force acting from the side of Hindústán could bring him to action. The news he received of the preparations in Gújarát and on the part of Sindia, for combined operations from the southward, offered the only prospect of effecting anything

---

* Notes on the War in India, Vol. III., 23.

† In my last lecture I referred to criticisms of General Brialmont and others on the campaign against Sindia and the Bhonsla. The plan of the campaign of 1804-5 seems much more open to criticism, because Holkar, having no ally to consult, was free to move in any direction which might seem best to him.

‡ 3rd N. C. 2/8, 2,21 (a new Regt.)   Lieut.-Col. Don's report, Notes on the War in India, Vol. III., 162.

§ The Fort with a territory worth 60,000 rupees yearly was ceded in 1791 to Túkají Holkar by the Rája of Jaipúr.

against Holkar's dominions at that season. Consequently the Commander-in-Chief determined to withdraw his main force into cantonments for the hot season, leaving Col. Monson with a strong detachment of Native Troops* to prevent the return of Holkar to the northward. On 18th May, General Lake marched from Náwái and reached Ágra on 7th June, after suffering greatly from the hot winds. On one day, 30th May, as many as 19 Europeans died from the heat out of his four weak regiments; and on the 2nd June even a larger number, whilst 250 native followers were said to have died on the same day.

Arrived at Ágra the army was broken up; the three regiments of British cavalry going on to Káhnpúr and the rest to various stations.

Without questioning the soundness of General Lake's decision to withdraw his main force from the field during the hot weather, it can hardly be denied that his entire dispersion of it was a mistake, and we shall shortly see that it led to serious consequences, since it left him unable to prevent an irruption of the Maráthás into the Doáb.

In May there occurred a disaster in Bundelkhand. Lieut.-Col. Fawcett (who was successor of Lieut.-Colonel Powell in command) was in camp at Kúnch, and had detached a force of 7 companies N. I., and 50 artillerymen, to reduce the small fort of Bela, about 8 miles off. This little force was further broken up, and the result was that Amír Khán, a freebooter who had been incited by Holkar to invade Bundelkhand, and of whom we shall presently hear more, fell upon two companies and destroyed them, as well as the artillerymen who were carrying on the siege of the fort, and captured 5 guns. This so much alarmed Col. Fawcett that he retired up the Betwa, leaving Bundelkhand open to the enemy. He was consequently removed from his command and Lieut.-Colonel Martindell appointed to succeed him; Bundelkhand was not finally subdued until 1809.

We now revert to Lieut.-Col. Monson's operations. On the 2nd June he was joined at Kotah by Lieut. Col. Don, who left a garrison in Rampura. A detachment of Sindia's cavalry under Bápújí Sindia joined him about the same time.

* 2/2nd, 2/8th, 1/12th, 2/12th, 2/21st, 2 comp. 2nd Bn. Artillery, Irr. Horse (Lieut. Lucan) and 6 galloper guns. Artillery, two 12-pounders in addition to the 10 battalion guns.

What the precise instructions given to Col. Monson were I have not been able to ascertain. The narrative in the "Notes relative, etc., etc." (III., 25,) merely says the Commander-in-Chief "directed him to form such a disposition of his force as should completely obstruct the return of Holkar to Hindústán." Sindia, whose force should, as well as that of Col. Murray, have co-operated with Monson's, does not appear to have done much. We hear nothing of him until a body of his troops under Sadásheo Rá,o appears on the scene at Khushyál Garh. Col. Murray does indeed appear to have made some forward movement, but how far it went I cannot ascertain. It is probable that, finding Sindia was inactive, he hesitated to carry out General Wellesley's orders. Napier says he was remarkable for indecision.* Meanwhile Col. Monson was moving South.

On 2nd July he captured, by escalade, the strong fort of Hinglazgarh, about 40 miles south of Kotah. His camp was then at Souára, and he stated in his report that Holkar, with the whole of his cavalry, infantry and guns, was within about 40 miles. Holkar was in fact near Rampura a small town west of the Chambal, not more than 30 miles off. In the days following the capture of Hinglazgarh, Col. Monson moved on, and on the 7th July, being then probably at Bhanpura, he heard that Holkar had crossed the Chambal with his infantry and guns.

Colonel Monson was now in a critical position. He had about 3000 infantry with 10 or 12 guns, and a body of irregular horse,

---

* In justice to Col. Murray it ought to be added that his orders were perplexing. Gen. Wellesley wrote as above mentioned on 7th May, but on 13th he wrote again saying that his advices from Gen. Lake's camp indicated an intention to delay the attack upon Holkar until the rains; and therefore at present Col. Murray was not to pass the frontier lest he "should be exposed singly to Holkar's operations." On 17th he is still unable to give any positive instructions, but says Col. Murray will "do well to have an eye towards Ujain." It was not till 22nd May that he writes "you may now proceed to carry into execution, as soon as you please, my instructions of 7th inst. It is probable that this letter would not reach Col. Murray before 27th May.

Supposing Murray to have been already near Banswáda he would be upwards of 100 miles from Ujain. Gen. Wellesley recommends him to join Bápújí Sindia as soon as possible, if he had not gone towards Gen. Lake. Now Holkar's force would be on the flank of his line of march, if Col. Murray had moved direct towards Ujain, and it is not surprising that under the circumstances he should have been cautious. He occupied Indúr on 21th August.

Bápújí Sindia (Daulat Rá,o's commander) was stated to be between Holkar (who was near Ratlám) and Mír Khán (who was about Bhopál) and Gen. Wellesley says the Sardar "does not much like his situation." Desp. II, 263.

In fact both Gen. Lake in detaching Monson without precise instructions, and Major-General Wellesley in his orders to Murray, seem to have acted injudiciously. The latter in a letter to Major Malcolm, 21th August, remarks, "I do not think the Commander-in-Chief "or I have carried on the war so well by deputies as we did ourselves." The failure does not appear to have been altogether due to the deputies. Murray commanded in South Valencia in 1813, see Napier, Bk. XX., Ch. IV.

with six "gallopers," whilst Holkar was in front of him with a large force of horse, foot, and artillery. Monson's first impulse was to attack, and there is no doubt that this would have been his wiser course. He at first moved forward, but then lost confidence and decided to retreat to the Mokandara Pass. The Mokandara Pass is a narrow winding passage, through a treble line of hills about two miles wide, which is formed by the outcrop of some of the sandstone beds in the Málwá Plateau. The direction of the strike is north-west and south-east. The pass is about 30 miles south of Kotah, and Colonel Monson's camp on 7th July was at about the same distance beyond the pass.

Having decided to retreat, Monson sent off his baggage and stores at 4. a.m. on 8th July to Sonára, and remained in order of battle on his ground till 11 a.m., awaiting attack. He then marched, leaving his cavalry under Lieut Lucan to cover his retreat to Sonára. Lieut. Lucan's force was soon attacked by Holkar's cavalry, and dispersed owing to the treachery of Bápújí. At 4. a.m. on 9th he again marched, and reached the pass at noon unmolested.

It is worthy of notice that Hinglazgarh, the capture of which had been represented as so important, does not seem to have been of any value as a point of support or pivot of operation.

On the 10th, Holkar made several ineffectual attacks on the pass with a large force of cavalry. Shortly after these attacks had been repulsed, Holkar was joined by his infantry and guns, and Monson fearing to be cut off from Kotah (by another pass at Ghatoli, 8 or 9 miles to his right) determined to retreat further. He marched on 11th, and reached Kotah early on 12th July, but the Rája refused either to admit him into the town or to give him any provisions. To add to his difficulties, the rains, which had set in with violence on 10th, now became incessant, and the country became so heavy that the Gámach Ghát on the Chambal river (only 7 miles from Kotah) was not reached till the morning of the 13th. On that day the river was in flood, and though it was crossed next day a halt had to be made to obtain supplies from Patan.

On 15th July, Monson was ready to march, but the rain rendered it impossible to move the guns so that he was forced to halt, and by the morning of the 16th they were so imbedded in the mud that it was impossible to move them. No provisions were left, and Col.

Monson was therefore obliged to spike the guns and abandon them.* On reaching the Mej River next day, near the entrance to the Lakeri Pass, it was impassable, and though Col. Monson was able to send the European artillerymen over upon elephants on the 18th, it was not until the 26th that he got the whole of his force over the stream. (9 days delay.) It is surprising that Holkar did not take advantage of this obstacle to destroy the whole detachment. A large body of his cavalry did indeed attack on 24th July, but was beaten off. The Lakeri Pass is somewhat similar to that of Mokandara and its northern outlet is about 18 miles from Rampura of Tonk. By the 29th July the force was collected at Rampura, but without guns, and having lost nearly all its camp equipage.

At Rampura Col. Monson received orders from General Lake not to fall back beyond Kotah, which he had already left 45 miles behind. Even if he had received these orders sooner it would have been to no purpose, but now he was not in a position to maintain himself even at Rampura. He had no provisions, and his force was no longer able to keep the field. Everything pointed to the necessity of retiring, say to Biána, where he would have found a strong position and could have received support from Ágra. Posted there he might still have fulfilled the task assigned to him (of excluding Holkar from Hindústán) to some extent. Twenty miles from Rampura his road crossed the Banás, now a formidable river, and his first care should have been to provide for passing the river, and to take advantage of Holkar's negligent pursuit to do so while still unmolested. Instead of this Colonel Monson remained at Rampura for more than three weeks, and when he at length moved it was without any preparation for crossing the Banás.

He had, on 14th August, received a re-inforcement of two battalions N.I., and six guns. He left in Rampura a garrison of a battalion-and-a-half of N.I. and four of the guns. With the remainder of his force, 5½ battalions and two guns,† he marched on the 21st August for Khushyálgarh, and on the morning of the 22nd was stopped by the Banás. Holkar had now come up in force, and the operation of crossing the river became very critical. On the 23rd it was impassable, but by good luck three boats were found in which the treasure and an escort of six companies was sent over. Next day

---

* He sent to the Rája of Búndi to take charge of them.
† 2/2, 1/9, 1/14, 1/12, 2/12, 6 companies 21st N.I., and 2 howitzers.

the river was fordable, and the enemy began to cross right and left, while Monson was crossing in the centre. The result was that the British had to abandon their two howitzers and all their baggage, and retreat to Khushyálgarh, harrassed by the enemy.

It is not necessary to pursue the retreat of Monson in further detail. Suffice it to say that on 27th and 28th August he moved in a hollow square, and fortunately produced so much moral effect by repulsing the Maráthá attacks, that, though all order was lost on leaving Biána in the night of 28th, the enemy were so much awed that no attacks of importance were afterwards made; and the survivors were able to straggle into Ágra on 31st August. In this retreat twenty two European officers were killed, and a large number of sepoys. The prisoners were shockingly treated by Holkar; many who refused to enter his service had their noses and right hands cut off.

Whilst all this was going on, Colonel Murray on 24th August (on which day Monson was at the Banás) occupied Indúr without opposition.*

So far however, the failure of Monson more than balanced any success achieved by Murray. Holkar, flushed with success, was ready to invade the newly conquered territory and the Commander-in-Chief with his army distributed in contonments was in no position to hinder him. Moreover the Ját Rája of Bhartpúr forsook our alliance, and joined with Holkar.

General Lake now collected his army in haste, and on 27th September it was assembled in camp at the Sikandra, near Ágra†. It consisted of 11 battalions (the 76th being still the only European one except two companies of the 22nd) and seven regiments of cavalry including as before the 8th, 27th and 29th Light Dragoons. It was organised in four infantry brigades (one in reserve) and two brigades of cavalry.

At this time Holkar was at Mathra, which he occupied on the 15th September.

On 1st October General Lake marched from the Sikandra towards Mathra. Holkar designed to seize Dehli before the Commander-in-Chief could arrive,‡ and with this object he despatched thither his

---

* See Wellesley on Monson, Wellington Despatches, II., 384, to Lieut.-Col. Wallace.

† See order of Brigading. Stubbs, I. 249.

‡ The force in Dehli was 3½ battalions of Native Infantry, 1,200 Matchlock men.

infantry and guns, while with his cavalry remained to amuse the British. On the first day's march no enemy was seen, but after that the Marátbá horse hung about the columns of march. From the 4th to the 12th the army was at Mathra, on the 7th October and again on the 10th, attempts were made to bring the enemy to action near Aríng, about 7 miles from Mathra, but without success. The march was resumed on the 12th October, and Dehli reached on the 18th.

Meantime the Resident, Lt.-Col. Ochterlony, and Lieut.-Col. Burn who commanded the troops, had been making a good resistance. On the news of Holkar's approach Ochterlony called in Lieut.-Col. Burn from Saháranpúr. He arrived with his battalion on 7th. On the 9th the Márathás erected a four-gun battery to breach the south west* angle of the city wall. A breach threatened soon to become practicable, and Col. Burn therefore made a sortie on 10th, and succeeded in spiking the guns. The enemy then threw up another battery and breached the curtain below the Túrkmán and Ájmír gates. This breach was retrenched on the 12th. On 14th October, a general cannonade was opened, under cover of which an attempt was made to escalade the city wall near the Lahor gate, but it was repulsed and the enemy had to leave his ladders behind. Before morning of the 15th the enemy had withdrawn, and made a circuitous retreat to the southwards through the hills of Gúrgáon.

Although no very systematic attack was made, still the enormous extent of the walls (7 miles in circumference) and their ruinous state at that time, together with the very small force at the disposal of Col. Burn, combined to render this defence of Dehli a memorable one. The name of the gallant commander is perpetuated to the present day in the Burn bastion.

During the month of October certain successes were obtained against Holkar in the Dakhan. Lieut.-Col. Wallace took Chandúr on the 12th, and on the 17th, having left a garrison there, he marched for Gálna, which he took on 25th; some smaller forts were taken about the same time.† These successes placed the whole of Holkar's territories in the Dakhan in British hands, as Colonel Murray's capture of Indúr had previously done for the most important part of his Málwá territory.

---

* S.E. in original report. But this is evidently a mistake.
† Chandúr, Notes III., App. D. p. 12. Galna, Notes, p. 245.

Reverting now to Dehli. On the 29th October, Holkar, who had been hovering about with his cavalry, suddenly crossed the Jamna between Pánipat and Dehli into the Doáb. Lieut.-Col. Burn had left Dehli on 26th to return with his battalion to Saháranpúr. Holkar overtook him and blockaded him in the fort of Shámli, a town about 64 miles north by east of Dehli.

On the 31st October General Lake crossed the Jamna in pursuit, with 6 regiments of cavalry and the reserve brigade of infantry under Lieut.-Col. Don, and commenced one of the most remarkable marches on record.

Major-General Fraser was to march with the rest of the army in persuit of the enemy's infantry and guns, which had retired towards Díg.

General Lake reached Shámli on 3rd, having marched 30 miles on the previous day, and relieved Colonel Burn. His subsequent march through Mahmadpúr, Barnáwa, Khataulí, Mírat, Hápar, Khásganj to Farakhábád, is laid down on the map which I have here.* The enemy always kept 25 or 30 miles ahead, burning and destroying as he went along. On the 16th however Aliganj was reached and found still burning, whilst Holkar was said to be at Farakhábád 26 miles ahead. Upon this information General Lake determined to make a night march to surprise the enemy. He accordingly marched at 9. p.m. with his two cavalry brigades and Horse Artillery.† Just as they were mounting news was received of a victory at Díg gained by Major-General Fraser over the infantry who had retired from Dehli.

Encouraged by this good news the cavalry pushed cheerfully on, and at sunrise on the 17th November reached the enemy's camp.

They found the horses still picketed while the men, wrapped in their blankets, slept beside them. No outposts of any sort seem to have been posted, and the sleepers were rudely awakened by the grape of the Horse Artillery and the "galloper" guns. The first brigade then charged under Lieut.-Colonel Vandeleur, the 8th Light Dragoons leading, and a party of the 8th completely destroyed a body of the enemy's infantry. Unfortunately an ammunition

---

* *Plate* VI.

† Notes on the War in India, App. D. 234, 1st Brigade Lieut.-Colonel Vandeleur, 8th Light Dragoons, 1st and 6th Native Cavalry. 2nd Brigade Lieut.-Colonel Need, 27th and 0th Light Dragoons and 4th Native Cavalry. Horse Artillery, Captain O. Brown.

tumbrill had exploded, just as the attack took place, and alarmed Holkar, who galloped off with a small party of horse and escaped in the direction of Mainpúri. The British cavalry continued the pursuit for 10 miles, cutting up great numbers of the enemy. The march of the previous day and night having been just 50 miles, this made a total of 70 miles within 24 hours. Considering that this feat was performed at the end of eighteen days in which 324 miles* had been covered, and under the sun of India, which even in the middle of November is still powerful, it must be held to be a very ex traordinary performance. All Holkar's cattle and baggage were taken, and 3000 men killed, whilst the completeness of the panic is shown by the absurdly small loss of the British; 2 killed and 18 wounded. The number of the Marátha Horse has been estimated at many thousand, by some as high as 60,000. The enemy's force was completely dispersed and fled across the Jamna towards Bhartpúr.

Farakhábád was already at this time a British military station, and the inhabitants, on the approach of the Maráthás, took refuge in the fort of Fatehgarh.

After this success General Lake halted for two days before continuing his march to Díg.

The victory gained by Major-General Fraser has been already alluded to. He marched from Dehli on 5th November. On the 10th he arrived at Govardhan, about 8 miles from Díg, where he was joined by the 1st Bengal European Regiment.†

Díg is a fortified town standing on a rocky site 20 miles east of Mathra, it then belonged, as it still does, to the Rája of Bhartpúr.

To the south lies, at a distance of about 2½ miles, the large village of Kasba Au, standing on a somewhat elevated site, and 1½ miles east of Kasba Au is the village of Umrah. General Fraser's camp on the night of the 11th was near the village of Bheij, 2½ miles east of Díg. Between Díg and Bheij was a marsh extending in a south-east direction between Bheij and Umrah. The enemy, 24 battalions and a considerable mass of horse with a large train of powerful artillery, was encamped between the fortress and the village of Au, which protected his left.

Major-General Fraser had only 7½ battalions of infantry (two of

---

* Average 19 miles a day including the day halted at Shámlí. This is measured from the Atlas sheets, and is no doubt less than the truth.

† Now the 101st. The detachment numbered 261, see Notes on the War in India, &c., III., 5.

them European), two regiments of native cavalry, in all less than 6,000 men, with 20 light guns, yet he did not hesitate to attack.

He formed in two columns, infantry on the right, cavalry on the left, with the artillery belonging to it on the reverse of each column, and in this order marched round the marsh by the south of Umrah. Arrived at Au, he formed up his infantry in two brigade lines. He placed the cavalry on his left to protect that flank against the enemy's horse. The ground between Umrah and Au was covered with high crops, which sheltered the advance to some extent, but nevertheless the columns were observed and fired into. As soon as the lines were formed the village was attacked and carried.

A part of the enemy's artillery had been posted within the swamp in a sort of cul-de-sac, from which they had fired on the British camp. These guns, with those in the main line, now brought a convergent fire to bear on the British force as it issued from the village of Au, and caused considerable loss. General Fraser fell here severely wounded. Brigadier-General Monson, however, took the command, drove the enemy from all his positions, and pursued him under the guns of the fortress. The results of the action were that about 2000 of the enemy were killed, and a large number driven into the marshes and drowned, while 87 guns of various calibre were taken. The victory was not achieved without considerable loss, showing that the enemy fought well. It amounted to 651 killed and wounded. This is about 11 per cent. of the force engaged ; more if we deduct for two battalions left to guard the baggage. Major-General Fraser died at Mathra on the 24th November, from the effects of his wounds.

General Lake marched from Farakhábád on the 20th November, and arrived before Dig on the 11th December.* The remains of Holkar's army had taken refuge in the town after their defeat by General Fraser, and Holkar himself had fled thither from Farakh- ábád. It was therefore necessary to reduce the place.

You will recollect that a treaty had been made with the Bhartpúr Rája, but the defeat of Monson caused his defection, and in the battle of Dig, not only did a body of his horse take part against us, but the guns of the fort fired on our troops, killing officers and men.

---

* He passed Hathras, then a strongly fortified town belonging to a Jat Rája, Dyar Rám, and Mudsan, another strong place belonging to Bagwán Sing of Sarsní.

General Lake spent some days in reconnoitering and waiting for Colonel Don's brigade to come up with a battering train from Ágra.

The town of Díg is of considerable size, about 1½ miles by 1 mile and the circuit of the walls is 4¾ miles. It is surrounded by lofty walls with round bastions connected by earthen ramparts. Within the town is a citadel about 150 yards square, with ramparts 70 to 100 feet high and 20 to 50 feet thick, surrounded by a wet ditch. At the time of the attack the town walls mounted 31 guns of all sizes, from 74-pounders to 4-pounders.

The point chosen for attack was the south-west angle which is formed by a small enclosed work called the Sháh Búrj, about 50 yards square, having an exposed masonry wall 36 feet high which could be breached from a distance. Five hundred yards south of this is a detached work called Gopál Garh.

On 13th December, General Lake took up a position west of the fortress, and the same night trenches were opened. The work does not appear to have been very skilfully conducted,* and the enemy was in sufficient force outside the place to cause loss and annoyance and impede progress. However, by the night of 23rd December a practicable breach had been formed and was successfully stormed.

During the night of the 24th December the enemy evacuated the citadel, thus leaving the whole place in the hands of the British. The loss in the siege amounted to 43 killed and 184 wounded, 2 European officers amongst the former, and 13 amongst the latter.

It was fortunate for General Lake that the wall of the Sháh Búrj was capable of being breached from a distance. His batteries were 800 yards from the place. He was totally wanting in proper equipment for a regular siege.† Moreover the enemy neglected the simplest precautions, neither making any attempt to repair the breach nor to stockade or retrench it in any way. It is probable that the ease with which success was obtained at Díg had a share in bringing about the serious defeat which the General was shortly to experience before the virgin fortress of Bhartpúr.

Having made some arrangements for the security of Díg, in which he left the 1/4th Native Infantry as garrison, General Lake

---

* The outwork called Gopál-garh, which prolonged the line of fort attacked, should have been first captured.

† A journal of the siege is in the British Indian Military Repository, Vol. II. (1823), p. 452,

marched for Bhartpúr on 28th December, and prepared to attack it. He was joined on the way by the 75th Regiment, and a supply of stores.

The general situation at the end of 1804 was this :—

Holkar, though defeated whenever he could be brought to action, still had a large force with him, principally or almost entirely horse. His capital, Indúr, and the adjoining territory in Málwa, were occupied by the Bombay force, formerly under Colonel Murray, and now commanded by Major-General Richard Jones. The garrison left by General Lake in Rampura, had been well commanded* and had kept open the line of approach of the Bombay force, which was now moving north to join the Commander-in-Chief.†

The Rája of Bhartpúr having joined Holkar, his fortified capital, as well as his other forts, such as Khumber, Wer, &c., served Holkar as pivots for his marauding operations and refuges in case of defeat.‡

Major-General Wellesley, in his instructions to Colonel Murray, had forbidden him to engage in sieges whilst Holkar was still in the field, and in a letter to the Commander-in-Chief himself, dated 27th May, 1804, General Wellesley strongly urges the necessity of giving " this description of freebooter " no rest, but pressing him with one or two light corps until his force melted away.

If the circumstances of the case justified a siege of Bhartpúr at all, it should at least have been undertaken with sufficient force and a proper equipment. The town has a perimeter of about five miles; it is surrounded by a great mound, rather than by walls, of mud; it has a wet ditch, and it stands in a plain which at that time was covered with pools of water.

. It contained a numerous garrison, about 50,000 men, mounted a large number of guns on earthen bastions, and Holkar was under the walls with a large force.

The Commander-in-Chief commenced the siege on 2nd January, 1805 with 7,800 men, all told. He had only six 18-pounders and eight 5½ inch and 8-inch mortars.§   It was not till the 17th that he was re-inforced by three battalions of Native Infantry.‖

---

* By Capt. Hutchinson, Bengal Artillery.   † It arrived at Bhartpúr 11th February.
‡ Wellington Despatches, Owen's selection, 423.
§ Two 24-pounders and a scanty supply of ammunition were brought from Díg on 14th Jan.
‖ The Bombay column did not arrive till 11th February, by which time the siege *ought to* have been over.

There was scarcely any engineering equipment at all, and the engineer branch of the service was represented at first by three officers only,* and those not of sufficient rank and experience to carry the necessary weight. Attached to the Engineers were three companies of pioneers.

Into the details of the siege time does not permit me to enter,† I can only briefly mention the principal facts.

The army encamped near Bhartpúr on 2nd January, 1805; a battery was begun on the 5th, 700 yards from the Anah gate.‡ On the 8th a breach in the curtain, about 350 yards north of the gate, was pronounced practicable, *having been viewed through telescopes.* On the 9th the enemy stockaded and built up the breach, and that night a storm was attempted and repulsed with a loss of 5 officers and 64 men killed, 23 officers and 364 men wounded. No approaches of any sort had been made. On the 16th a second breach was made, about 150 yards south of the same gate. From the 17th the enemy were busy stockading this breach till the 20th, when a storm was attempted. This attempt cost the British 3 officers and 53 men killed, 15 officers and 477 men wounded. On this occasion it was intended to pass the wet ditch by portable bridges. The notable expedient had been adopted of sending three native troopers to ascertain the width of the ditch. They gallopped to the edge, pretending to desert, viewed it, and reported it to be 28 feet wide. The bridges naturally turned out to be much too short and, the water being 8 feet deep, the stormers were helplessly massacred on the counterscarp.

On the 4th February, a month after the begining of the siege, a parallel was at last opened. On the 6th, the camp was shifted ; partly for sanitary reasons, partly because it was now intended to make a breach in another place. On the 11th a new breach was formed, about 150 yards south of the Anah gate, but no trenches had as yet been made to conduct the stormers from the battery, which was 430 yards from the breach. By the 20th February, when the trenches had been made and the assault was delivered, the breach had naturally been strongly retrenched.

---

* Lieuts. Thomas Robertson, Thomas Wood, H. W. Carmichael Smyth. Lieuts. Richard Tickell and William Cowper (Bombay) joined later.

† Plan of Bhartpúr, surveyed in 1857-58, under Surveyor General of India ; scale, 8 inches to a mile.

‡ Journal of the siege is in the British Indian Military Repository, vol, V. (1827), p. 1—811,

On this occasion three columns were formed. One[1] was to storm the Bhím Naráyan Gate, a mile to the right of the breach, which was reported easy of access. Another[2] was to drive the enemy from the glacis on the right of the breach (he had made a sortie in the morning and held the advanced trench some time); while the third was the real column of assault on the left[3].

Of these the centre column, under Captain Grant of the 86th, alone performed its task. It drove in the enemy and took his guns, eleven in number. The right column failed even to reach the point of attack. The assault by the left column failed disgracefully. Of all the European troops contained in it the companies of the 22nd Regiment alone responded to the order to advance. The other regiments, panic-struck by some idea of a mine, refused to advance, and not even the gallant example of the 12th Native Infantry which, led by Colonel Don, planted its colours on a tower to the right of the breach, would induce them to move. This failure cost 1 officer and 156 men killed, 22 officers and 692 men wounded.

Next day the Commander-in-Chief addressed the troops on parade, in terms of affectionate right, expressing his sorrow that by not following their officers they had lost the laurels which they had gained on so many occasions. He gave them an opportunity of retrieving their reputation by volunteering. Upon this every man stepped forward. Lieut. Templeton of the 86th offered to lead the forlorn hope, for which 200 men were selected, and a fresh storming party was organized for the same afternoon.* But though this renewed attack was made with determined gallantry, it met with no better success than the last; and, after a prolonged effort, had to withdraw with a loss of six officers and 101 non-commissioned officers and men killed, 25 officers and 730 men wounded.

Losses in the four assaults of Bhartpúr, not including the trenchwork.

	OFFICERS.		MEN.	
	Killed.	Wounded.	Killed.	Wounded.
1st Assault	5	23	64	364
2nd ,,	3	15	53	477
3rd ,,	1	22	156	692
4th ,,	6	25	101	730
Totals	15	85	374	2263

[1] 65th Regiment 300 men, 1st Battalion Bo. Grenadiers, 1/3 Bo. [2] 86th Regiment 200 men, 1/8 Native Infantry. [3] His Majesty's 22nd Regiment (2 companies), 75th and 76th Regiments, the Bengal European Regiment, 1/12th N. I., 2/12th N. I., and 1/15th N. I.
* His Majesty's 65th, 76th, 86th and 22nd Regiments, 1/2nd, 2/15th Native Infantry and the Bombay Grenadiers.

With this attempt ended the active operations against Bhartpúr. On the night of the 22nd and 23rd the guns were withdrawn and the trenches abandoned. Next day the enemy triumphantly fired the batteries. On the 24th the army withdrew to a position 6 miles north west of the city, covering the roads to Ágra, Mathra and Dig.

The causes of this disastrous failure, by which the army lost the service of more than 100 officers and 3,000 men, out of a total effective of not more than 12,100 men, are sufficiently obvious. General Lake complained that "neither the abilities, knowledge, nor experience" of his engineers "were adequate to the occasion"* thus condemning himself for want of judgment in selecting them.

The journal of the siege records that on the 2nd January, as the Commanding Officers of Artillery and Engineers were on their way to a first reconnaissance, they were overtaken by General Lake, who asked "will the battery be ready to-night ? "† and this impatient question gives the clue to the whole causes of the failure. The general was evidently totally ignorant of the requirements of a successful siege, and, having no officer of sufficient authority to obtain a hearing, wasted the lives of his men in attempting what, under the conditions, was impossible.

Whilst the siege was going on, a remarkable cavalry operation took place in Bundelkhand. On the 7th February, Amír Khán (the freebooter who opposed Colonel Powell in Bundelkhand) quitted Holkar's camp and crossed the Jamna with a large body of horse. Next day General Lake despatched Major-General Smith, with 1,800 men (the bulk of his cavalry) in pursuit. The pursuit was so active that Amír Khán (though he burnt the cantonments at Moradábád) had not time to do much mischief in the country, He was at last overtaken on the 2nd March at Afzalgarh, near Sherkot on the Rámganga.

His cavalry were dispersed, and a small body of infantry destroyed. In this action Skinner's Horse (now the 1st Bengal Cavalry) took part. On the 11th March, Amír Khán was again surprised at Chandpúr near Amroha, by Captain Murray. He fled back to Bhartpúr, and shortly after into Bundelkhand. Major-General

---

* Commander-in-Chief to Govenor General, 1st July, 1805, Repository, V. 158.
† The officer's reply was " how is it possible ?" to which the general rejoined " then it shall be ready to-morrow night, and you must work harder, and get more men." See Owen's Selections, 435, for Major-General Wellesley's opinion.

Smith rejoined the Commander-in-Chief on the 23rd March, having covered 700 miles in 43 days.

General Lake's defeat before Bhartpúr, added to Monson's disaster, bore the usual fruit of defeats in Asia. Every one began to think that the Company's ikbál was gone.* The Rája of Bhartpúr did indeed still dread Lake's determination, which was evinced by continued (though tardy) preparations to resume the siege with a proper provision of stores.† Early in March the news of the General having been raised to the peerage was received, and the Rája took advantage of this opportunity to open negociations. It is probable that he was rather tired of his Maráthá allies, who lived on his country, and, as shewn by Holkar when his camp was occasionally beat up by the British, as well as by Amír Khán, could do nothing but run away when attacked. But Sindia, who had never agreed to the arrangements about the cession of Gwáliár, which were demanded from him as part of the treaty of Surji Anjangáon,‡ was now emboldened to assume a threatening attitude. Soon after Monson's disaster he, instigated by his minister Rá,o Ghatkai, addressed a defiant letter to the Governor-General. This letter was intrusted to a wakíl who kept it for several months, until he was encouraged by our disaster before Bhartpúr to present it.

Early in January, 1805, Sindia, who had been at Burhánpúr, and had promised to go to Újain, with a view to co-operating against Holkar, moved instead towards Bhopál, much to the alarm of that friendly state. On 22nd March, he announced to his Resident his intention of marching to Bhartpúr with the view of mediating, at the head of his army, between the Rája and the British Government.

On the 29th March, he was actually at Sabalgarh, south of the Chambal River, only about 45 miles south-west of Dholpúr.

The position of affairs was therefore serious. Sindia was apparently on the point of becoming actively hostile, Holkar was still in the field, and the Rája of Bhartpúr still unsubdued. Lord Lake, however, with characteristic determination, showed no signs of haste to treat with Bhartpúr, but on the contrary "thought proper to

---

* See Gen. Wellesley, on 13th January, 1805. Owen, 434.
† See journal as above "Making fascines," 20th February to 9th April, daily entry.
‡ In this he seems to have been right. See Major-General Wellesley to Major Malcolm. Owen, 388, 393, 399.

"withold every encouragement to his advances * * * until he should be well assured of his compliance with every concession " required of him.

On the 8th April, a new battering train and supply of stores having arrived, Lord Lake took up a fresh position to resume the siege. The Rája then submitted to the terms required, and a new treaty was signed on the 11th.

A few days before this (2nd April) Lord Lake with his cavalry surprised Holkar in his camp near Bhartpúr, and killed a large number of his men in a pursuit of 7 miles. Holkar now retired across the Chambal with the remnant of his army, about 13,000 men and twenty or thirty guns. On 15th April, he joined Sindia in his camp at Sabalgarh. Bápújí Sindia and Amír Khán arrived there on 11th and 14th respectively.

On 21st April, Lord Lake left Bhartpúr, and marched to Dholpúr. He crossed the Chambal on the 30th April, and joined Colonel Martindale,* who had been ordered from Bundelkhand with over 9,000 men to watch Sindia, and was in camp at Jatáwhar, about 8 miles S.S.E. of the present Chambal Railway Bridge. At the news of Lord Lake's approach Sindia retired towards Kotah, and several of his lesser confederates deserted to the British. Lord Lake's army, which now contained nearly 18,000 regulars, was brought up by this means to nearly 30,000 men.

On the 10th May, the Bombay force marched for Rampura, and on the 20th, Colonel Martindale's detachment moved off for Bundelkhand.

In the beginning of June, Lord Lake† got his army into cantonments. The 75th and 76th Regts., with the Company's Europeans, went to Fatehpúr Síkrí, and the rest of the army to Ágra and Mathra. The three regiments of dragoons‡ occupied the Sikandra.

Cantoned in this position, the army was ready to take the field at very short notice. Had a similar disposition been made in the previous year, it would probably have enabled Lord Lake to rescue Monson's detachment, and to prevent Holkar's irruption into the Doáb.

---

* Colonel Martindale had arrived here from Bundelkhand on 5th April. He had 10 battalions, 3½ squadrons, 20 guns, and some irregulars.
† He left Jatáwhar on 26th May.
‡ A change of numbers occurred about this time. The former 27th and 29th Dragoons became 24th and 25th. Thorn, 461.

The camp of Mr. Jenkins, the Resident at Sindia's court, had been assailed and plundered early in 1805 by some of Sindia's people, and the Resident had been unable to obtain redress. He had requested his *congé* in vain, Sindia being no doubt afraid that his departure would be the signal for war. In June, Lord Lake wrote to Siudia demanding the dismissal of Mr. Jenkins within 10 days, under a threat of war should he refuse. Sindia replied that he only awaited the arrival of a successor. Holkar and Sindia had about the same time moved west, towards Ájmír. Shortly after, advances were made by Sindia which enabled Lord Lake to reply that no negociations could go on until the Resident was permitted to leave. Mr. Jenkins was then permitted to take his departure with suitable honours.* Everything was now in a fair way towards adjustment, when an event occurred which frustrated Lord Lake's plans.

This was the recall of the Marquess Wellesley, and the arrival of the Marquess Cornwallis, with a peace-at-any-price policy.

Lord Cornwallis had held the office of Governor-General with distinction from 1786-93. He now returned to India, broken in health, and pledged to the Directors to overturn the policy of his predecessor.

On the 19th September, he wrote to Lord Lake to the following effect. He was prepared to compromise, or even abandon, the demand which had been so repeatedly and urgently made on Sindia, for the release of the British Residency.* He was prepared, as his predecessor had been, to restore Gohad and Gwáliár, Sindia giving up his pensions and jághírs under the treaty of Surji Anjangáon. He considered the possession of Dehli very unfortunate and would restore it to Sindia, who was to be allowed to re-establish Maráthá power in Hindústán. Lord Wellesley had made the Chambal our frontier towards Central India. He was prepared to withdraw to the line of the Jamna, and to abandon all the minor chiefs between these rivers, with whom defensive alliances had been lately formed. Dholpúr and other districts were to be given back to Sindia, and the Rája of Jaipúr was to be left to settle with him as best he could.

In sending this letter to Lord Lake, the Governor-General enclosed one for Sindia to the same effect. Lord Lake witheld this letter,

---

* Lord Wellesley had now made up his mind to restore Gohad and Gwáliár.
† Mill, VI., 525. Marshman, II., 187.

pending the reply to a remonstrance* which he addressed to Lord Cornwallis. Before it could reach him the Governor-General was dead.†

On the death of Lord Cornwallis, Sir George Barlow, a Bengal civilian of mediocre abilities, became acting Governor-General. He had energetically assisted Lord Wellesley in his policy, but now, having found that it was unacceptable in Leadenhall Street, was just as eager to undo it. He even went beyond anything that Lord Cornwallis would have sanctioned, for he held that anarchy in the native states was a guarantee of the security of British India..‡

Fortunately Lord Lake's negociations with Sindia were so far advanced, that they were not very materially influenced in their conclusion by the change of policy.|| With Holkar it was different.

Holkar and Amír Khán having quitted Sindia, proceeded to Ájmír. Holkar collected an army of about 12,000 horse, 3,000 foot, and 30 guns, and marched northward in September (after vainly trying to induce the Rája of Jaipúr to join him), with a view of gaining the Sikh chieftains of Sirhind (Patiálá, Nábha, Jhínd, &c.,) over to his side. His line of march was through Shekawatti, skirting Alwar and Rewári to Dádri, in Jhajhar, where he left his infantry, guns, and 1,000 horse to harry the British territories. He himself went on towards Patiálá.

Lord Lake was instantly in motion. On 10th October, the troops at Ágra and Fatehpúr marched for Mathra. The Bombay Division from Rampura was directed on Shekawatti, a force was sent towards Saháranpúr, and another to Rewári to protect the Doáb, whilst Lord Lake himself started in direct pursuit, with 5 regiments, (18 squadrons) of cavalry, the reserve brigade of infantry, and the Horse Artillery.

There is little more to be said about this part of the campaign. The march was not very rapid, except for two or three days at the end. It is remarkable chiefly as being the first occasion on which the Satlaj was crossed by a British force. The spectacle of Holkar flying before the British was not one calculated to enlist the Sikhs on his side. Holkar was therefore obliged to sue for peace. Very favourable terms were granted. He renounced all claims on the territory north of the Chambal and on Bundelkhand and, like Sindia,

<hr/>

* Abstract, see Mill, VI. 520.   † Died at Gházipur, 5th October, 1805.   ‡ Mill, VI., 531.
|| The renunciation of right to contract treaties with Rajpút chiefs was a serious exception.

agreed not to employ Europeans without the consent of the British Government. He was to relinquish all rights to Rampura (of Tonk) and all claims on the Rája of Búndi, and he was to return to his own territories by a defined route, without injuring the territories of the Company or its allies. On the other hand he was to receive back the forts and territories taken from him south of the Taptí and Godávari.

Sir G. Barlow altered this treaty when ratifying it, and alledging that they would be the cause of troubles and expense, left to Holkar the territories north of Chambal.* But he did worse. In spite of the remonstrances of Lord Lake, he deliberately made over to Holkar's vengeance the friendly Rájas of Búndi† and Jaipúr. It was not long in falling on them. Holkar should have been ordered to accompany, or precede. the British Army on return to Hindústán. Instead of this he was left to follow, and no sooner was the Commander-in-Chief across the Satlaj, than he began to pillage the Sikhs. Harriáua had been granted to one Abdul Sanad for his services. Holkar ravaged the country, and levied contributions on it. Lord Lake requested Sir G. Barlow to defer his renunciation of the Jaipúr alliance until Holkar should have gone home. But Sir George insisted on declaring the renunciation immediately, for fear the British Government might have to resent Holkar's proceedings. Holkar responded by extorting 18 lakhs of rupees from the unfortunate Rája, after which he proceeded to punish the Rája of Búndi for the assistance he had given to Colonel Monson.

Thus were the advantage gained by so much exertions and hard fighting frittered away by the weakness of Lord Wellesley's successor. Worse still, the good name of England was stained, and confidence in British good faith rudely shaken. Lord Lake had shortly after to receive at Dehli,‡ from the mouth of one of his agents, the bitter reproaches of the Rája of Jaipúr, reproaches rendered all the more bitter by the consciousness that they were well deserved.

Central India was abandoned to a state of anarchy, and when at last Lord Hastings had to re-settle affairs in 1817, an army of 100,000 men was required for the purpose.

---

* He did the same with Sindia.   † Who had helped Monson in his distress.
‡ Mill, Book VI., 541.

Note.—The events of 1805 have certain points of resemblance to those of 1881. In 1805, as in 1881, we had just closed a series of successful military operations and greatly extended our influence and obligations. In both cases we hastened to withdraw, as if alarmed at our own daring. In 1805 Dehli was considered an embarrassment, though we did not absolutely throw it away, like Kandahar in 1881. Then, as in 1881, it was asserted that we could not find a more advantageous frontier than a river, and the Jamna was the prototype of the Indus. Then, as of late, arguments for withdrawal were sought in finance, and page upon page of figures may be found purporting to prove that, far from being a source of strength, the acquisitions of the Marquess Wellesley were no better than a positive loss. *

H. H. J.

---

* Mill, Book VI., Chap. 13.

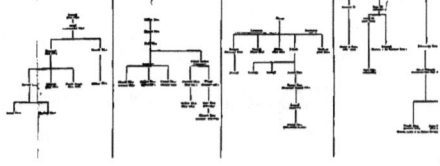

Appendix II.

CHRONOLOGY OF THE CAMPAIGNS.

1802.	
Dec. 31	Treaty of Bassain.
1803.	
February	Madras force concentrated at Harihar under Lieut.-General Stuart, Commander-in-Chief in Madras.
April 20	Major-General Wellesley enters Púna.

CAMPAIGN AGAINST SINDIA AND THE BHONSLA.

Aug. 7	General Lake marches from Káhupúr.
8	Major-General Wellesley takes Ahmadnagar.
21	Lieut.-Colonel Murray marches from Baroda.
29	General Lake's action before Aligarh.
„	Lieut.-Colonel Murray takes Bharuch.
Sept. 4	General Lake captures Aligarh.
11	„ „ gains the battle of Dehli.
14	„ „ enters Dehli
17	Lieut.-Colonel Woolington takes Powangarh.
18	Colonel Harcourt takes Jagannáth.
21	„ „ „ Bálásúr.
23	Major-General Wellesley gains Battle Assaye.
24	General Lake Marches from Dehli for Ágra.
Oct. 4	„ „ arrives before Ágra.
10	„ „ wins action before Ágra.
„	Colonel Powell defeats Shamshír Bahádhar in Bundelkhand.
14	Colonel Powell takes Barabatti.
17	Fort of Ágra capitulates to General Lake.
21	Assirgarh surrenders to Colonel Stevenson.
27	General Lake leaves Ágra.
Nov. 1	„ „ gains Battle of Laswárí.
2	Colonel Harcourt occupies the defile of Bermuth.
8	„ „ marches from Laswárí.
14	General Lake concludes treaties with Jaipúr, Alwar, and Johdpúr.
23	Suspension of hostilities in the Dakhan agreed to between Sindia and Major-General Wellesley.
28	Major-General Wellesley gains battle of Argáon.
Dec. 4	Colonel Powell takes Kálpí.
14	Major-General Wellesley takes Gáwilgarh.
„	„ „ makes peace with Rája of Berá.
21	General Lake detaches Lieut.-Colonel White to Gwáliár.
27	„ „ reaches Biána.
30	Major-General Wellesley makes peace with Sindia at Surjí Anjangáon.
1804.	
Feb. 4	Fot of Gwáliár surrendered to Lieut.-Colonel White.
27	Sindia becomes a party to a treaty of alliance between British Government, the Peshwá, and the Nizam.

Campaign against Holkar.

1804

Feb.	9	General Lake moves from Biána.
April	17	„ „ at Dosa.
	„	„ „ detaches Monson to Jaipúr.
May	15	Lieut.-Colonel Don takes Rampura of Tonk.
	„	Holkar retires behind the Chambal.
June	2	Lieut.-Colonel Don joins Monson at Kotah.
	6	General Lake reaches Ágra, and his army goes into cantonments.
July	2	Monson takes Hinglasgarh.
	„	„ moves to Pipla.
	„	„ „ Gurrats.
	8	„ retreats through Sonára.
	9	„ at Mokandara.
	10	Holkar attacks Monson.
	30	Monson reaches Rampura.
Aug.	21	„ leaves Rampura.
	24	Murray occupies Judúr.
	31	Monson reaches Ágra.
Sept.	27	General Lake at Sikandra.
Oct.	1	„ „ marches for Dehli.
	14	Attempted storm of Dehli by Holkar.
	31	General Lake crosses the Jamna in pursuit of Holkar.
Nov.	5	Major-General Fraser leaves Dehli.
	13	„ „ gains the Battle of Díg.
	17	General Lake routes Holkar at Farukábád.
Dec.	24	Capture of Díg.

1805.

Jan.	2	Siege of Bhartpúr opened.
	9	First assault of Bhartpúr.
	20	Second „ „
Feb.	20	Third „ „
	21	Fourth „ „
	23	Siege raised.
March	2	Amír Khán defeated by Major-General Smith at Afzalgarh.
April	11	Peace signed with Rája of Bhartpúr.
	30	Lord Lake in camp at Jatáwhar.
June		„ „ cantons his army at Ágra and Mathra.
Oct.	10	„ „ marches for Mathra.
Dec.	2	„ „ reaches Ludiána.
	9	„ „ at the Beás.
	25	Holkar makes peace.
	31	Review of Lord Lake's army on the banks of the Beás.

1806.

Jan.	9	Lord Lake begins his return march.

Appendix III.

NOTE ON THE BATTLE OF DEHLI.

I have had some difficulty in ascertaining the actual position of the battle-field. The name given to it is misleading, and there is actually a pillar not far below Patparganj, with an inscription to the effect that it marks the field of battle, which would seem at first sight to be very strong evidence. But this did not agree with the mileage given in the itineraries of the march.

The original despatch of the Commander-in-Chief (printed in Bengal Papers) does not mention the name of any of the villages on the battlefield, nor does the accompanying sketch of the action give any names. Moreover, this sketch is not to any scale.

The narrative of the Governor-General (Bengal Papers, page 248) states that the army made a short march to the west of Sikandrábád on the 10th, and that on the 11th it made a march of 18 miles to its encampment *near the Jehnah nullah (about six miles from Dehli)* before the action. The Governor-General adds that the battle was fought within view of the minarets of Dehli. Major Thorn, who was not present at the battle—his regiment, the 29th Light Dragoons, having been detached as mentioned in the text—also mentions the minarets, and says that after the battle the whole army encamped on the banks of the Jamna, opposite to Dehli.

But the "Survey of the Route of General Lake's Army," by Lieut. Carmichael Smyth (see list of authorities), shows that neither the Governor-General nor Major Thorn is correct. On this survey each halting-place is marked by a sketch of a double-poled tent and a Union Jack with date of the camp. The distances, as measured from this map, have been compared with those on the modern maps of the same country, and with the table of marches in Henley's Code.

These all agree very well together. What was the main road of that day runs in this part much nearer the Jamna than the present Grand Trunk road, and the crossing of the Hindan was at a point about nine miles below Ghází-ud-dín-nagar. This old road runs through Sikandrábád and Súrajpur, and by Saddarpúr and Chalera to Patparganj and Dehli. The crossing of the Hindan or Jenah nullah was about eleven miles from Dehli, instead of six only.

From a careful comparison of the maps and distances, I am led to believe that the actual position of the battle was as shewn in *Plate V.*, and that the villages on the Marátbá line of battle were Saddarpúr, Agápúr and Baraula, while a village with square enclosure (shewn on the sketch) in front of the enemy's line, and where the Commander-in-Chief formed up his infantry line, was Sarai.

The survey of the route shows the distance from the halting-ground of the 10th to the first camp of the 11th, on the Hindan, to have been a good twenty miles, and the camp, after the action between Chalera and Hoshigarpur, about three miles further on. This second camp was still nearly six miles distant from Patparganj, and nearly niue from Dehli.

No doubt the minarets would be visible, as the intervening country is perfectly flat. They are visible from near the present Grand Trunk Road crossing, and the distance is about the same.

I am at a loss how to account for the pillar near Patparganj. Perhaps some one of my brother-officers, who may be serving in that part of India, would send me some information about it. I have been disappointed in my endeavours to get the matter investigated on the spot, owing to the frequent moves of officers in India.

Appendix IV.

NOTE ON MARCHES IN THE MARÁTHÁ CAMPAIGNS.

The late Sir George Pomeroy-Colley, in a lecture on Marches, delivered on 31st January, 1873, at the Royal United Service Institution, spoke as follows:—
"I believe that the records of our Indian wars, of Lord Lake's Maráthá "campaigns, and, more recently, of some of the flying columns during the "mutiny, contain the most remarkable examples of such feats. Unfortunately, "from the difficulty of finding the places on the map, and identifying names, "it is often impossible to verify them."

It seems, therefore, that a more particular notice of some of these marches than the limits of the text would admit of may not be devoid of interest.

The three really remarkable marches in the campaigns are:—

1. Major-General Wellesley's in October and November, 1803.

2. General Lake's, in pursuit of Holkar, in November, 1804.

3. Major-General Smith's, in pursuit of Amír Khán, in February and the beginning of March, 1805.

The first of these is probably the most remarkable, as it was performed by a whole army, with guns and impedimenta; but I regret to say, I have not been able, even with the assistance kindly afforded to me by Mr. Saunders, to lay down its course on the map. As stated in the text, the names are very inaccurately given in the despatches of the Major-General, and many despatches have no local date at all. But, in the hope that some of my brother officers, who may be employed in that part of the Dakhan, may be inclined to look the route up on the ground, a table is annexed of such halting-places as are given, together with references.

The second march is shown on the diagram (*Plate* VI.), which gives the sheets of the Indian Atlas on which it can be traced. The distances in the annexed table have been measured from the Atlas sheets, on a scale of 4 miles to 1 inch, and are, therefore, less than the actual distances covered.

The force consisted of three brigades of cavalry and the reserve brigade of infantry, under Lieut.-Colonel P. Don.

The third march was performed by cavalry only, with horse artillery.* Its course can be traced with tolerable accuracy on the sheets of the Indian Atlas, Nos. 49, 58, 66, 67, and 68, and from them the distances given in the following table have been taken. They are, therefore, somewhat under the actual distances covered.

---

* 8th, 27th, and 29th Light Dragoons; 1st, 3rd, and 6th Bengal Cavalry, and Horse Artillery.

TABLE I.

MARCH OF MAJOR-GENERAL HON. A. WELLESLEY, BETWEEN THE BATTLES OF ASSAYE AND ARGAUM.

1803.	Place of Camp.	Authority.	Remarks and References to Sheet of Indian Atlas.
Sept. 23	Assaye.		Defeated the Confederate Rájas.
24	Halt at Assaye.	Well. Desp. I.,	
25	Ditto.		
26	Ditto.		References to Well. Desp.
27	Ditto.		are to Edition of 1834.
28	Ditto.		
29			
30			
Oct. 1			
2			
3	50 miles N. of Aurangabad	Do., Page 419	
4			
5			
6			
7	Waukory.	,, 429	
8	Ajanti.	,, 433	Sheet. 38.
9			
10	30 miles N. of Aurangabad	,, 434	
	Birkenholey.	,, 438	
11	Phoolmurry.	,, 441	Poolmurree.—Sheet 38.
12	Ditto.	Owen, 314	
13	Ditto.	Well. Desp. I., Page 443	
14	Ditto.	,, 446	"Halted on 14th & 15th,
15	Ditto.		and marched on 16th."
16	16 miles N. of Phoolmurry	,, 453	Well. Desp. I., 454.
17	Pahlood.	,, 454	
18	Adjuntee.	,, 456	
19			"Descended the Ghát."
20			Well. Desp. I., 469.
21	Ferdapoor.	,, 458	
22			
23	Ditto.	,, 462	
24	Ditto.	,, 468	
25	Adjuntee.	,, 466	
26	Pahlood.	,, 472	
27			
28	Phoolmurry	,, 475	
29	Aurangabad ?	,, 477	"Passed Aurangabad on
30			29th.—W.D. I., 481.
31	Naundair Warry, 4 kos) N.E. of Puttun.)	,, 477	"This is my second halt from the bottom of the Ferdapoor Ghaut ; the distance is, I believe, nearly 100 miles." Well. Desp. I., 477.

TABLE I *(Continued)*.

MARCH OF MAJOR-GENERAL HON. A. WELLESLEY, BETWEEN THE BATTLES OF
ASSAYE AND ARGAUM. *(Continued)*.

1803.	Place of Camp.	Authority.	Remarks and References to Sheet of Indian Atlas.
Nov. 1	Cheesekair.	Well. Desp. I., Page 400	
2	Ditto.	Do., 481	
3			
4			
5			
6			
7			
8			
9	Chitchooly.	,, 491	Sheet 55.
10			
11	Jaum.	,, 494	Sheet 55.
12			
13			
14			
15			
16			
17			
18			
19	Iwankoad on the Payn Gunga.	,, 511	
20			
21			
22			
23	Rajoorah.	,, 514	Sheet 55?
24			
25			"Descended the Ghauts." Well. Desp. I., 528.
26			
27			
28			
29	Parterly.		Battle of Argaum.— Sheet 54.
30	Ditto.	,, 528	

The halting places are taken from the dates of letters and reports in the Wellington Despatches.

Suggestions by Mr. Saunders.

Parterly is Patoolla on Indian Atlas ; now called Pathulda.

Ferdapoor seems to be Farhadpur in sheet 38, latitude 30° 35′, at foot of Ajanta Pass.

Naundair is Nandoor on sheet 38 ; 4 kos N.E. of Puttun.

Pahlood is Pilode on Scott's map of the Peninsula, and corresponds with Podwuth on the Indian Atlas, sheet 38.

Cheesekair. Scott has Cheetchkaira on the road between Poolmurree and Ajanta.

Chitchooly and Jaum are on the northern edge of the hills south of Ballapoor.

Rajoorah Pass is said in the Berar Gazetteer to be the Ghát south of Pathoor, S.E. of Ballapoor, but is differently placed on Scott's map.

TABLE II.
MARCH OF GENERAL LAKE IN PURSUIT OF HOLKAR.

1804.	From	To	Miles.	Remarks.
Oct. 31	Dehli ...	Loní ...	10	
Nov. 1	Loní ...	Bághpat ...	14	
2	Bághpat ...	Kándla ...	27	
3	Kándla ...	Shámlí ...	11	Relieved Colonel Burn.
4	Halt.			
5	Shámlí ...	Mahmadpúr	12	
6	Mahmadpúr	Barnáwa ...	19	
7	Barnáwa ...	Khataulí ...	25	
8	Khataulí ...	Mirat * ...	21	* Became a cantonment in 1809.
9	Mírat ...	Hápar ...	20	
10	Hápar ...	Málágarh ...	19	
11	Málágarh ...	Shikárpur ...	18	Crossed the Kálí Nadí.
12	Shikárpur ...	Pilhannah ...	20	Passed Fort of Komona.
13	Pilhannah ...	Koriya Ganj	18	
14	Koriya Ganj	Khasganj ...	23	
15	Khasganj ...	Sirpura ...	19	
16	Sirpura ...	Aliganj ...	23	
17	Aliganj ...	Farakhábád	26	In addition, pursuit 10 miles out (Thorn, 391), making 46 miles.

Total 325 miles in eighteen days, or average of 18 miles a day, including the halt. The Infantry Brigade was at Aliganj on 16th.

FORCE.—His Majesty's 8th, 27th, and 29th Light Dragoons; 1st, 4th, and 6th Native Cavalry, and the Horse Artillery. Also the Reserve Brigade of Infantry under Lieut.-Colonel Don, consisting of 2 companies of His Majesty's 22nd Regiment, and 3 battalions of Native Infantry, viz.:—1st and 2nd battalions of 12th Native Infantry, and 2nd battalion of 21st Native Infantry.

TABLE III.

MARCH OF MAJOR-GENERAL SMITH IN PURSUIT OF AMÍR KHÁN.

1805.	From	To	Distance Miles.	See Thorn, p.431, and Stubbs I., 297.
Feb. 8	Bhartpúr ...	Mathra	26	
9	Mathra ...	Camp in the Doáb	3	
10	Camp ...	7 miles N.E. Joár	18	
11		Aligarh	20	
12	Aligarh ...	Near Komona ...	16	
13	Komona ...	Pánagarh ...	22	
14	Panagarh ...	Púth	24	
15	Púth ...	Garmaktesar and Komadána Ghat	13 ?	Where is Komadána ?
16	Halt.			
17	Komadána...	Amroha... ...	25	
18	Amroha ...	Moradabad ...	21	
19	Halt.			
20	Moradabad	Rámpúr	—	
21	Rámpúr ...	Chappara ...	23	
22	Chappara ...	Shergarh ...	—	
23	Halt.			
24	Do.			
25	Shergarh ...	Milak	23	
26	Halt.			
27	Milak ...	Moradabad ...	34	
28	Moradabad	Kánt	21	
March 1	Kánt ...	Badáli	—	
2	Badáli ...	Afzalgarh and Skerkot ...	—	} Passed Skerkot defeated Amír Khán, and returned to Skerkot.
3	Halt.			
4	Sherkot ...	Shergarh ...	19 ?	
5	Shergarh ...	Moradabad ...	19 ?	
6	Moradabad	Ganahan river ...	9	
7	Ganahan riv.	Chandausé ...	34	
8	Chandausé..	Rámganga river	23	
9	Rámganga...	On Chandausi rd.	20	
10	Camp ...	3 kos from Sambhal ...	14	
11	Halt.			
12	Camp ...	Amroha	33	
13	Halt.			
14	Amroha ...	Komadána ...	22	
15 & 16	Komadána .	Bahádurganj ...	} 35	Crossing the Ganges.
17	Bahádurganj	Jehángírábád ...		
18	Jehángírábád	Komona... ...	22	
19	Komona ...	Koel	21	
20	Koel ...	Beyond Joar ...	26	
21	Joar ...	Mathra	16	
22	Mathra ...	No name given...	} 26	
23	Camp 22nd	Bhartpúr ...		

FORCE.—8th, 27th, and 29th Light Dragoons ; 1st, 3rd, and 6th Bengal Cavalry ; Horse Artillery.—About 1,800 men in all.

Appendix V.

AUTHORITIES CONSULTED.

In many cases the authority is indicated in the foot notes, and a list of the full titles of the various works is given below. I must specially acknowledge the assistance I have received in the topography from Mr. Trelawny Saunders, Geographer to the India Office.

LIST OF AUTHORITIES.

Wellington Despatches, Vols. I. and II.

Thornton's Gazetteer of India.

Mill's History of British India, third edition, Vol. VI.

History of the Mahrattas, by James Grant Duff, Esq., 3 Vols., London, 1826.

Geology of India, Medlicott and Blanford.

A Sketch of the Mountains and River Basins of India, by Trelawny Saunders, Geographer, India Office.

Elphinstone's History of India, original edition, 1841.

History of the Bengal Artillery, by Major Francis Stubbs.

Military Repository, No. 2 and No. 3. (This book is in the India Office Library).

Thorn's Memoir of the War in India, (India Office Library, No. 11.)., from 1803 to 1806.

Notes relative to the late Transactions in the Marhatta Empire. (3 volumes in red Morocco; in Political Department of India Office; presented to the Court of Directors by the Marquess Wellesley.)

Bengal, also Fort St. George and Bombay Papers, presented to the House of Commons. Printed by order of the House of Commons, 5th and 22nd of June, 1804. (Record Department, India Office, No. 32.)

Accounts and Papers, X. of 1805, XVI. of 1806. (House of Commons Library).

Marshman's History of India.

A Selection from the Wellington Despatches, by Sidney J. Owen.

Survey of the Route of H.E. General Lake's Army in 1803 and 1804. By Lieut. Carmichael Smyth; original forwarded to Court of Directors. (In Geographical Department of India Office).

Plan of Campaign proposed by H.E. General Lake, with Remarks by the Governor-General, and Explanations by the Commander-in-Chief. Manuscript in Military Department, Calcutta. (Referred to in the printed Bengal Papers, at pages 156 and 159.)

Siege of Bhartpúr. Creighton. (India Office.)

Malcolm's History of India. (India Office.)

Despatches of the Marquess Wellesley, Vols. III. and IV.

Text-book of Indian History, with Geographical Notes, Genealogical Tables, etc. The Rev. G. A. Pope, London, 1880.

Memoirs of John Shipp, late a Lieutenant in H.M. 87th Regiment, 3 Vols. (in R.U.S.I. Library)

Route March of the Army under the personal command of the Commander-in-Chief. Appendix to Abstract of General Orders and Regulations in force in H. E. I. C. army on the Bengal Establishment to 1st February, 1812. (This book is in Military Department of India Office).

Appendix VI.

TABLE OF LOSSES IN THE DIFFERENT ACTIONS.

Name of Action.	Force Engaged.	Killed and Wounded, and Missing.	Per-centage of Losses.
Battle of Dehli ...	about 4,500	461	10
,, Assaye	,, 8,000	1,566	nearly 20
., Agra	,, 4,600	229	5
,, Laswárí ...	,, 8,000	822	over 10
,, Argaum ...	,, 13,000	339	under 3
,, Díg ...	under 6,000	651	11
Four Assaults of Bhartpúr	12,100	3,000	25

LIST OF APPENDICES.

LIST OF MAPS, &c.

INDIA,

SYSTEMS, &c.

LUDIANA

TRIP
NIRA
DEH

ALVAR   LASWA
MATHRA
JAIPUR BHARTPUR

JODHPUR

LUNI R.   S. R.   CI
ARVALI HILLS
TONK
CHAMBAL

MT ABU   UDAIPUR   KOTAH   RAJMAHAL

MAHI

JJAIR   BHOPA
VINDHY   INDUR N.R
BARODA   SATPURA   NARMAD RAN
SURAT   TAPTI   ASSIRCARH   AWILCARH   CALCUTTA
BURHANPUR ELICHPUR
KHANDESH   SIR   AMRA
GULF OF KHAMBIT   RAITHAL WADI
NORTHER   AJANTA ASSAYE
AURANGABAD
ALNA

BASSAIN
KALIYAN JUNAR   COD
BOMBAY   AHMADNAGAR
PUN   PEN
JINJIRA
BANKOT   SATTARA   BIDAR

GOLKONDA
SOLAPUR   BIJAPUR KISTNA
BELGAUM   MUDGAL D. R.
GOA
CAPE RAMAS   PEN
HARIHAR

SUR
MANCALUR   BANGALUR
SERINGAPATAM   O AN INCH
MAISUR   200   300   400 MILES
NILGIRI   KAVA

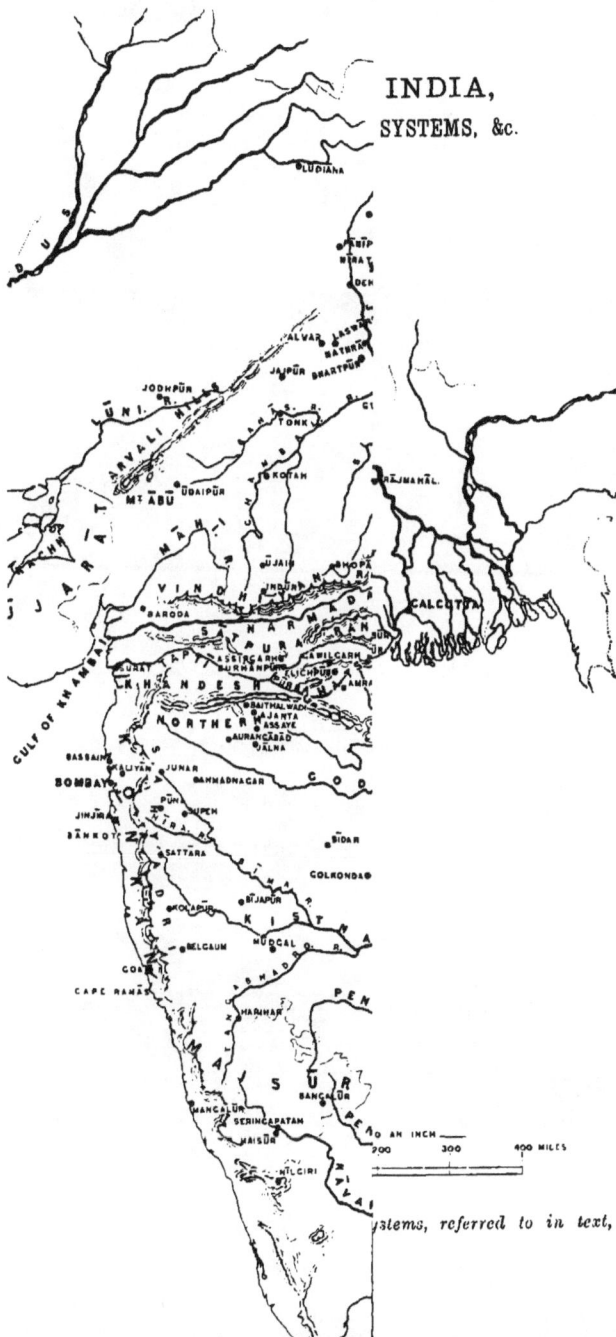

ystems, referred to in text,

D U S

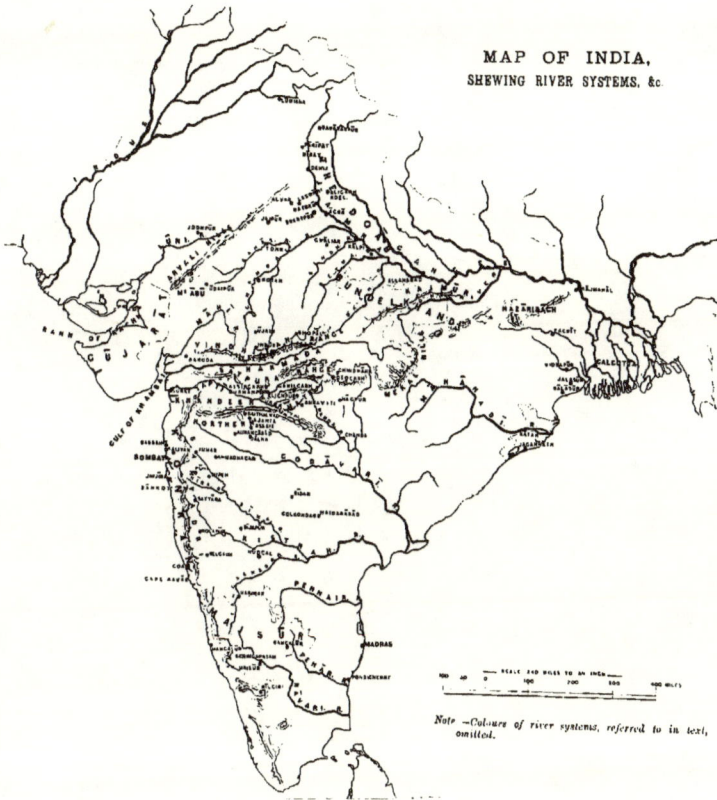

MAP OF INDIA,
SHEWING RIVER SYSTEMS, &c.

Note —Colours of river systems, referred to in text, omitted.

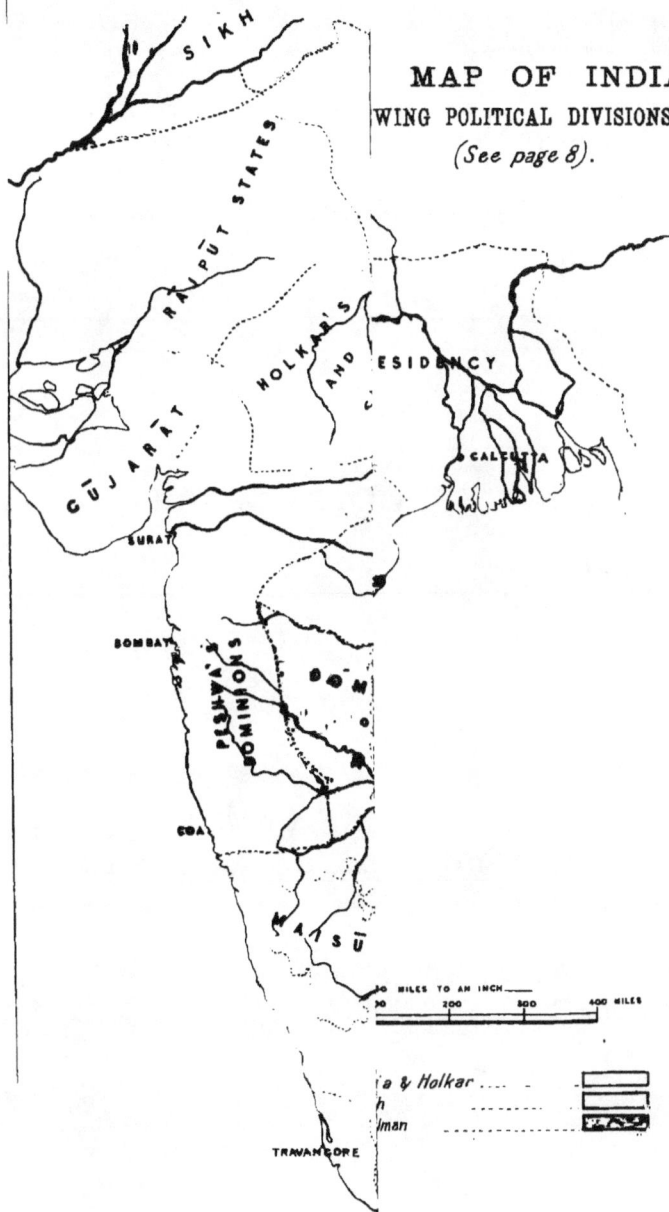

SIKH

RAJPŪT STATES

MAP OF INDIA,

WING POLITICAL DIVISIONS IN 1803.

(See page 8).

HOLKAR'S

AND

ESIDENCY

GŪJARĀT

SURAT

CALCUTTA

BOMBAY

PESHWA'S DOMINIONS

O M

COA

GOA

AISŪ

MILES TO AN INCH

200   300   400 MILES

a & Holkar . . . .
h
Iman

TRAVANCORE

MAP OF INDIA,
SHEWING POLITICAL DIVISIONS IN 1803.
(See page 8).

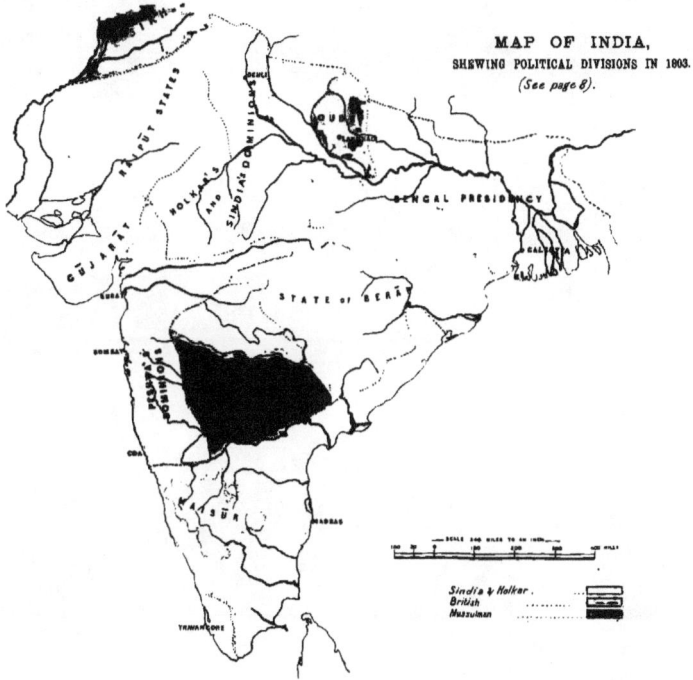

Sindia & Holkar.
British
Musulman

THEATRE OF WAR
IN 1804 TO 1806.

LŪDIĀNA

PATIĀLA

SAHĀRANPUR

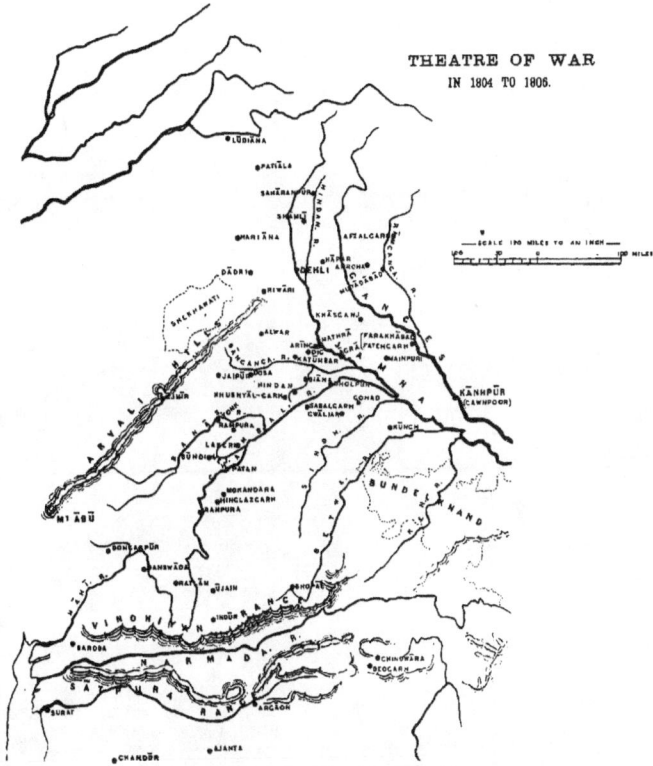

THEATRE OF WAR
IN 1804 TO 1806.

L ORDER OF BATTLE, MARCH ANDED BY

XCELLENCY ⟩ LAKE.

Camp at Secu⟩

(*Fro*

Front

att. I.	6 Comp. 16th N.I.	1st Batt. 2nd N.I.	1st Batt. 14th N.I.	4 Comp. 17th N.I.	His Majesty's 76th Regt.	1st Batt. 4th N.I.
ol. .	Lt.-Col. White.	Major Kergan.	Lt.-Col. McKulloch.	Capt. Bagshaw.	Major Mc Leod.	Lt.-Col. Brown.

4th Brigade : Lt.-Col. Pow.de : Hon. Lt.-Col. Monson.
Major of Brigade : Capt. Brigade : Lt. Ritso.
Duncan. ledge. -Mr. of Brigade : Capt. Berry, 4th N.I.
Actg. Qr. Mr. of Brigade ; L⟩

	4th Brigad		1st Brigade.
Left Wing Artillery, Capt. Green, Commanding.	3 6-pounders. 3 Tumbrils.	ng y, 1son, ing.	1 5½-inch Howitzer. 3 6-pounders. 4 Tumbrils.

LEFT WING.   WING.

Jeneral St. John, Commanding.   *e, Commanding.
of Brigade, Lieut. Coxon.   *, Capt. Scott.
le-Camp, Lieut. Wilson.   *pt. Brietzicke.
                        Lt.-Col Capt. Mc Gregor.
                        Arti
                        A
                        Qua

, and   Engin
attle.   *issary of Ordnance*
                   Grain Department.

HEAD

rigade, Col. St. Leger, Comdg. Cavalry.   3rd Brigade, Col. Macan.
Capt. Rose. Aide-de-Camp, Lt. Gore.   M. B., Lt. Macan, 27th Dragoons.
Qr. Mr., Lt. Johnson, 2nd N. Cavalry.   Acting Qr. Mr., Lt, Shubrick.

xn.   Lt.-Col. Need.   Major Mounsey. | Lt.-Col. McGregor. Hon. Lt.-Col. Carlton

avalry. H.M. 27th Dragoons.   6th N. Cavalry. | 4th N. Cavalry.   H.M. 29th Dragoons.

GENERAL ORDER OF BATTLE, MARCH AND ENCAMPMENT OF THE ARMY COMMANDED BY

HIS EXCELLENCY GENERAL GERARD LAKE.

Camp at Secundra, August 26th, 1803.

(From Thorn's History.)

Front Line of Infantry.

2nd Batt. 6th N. I. | 1st Batt. 12th N. I. | 2nd Batt. 4th N. I. | 8 Comp. 16th N.I. | 1st Batt. 2nd N. I. | 1st Batt. 14th N. I. | 2nd Batt. 2nd N. I. | 1st Batt. 16th N. I. | 2nd Batt. 16th N.I. | 2nd Batt. 12th N.I. | 4 Comp. 4th N.I. | His Majesty's 27th N. I. | 1st Batt. 76th Regt. | 1st Batt. 6th N.I.

Major Bassett. | Lt.-Col. Palmer. | Lt.-Col. Ashe. | Lt.-Col. White. | Major Krepan. | Lt.-Col. McKulluch. | Lt.-Col. Blair. | Major Forbes. | Major Holdane. | Major Oehterlong. | Major Edwards. | Capt. Bagshaw. | Major Mc Leod. | Lt.-Col. Brown.

2nd Brigade : Col. Clarke.
Major of Brigade :
Qr. Mr. of Brigade : Capt. Duncan.

4th Brigade : Lt.-Col. Powell.
Major of Brigade : Capt. Cumberledge.
Acty. Qr. Mr. of Brigade ; Lt. Pester.

3rd Brigade : Col. McDonald.
Major of Brigade . Capt. Christie.
Acty. Qr..Mr. of Brigade : Capt. Wallis.

1st Brigade : Hon. Lt.-Col. Monson.
Major of Brigade : Lt. Bittn.
Actg. Qr.-Mr. of Brigade : Capt. Berry, 4th N.I.

2nd Brigade.
1 5½-inch Howitzer.
2 12-pounders.
3 Tumbrils.

Left Wing Artillery, Capt. Green, Commanding.

4th Brigade.
3 6-pounders.
3 Tumbrils.

3rd Brigade.
2 12-pounders (reserve).
6 6-pounders.
1 5½-inch Howitzer.
9 Tumbrils.

Right Wing Artillery, Capt. Robinson, Commanding.

1st Brigade.
1 5½-inch Howitzer.
3 6-pounders.
4 Tumbrils.

LEFT WING.
Hon. Major-General St. John, Commanding.
Major of Brigade, Lieut. Caron.
Aide-de-Camp, Lieut. Wilson.

PARK.
Lt.-Col. Horsford, Commanding Artillery.
Adjutant, Lt. Butler.
Quartermaster, Lt. Brown.

RIGHT WING.
Major-General Ware, Commanding.
Major of Brigade, Capt. Scott.
Aide-de-Camp, Capt. Brietzcke.
Persian Interpreter, Capt. Mc Gregor.

Heavy Train, Carts, and Bazaars, Baggage, Cattle.

Engineer and Pioneer Corps.
Capt. Wood.
Lt. Swinton.
Lt. Forrest.

Commissary of Ordnance and Grain Department.

HEAD   QUARTERS.

2nd Brigade, Col. St. Leger, Comdg. Cavalry.
M. B., Capt. Ross. Aide-de-Camp, Lt. Gore.
Acty. Qr. Mr., Lt. Johnson, 2nd N. Cavalry.

1st Brigade, Lt.-Col. Vandeleur.
H.B., Lieut. Bolton.
Acting Qr. Mr. Brigade,

3rd Brigade, Col. Macan.
M. B., Lt. Macan, 27th Dragoons.
Acting Qr. Mr., Lt. Shubrick.

Capt. Brown. | Lt. Col. Brown. | Lt.-Col. Need. | Major Mascary. | Lt. Col. Gordon. | Lt. Col. Vandeleur. | Major Middleton. | Lt.-Col. McGregor. | Hon. Lt.-Col. Carlton

Horse Artillery. | 2nd Reg. N. Cavalry. | H.M. 27th Dragoons. | 6th N? Cavalry. | 1st N. Cavalry. | H.M. 6th Dragoons. | 3rd N. Cavalry. | 4th N. Cavalry. | H.M. 29th Dragoons.

Front Line of Cavalry.

THE CAMPAIGNS OF LORD LAKE AGAINST THE MARÁTHÁS—1804-6.   Plate V.

BATTLE OF DEHLI.

Scale 2 miles to an inch ¹   ✗. Site of Battle of Dehli

Copied from a Map compiled in 1871 for use of Troops at Dehli Camp of Exercise

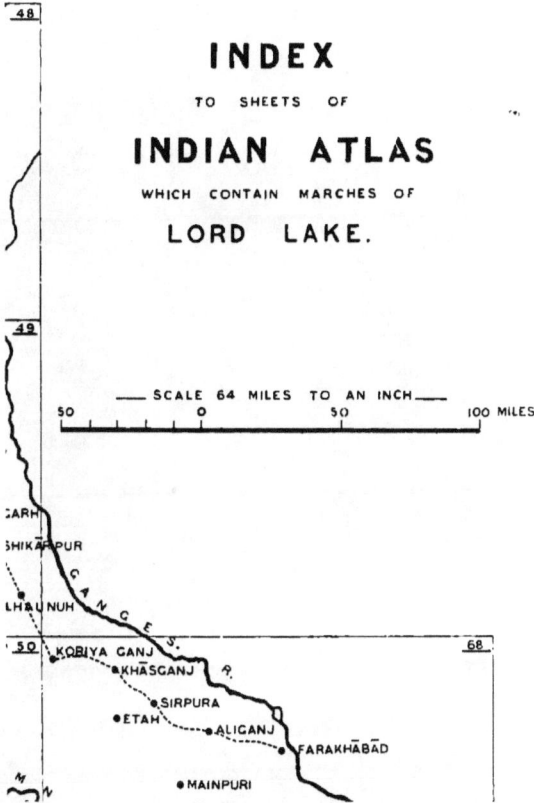

INDEX

TO SHEETS OF

INDIAN ATLAS

WHICH CONTAIN MARCHES OF

LORD LAKE.

THE CAMPAIGNS OF LORD LAKE AGAINST THE MARATHAS—1804-6.
BATTLE OF LASWÁRI.

Enlarged from Gwalior and Central India Topographical Survey, Sheets 16 & 21).

Plate VII

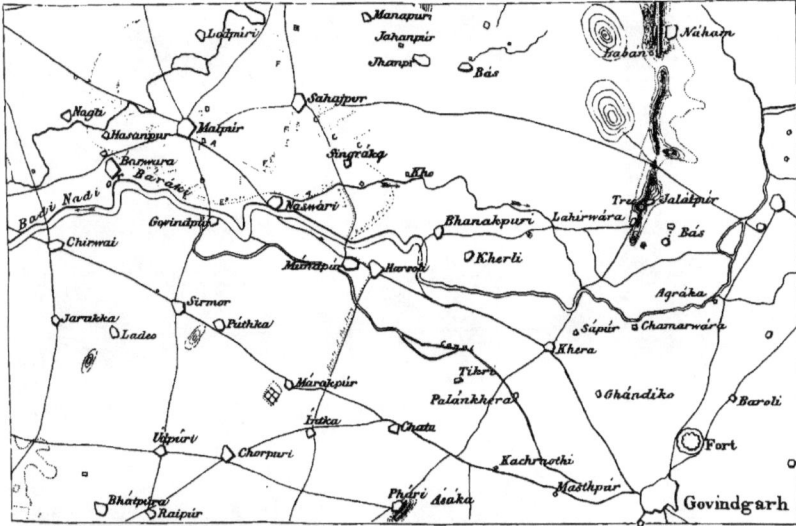

Manapuri
Ladmiri
Jahanpir
Jhanpi
Bás
Náham
Laban

Nagtú
Hasanpur
Malpir
Sahajpur
Singrákg
Kho
Tre
Jalálpúr

Banwara
Baráski
Nasári
Bhanakpuri
Lahirwára
Bás

Baki Nadí
Chirwai
Gorindpur
Mánápur
Harsoa
Kherli
Agráka

Jarakka
Ladeo
Sirmor
Pithka
Sápúr
Chamarwára
Khera

Marakpur
Canal
Tikrú
Palankherá
Ghándiko
Baroli

Utpúr
Intka
Chata
Kachrasthi
Fort

Bhátpúra
Raipúr
Phári
Asaka
Masthpúr
Govindgarh

NOTE:— AA —First position of the enemy when attacked by the British infantry.
BB —Second position.
RR —Route of the following columns from British for enemy's left.
CCC —Position of Cavalry brigades to attack AA.
FFF —Position of Cavalry brigades during attack on BB.
[—Maratha's artillery.
Backward arrows in a tank.

udeepoor
tree
Simboonaulke Serei

Bisswahree Bubbeea

n. Bilsooree
Juggernaut ke Seerei

Arrah

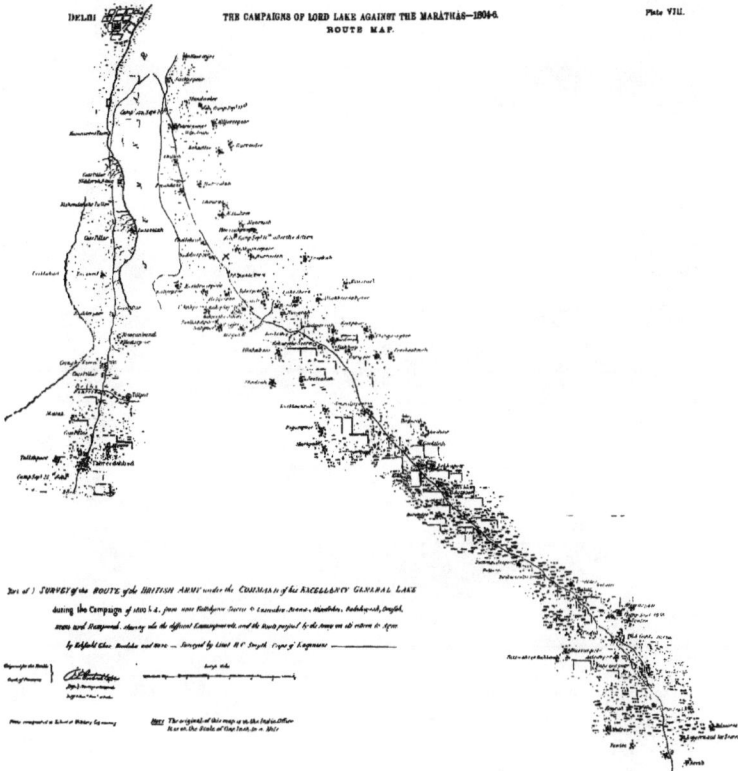

Part of a SURVEY of the ROUTE of the BRITISH ARMY under the COMMAND of his EXCELLENCY GENERAL LAKE
during the Campaign of 1805 &c.

BLASTING OPERATIONS

AT

TIMLIN'S NARROWS, BERMUDA,

In 1879-81,

By Lieutenant C. K. Wood, R.E.

(Communicated by the Commanding Royal Engineer, Bermuda.)

1879.

The work was first started on the 9th of September, 1879, in accordance with the wishes expressed by his Excellency the Governor.

Owing to unavoidable reasons the work had to be carried on at first from Boaz; and the men and boats were taken to and fro daily to the work at Timlin's Narrows, by the steam launch. The distance was great and much time and money was thus spent on the journey. In addition to this it was very hard work for the men, as we paraded at 7 a.m., and often did not get back to Boaz until 6 p.m., breaking off for about half-an-hour in the middle of the day for lunch, which they took with them; storms of rain were frequent, and the men had often to come home a long journey wet through to the skin. This was obviated, however, about the middle of October by the men being moved to Agar's Island, which is only about half-a-mile from Timlin's Narrows.

Owing to the late season of the year I received orders not to make any preliminary survey of the narrows channel and the reefs that bordered it, as it then existed, previous to blasting, but to commence blasting at once, as there was little time to spare. Accordingly the actual work done in 1879 cannot be recorded on any chart. I may, however, here remark that the soundings on Hinson's Island were almost identically the same as those on *Plate* I., which now accompanies this report, made from a survey taken in October 1880, the reason being that little or no work was done upon that side in 1879.

The reef, however, on the N.W. side of the channel had a sheer face on the channel side, there being only 3 or 4 feet over it at low water quite close to the buoy, and being in portions actually un-covered at low water. The rock on this reef was very hard, but being under-cut and full of holes on the channel side, it was very favourable for blasting, and the work progressed very rapidly. A single charge of 20 lbs. of gun-cotton often brought away three or four solid blocks of stone, weighing 3, 4, 5 and sometimes as much as 8 tons. Later on, however, we came on a softer vein, more like hard clay and shells; this was hard to work in, as not only did the charges not work to such good effect, but what work they did do was all broken into small rubble and sand instead of large blocks. On weighing we found that about 15 cubic feet of this rock went to 1 ton.

The boats used on the work were as follows:—1 cutter, 1 gig, 1 dinghy, 1 lighter. The cutter, a submarine mining boat, was used as a diving boat. The lighter, lent by the Admiralty, was fitted with a joggle in the stern and a strong winch amidships; she was used to haul up the *debris* and then remove it into deep water. The gig and dinghy were used to run the warps out to the buoy, and for general purposes ; they were both submarine mining boats.

The first thing done in the way of work was to lay out three strong moorings, with 7-cwt. sinkers attached, in deep water, in different directions, clear of the channel but adjacent to it, about 200 yards off. The object of these was to have three places to warp the lighter to, where she might lower away the *debris* well clear of the channel. The particular mooring, chosen to warp the lighter to, de-pended on the direction of the wind and tide. Other moorings, with only 5-cwt. sinkers, were also laid down, and used for getting and keeping in position the diving boat and lighter when at work, by means of warps leading to them.

The moorings being laid down and all stores collected, the blasting and removal of the *debris* commenced.

The charge cases were made of zinc cylinders manufactured for the purpose; the zinc stood well at such small depths of water. The charges were in three sizes, viz. :—5 lbs., 10 lbs., 20 lbs. The ex-plosive used was gun-cotton, with platinum wire detonators. The reasons why such small charges were used was that, owing to the rock being full of holes, as above described, and much shaken by blasting in former years, these charges were more economical, and had the additional advantage of not shattering the rock into small fragments as larger charges did. The largest charge used was one of 50 lbs., and this only once, when it broke the rock into such small pieces that I did not again attempt a large charge while the rock possessed the character and form above mentioned. Of course the best positions for the charges were chosen either in holes or cracks, or better still under overhanging projections. In the latter case they were placed by the diver in correct position; but often they could be lowered away from a boat and directed into correct position by the aid of a water-glass, without the assistance of a diver at all. The charges were invariably fired by 10 cells of a firing Leclanché battery.

The plan adopted for the removal of the large blocks of stone loosened by the blasting was as follows :—

The lighter was warped into position alongside the diving boat, only end on to it, with her stern next to the diving boat, and with a warp leading from the bow to the mooring buoy, as shown in *Fig.* 1., *Plate* II. The chain which leads from the winch over the stern joggle was then passed to the diver, down below, who placed it round the block of stone to be removed; when secure, the winch was worked till the stone was raised sufficiently from the bottom, then the lighter was warped away into deep water and the block was lowered; this being done the lighter was warped back into position for another stone.

In order to allow of the stone being lowered away without the assistance of divers the chain was arranged as follows :—

At the end of the chain was a large ring, through which the standing part was brought so as to form a loop; in the middle of this loop another chain was fastened on by a ring, which was called the tripping chain, see *Fig.* 2., *Plate* II.

By a glance at the figure it will be seen that when the loop is put round a block of stone, and the strain taken on the standing part which leads over the joggle to the winch, the loop is tightened and the stone held securely, and thus the stone may be raised by working the winch to a level with the top of the water, or, as was generally the case, to a level with the keel of the lighter.

To lower away the stone you have merely to take up the slack of the tripping chain and make it fast inboard, then walk back on the winch; this loosens the standing part, and the strain coming on the tripping chain gradually pulls the standing part through the ring, till the loop is large enough for the stone to fall out. This plan was never found to fail. Care, however, must be taken that the distance from the ring at the end of the chain to the tripping chain be less than the diameter of the stone, else the loop cannot be tightened on the stone.

In cases where the rock was mere rubble, a box holding about 22 cubic feet of stuff was lowered away and the diver filled it with rubble; the larger rubble being hoisted off the ground by the aid of a hook-rope, the hook of which was moused and a loop formed by passing the standing part through it, and guided into the box by the diver. The box was filled with very small stuff by the diver, using a galvanized iron bucket and ordinary garden hoe; he put the bucket between his knees, scraped the small stuff into it with the hoe, and then emptied it into the box. The box when full was raised by a winch, warped away, and emptied by a tripping chain attached to the bottom.

Owing however to the hard nature of the rock little or no box and bucket work was done in 1879.

Not only did the work progress very rapidly for the reason stated in the last paragraph, but, also, at first, owing to the shallowness of the water, I employed, simultaneously with the divers in proper dresses, two very excellent divers out of the Company, who worked without dresses or apparatus, putting chains round blocks and laying charges. These men could put the smaller chain round blocks of stone at a depth of 10 feet, and one of them could lay charges very satisfactory at about 15 feet.

The greatest number of cubic feet of *debris* ever removed in one day of eight hours work was 750 cubic feet. The average was about 270 cubic feet; when it came to box work with one diver at work, 6 boxes or 132 cubic feet could be removed daily. With two divers at work at once, 9 boxes or 198 cubic feet.

The daily average of men employed was :—

Making up charges	3
Steam launch	5
Timlin's Narrows	17
Total	25

When the party was moved to Agar's Island this number was reduced to 20 men, as the launch was not then required.

The number of days on which work was actually done at Timlin's Narrows was 50.

The amount of *debris* which was actually removed during this period and lowered away into deep water was 12,250 cubic feet.

It is estimated that about 7,750 cubic feet were loosened by blasting, but not removed, being left at the bottom as small stuff.

The amount of gun-cotton expended in 1879 was 550 lbs., the work done by this gun-cotton, as shewn above, was 22,000 cubic feet. The average work done by every pound of gun-cotton was 40 cubic feet of rock. This is large, but it is accounted for by the fact of the favourable condition of the rock, and also that from the previous work, years ago, many blocks of stone remained which had only to be removed, not blasted.

Owing to the detachment being required at Head-quarters, to go through the annual practice in submarine mining, the work was stopped on 29th November, 1879.

1880-1.

In accordance with General Order of the 27th September, 1880, the proposed detachment of the 28th Company, R.E., required for carrying on the work at Timlin's Narrows, was moved to Agar's Island on the 29th September.

The detachment of Royal Engineers consisted of : —

1 lieutenant, 1 sergeant, 1 first corporal, 1 bugler, 15 men. Total 1 officer and 18 men.

The men were quartered in a building called the cooper's shop, kindly lent by the Commissary General of Ordnance. The officer was quartered in a tent.

The boats employed were :—1 pinnace, 1 launch (pulling), 1 gig, 1 dinghy. The pinnace, a submarine mining boat, was used as a diving boat. The launch was lent by the Admiralty, and used as a lighter for removing the *debris* ; she was fitted with a suitable joggle, and a winch amidships ; this was the only boat they could lend us, but being very high out of the water and very large she was not so handy as the lighter lent in 1879 ; in strong breezes she was somewhat unmanageable, owing to her holding a good deal of wind. The gig was a submarine mining boat, used to take the party to and from Agar's to work, also in laying warps. The dinghy was hired by the late Colonial Surveyor, as there was no submarine mining boat available, and the work could not proceed without one; she was used for the same purposes as the gig. Most of the moorings having been laid down in 1879, a few new ones only were required. The launch and pinnace were kept moored in a sheltered position at Timlin's, the gig and dinghy at Agar's.

For the first few days the men were employed getting stones together and making an accurate survey of the reefs at Timlin's, soundings being taken every five feet.

A plan on a scale of 20 feet to one inch (*Plate* I.) is attached to this report, showing the soundings as taken in October, 1880, before commencing to blast.

This year we started on the N.W. side of the channel, where we had left off in 1879, but finding that all the hard rock had been removed as far back as it was intended to widen the channel, after firing a few charges I settled to commence work on the Hinson Island side.

The reason for abandoning the work on the N.W. side was twofold :—

1st.—Owing to the soft nature of the rock—a sort of hard clay and shells—it was all small stuff when blasted.

2nd.—As there was only a slight face of but three feet to work on the charges were not effective.

Accordingly I came to the conclusion that it was best to leave it till the last, then fire several charges over its surface to break it up, and then let the dredge cut through and remove it.

Having settled to start blasting on the Hinson Island side and to take off a corner of that shoal, it was necessary to determine the best spot at which to start. After a careful examination a very favourable spot was found, where the first charge might be laid. This was at a small re-entering angle of the shoal, about eighteen feet to the south of the White Channel buoy; the reasons for choosing this spot were very numerous, the chief of which were :—

1st.—It was the most projecting point of the shoal.

2nd.—In addition to there being a slight re-entering angle, there was a sheer face at that point of about three feet, a fall from fifteen feet on shoal to eighteen feet in channel.

3rd.—This was evidently a portion of hard rock jutting out, and a deep narrow crack ran up from the angle into the shoal.

We first put in a small charge of 10 lbs., which widened the crack sufficiently to enable us to put in a 5-lb. charge at about five feet from the end, and, following the crack up in this way, we eventually put in a large charge of 40 lbs., which turned a large portion of the rock into the channel in large blocks, leaving a face on the shoal of about five feet in depth, and a depth of water at its foot of eighteen feet at least; we then worked along the shoal to the south, being careful to keep a good face all the time, as in surface blasting with gun-cotton it is most essential to get a face to work on, otherwise a good deal of the force of the gun-cotton is expended uselessly.

In these operations the difference of work done by a charge against a face or on a slope was very marked.

In this way we worked along till we came out into deep water, about 85 feet from the White buoy, having taken a strip of shoal away about 15 feet in width, and that to a least depth of 15 feet H.W.

We now started to work back again to the White buoy, taking it back at starting only another five feet, but gradually getting broader, up to nearly 20 feet at the White buoy; in returning we were careful to put the charges so that we had always a re-entering angle, and in this way the charges worked to great advantage; indeed, we often cut in behind the rock, which gave better results still, as the next charge had three sides to work on. What is meant will be better understood by a glance at *Fig.* 3., *Plate* II.

The piece *ACD*, hatched from left to right in *Fig.* 3, shows the portion already deepened, the piece hatched from right to left shows that to be removed, *C* is the charge, and the dark hatching shows the probable crater; *AB* is a face varying in depth, and from *B* it runs out to nothing at *D*, which is the edge of the channel.

By putting the charge thus in the re-entering angle at the foot of the face we kept a face of about six or seven feet.

After firing a charge all the *debris* was removed to a depth of at least 15 feet before firing another charge; subsequent charges, however, often covered up our previous work with a foot or so of small *debris*, which we did not remove, as it would have been mere waste of time and money to clear this away by divers with box and bucket when the dredge was expected.

By this method we made certain that the rock was blasted and broken up all over to at least a depth of 18 feet, and it was intended that the dredge should, at the conclusion of the work, dredge this *debris* up.

The character of the rock along this shoal was on the whole of a soft nature, like that previously described, with veins of hard rock cropping up every now and then. The proportion of hard rock being very small, the chain described in the report on the operations in 1879, was very little used, and the *debris* was chiefly removed by the divers putting it into a box and then warping it away, as described in the report above referred to.

As in 1879, two divers could remove about 198 cubic feet, and when only one diver was at work six boxes or 132 cubic feet was about the average day's work. Owing to the removal of one of our divers for employment on the "Carolina Z," and his subsequent death, we had not a sufficient number to work two simultaneously, except just at first, and thus the work did not progress as fast as it might have done.

For this tolerably soft rock charges of 50 lbs. of gun-cotton were found most effective, they generally cut along the face about eight feet.

The cases for these charges were at first made of zinc, but latterly, having procured some empty six gallon oil cans, they were adapted as charge cases, and much time and money was thus saved. A tin plate was carefully soldered over the bung hole, care being taken to clean the iron well, in order that the solder might take on it. A circular hole, about five inches in diameter, was cut in the same end of the drum, to which was soldered securely a tin cylinder about six inches in diameter and four inches long, thus leaving a shoulder of half-an-inch all round at *a*, see *Fig*. 4., *Plate* II.

The primer was made as follows :—A tin tube was made about ten inches long and one and a half inch in diameter; about two inches from one end a flange plate was soldered on to this, and again about four inches from that another flange, also circular, was soldered; each flange was about six inches in diameter, so that it could just fit into the tin cylinder soldered on to the drum, see *Fig*. 5., *Plate* II. The flange *B* was not, however, slipped or soldered on till the very last thing. Through this tube two electric wires were led; these were held in position and the whole made water-tight by running a composition into the tube in a molten state; the composition consisted of pitch, parafin and tallow. The fuze and 2-lb. dry primer, all in a water-tight bag, were connected on to these wires with a water-tight joint at *C* The charge-case having been packed with gun-cotton discs and the primer above mentioned inserted, the flange *A* rested on the shoulder *a* of the drum; the tin cylinder was then packed tightly with damp clay, which forced the flange *A* on to the shoulder *a*, and prevented any fear of the solder touching and firing the charge. The flange B was then soldered on to the small tube containing the wires, the edges of the cylinder were turned over, the whole well soldered, and the charge was complete. This description of charge case worked very well.

Old chain or pieces of scrap iron were attached to the charge in order to sink it. The charges were sometimes fired by ten cells of a firing Leclanché battery, and at others by a quantity-dynamo.

The average number of men daily employed on the work up to the 12th of December was 20, made up as follows :—17 at Timlin's Narrows, 3 at Boaz making charges.

From the 12th December the average was 18, made up as follows :—16 at Timlin's Narrows, 2 at Boaz making charges.

From the 19th October to 31st March the total number of days lost, owing to bad weather, was about 30.

The actual number of hours of work done on the job was 17,430.

The number of cubic feet of *debris* actually removed into deep water was 11,700.

The amount estimated as blasted but not removed, being left at the bottom as small rubble and sand, was 11,300 cubic feet. This is the amount that could be removed by dredge without any further blasting.

The amount of gun-cotton expended upon the work up to the 31st March, 1881, was 1383 lbs. Thus the work done by 1 lb. of gun-cotton averaged $\frac{23000}{1383}$, or nearly 17 cubic feet.

Plate I. shows clearly the work done in 1880-1, the portion removed having a wash of yellow over it; as stated on the *Plate*, the soundings shown over the portion removed are not now probably correct, as *debris* has fallen upon it by successive charges. This was intended to be rapidly and cheaply removed to a depth of at least 17 or 18 feet by the dockyard dredge, but owing to her having been condemned by the Admiralty and broken up she was not available.

Very little work has been done on the N.W. side of the channel this year, and the weather has not permitted of a survey being made in time to show on *Plate* I. the work done.

In conclusion, seeing that 677 lbs. of gun-cotton are unexpended, I would propose to complete the blasting operations as originally intended, which the recent bad weather has prevented, viz., to cut away to a depth of 15 feet the remaining portion on Hinson Island, also as shown by red tint on *Plate* I., and also the corners of the reef on the N.W. side, as shown by red tint.

It is estimated the amount of cubic feet to be removed to carry this proposition out would be about 2,000 cubic feet.

Taking a day's work from previous data as 132 cubic feet, this would take about 16 working days.

As the stores are already in hand the only cost would be that of working pay; taking this as 6d. a foot the cost would be £50.

As a dredge cannot be obtained it might be worth while to try and remove the *debris* over the work already done with a spoon and bag, this would certainly be quicker than using a diver, and much less expensive if it could be managed.

C. K. WOOD, Lieut. R.E.,

Officer in Charge.

Agar's Island,
12th *April,* 1881.

APPENDIX I.

SHOWING TOTAL COST IN 1879.

The total cost in 1879 was as follows :—

	£	s.	d.
Working Pay	120	18	3
Local Bills	15	12	9
Admiralty Stores ...	19	0	0
Gun-cotton and Fuzes	75	0	0
	£230	11	0

The local bills included tin, zinc and solder for making the charge cases, chain, and small stores generally.

The Admiralty stores consisted of ropes for the warps used.

All the above sums of money were paid by the Colonial Government in 1879, with the exception of the gun-cotton and fuzes, which were lent from the submarine mining stores for the work at Timlin's Narrows and have been settled for in the accounts of 1880-1.

The average cost per cubic foot of *debris* actually removed into deep water was—

Working Pay	$2\frac{1}{4}d$. per cubic foot.
Stores	2d. ,,
Total	$4\frac{1}{4}d$. ,,

The average cost per cubic foot removed and blasted was :—

Working Pay   1¼d. per cubic foot

Stores   1¼d.   „

Total   2½d   „

C. K. W.

APPENDIX II.

Showing Total Cost in 1880-81.

The total cost of work done in 1880-81 was :—

	£	s.	d.
Working Pay	284	5	10
Local Bills	13	15	8
Stores, Ordnance Store Department	259	6	2
Total	£557	7	8

The local bills were for small stores, such as zinc, tin, solder, etc., purchased from Mr. Black.

The total of the bills for stores from Ordnance Store Department, paid for by the Colonial Government in 1880-81, was £430 8s. 4d.

But of these, 550 lbs. of gun-cotton and 143 fuzes, amounting to £75 0s. 0d. come against and are included in the expenditure for 1879.

677 lbs. of gun-cotton and 100 fuzes, amounting to £96 2s. 2d., are still in hand unexpended, making a total of £171 2s. 2d., which has to be deducted from £430 8s. 4d. in calculating the value of Ordnance Store Department Stores consumed up to 31st March, 1881.

The cost per cubic foot of *debris* actually removed was :—

Working Pay   5¾d. per cubic foot

Stores   5¾   „

Total say   1s.   „

The cost per cubic foot of stuff removed and blasted was :—

Working Pay   3d. per cubic foot

Stores   3d.   „

Total   6d.   „

This increase of cost per cubic foot is due, as previously stated, to the character of the rock having changed from hard rock, with favourable cracks and holes, to solid rock of a soft nature, causing—

1st.—A greater expenditure of gun-cotton per cubic foot removed.

2nd.—A much greater time and, consequently, expense in removing the *debris*.

C. K. W.

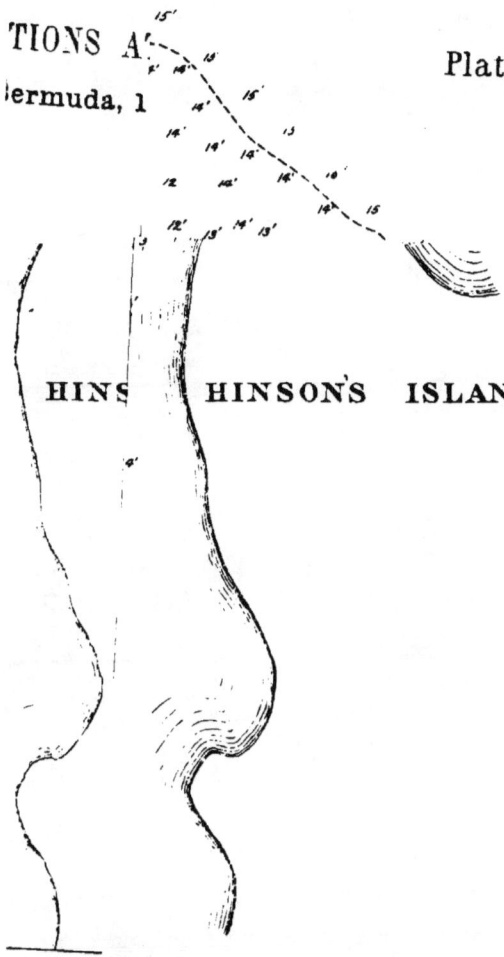

'TIONS A'

ermuda, 1

Plate I.

HINS HINSON'S ISLAND

BLASTING OPERATIONS AT TIMLIN'S NARROWS,
Bermuda, 1879-81.

Plate I.

SURVEY OF TIMLIN'S NARROWS

TAKEN OCTOBER, 1881.

By COLONEL AND LIEUT somet relating to 1880-81

The figures show depth of water in feet at M.W., soundings taken every 2 feet.
The dotted lines show 13 feet contour.

Bottom removed on 1879 . . . . . 14,350 cubic feet
Rock blasted but not removed 7,750
                                         _____
                              Total   20,100

Plan showing the position of the 15-foot fissure on the conclusion of the work on 31st March 1881.

The boundaries to the N.W. of the 15-feet C... are 1... up the channel sides were sloped at such portion. The rock was thoroughly then not properly met much less, except in the rubble falling in from lower chukart which it was pursued the dredge won't remove.

HINSONS ISLAND

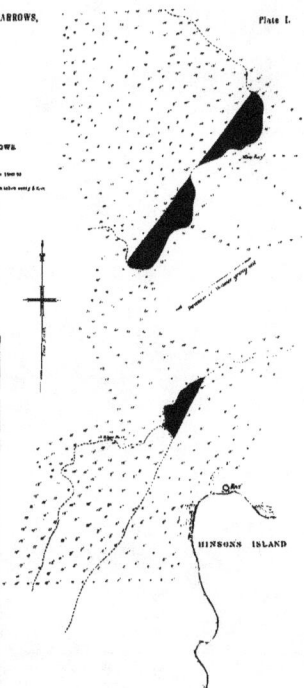

HINSONS ISLAND

Fig. 2.

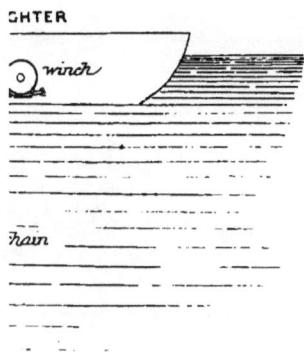

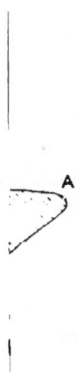

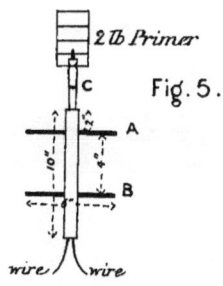

Fig. 5.

Bermuda, 1879-81.

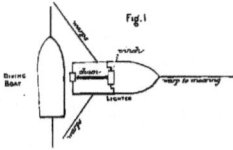

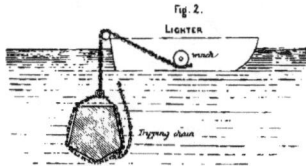

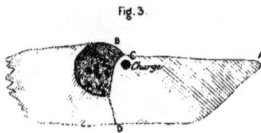

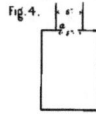

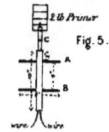

Fig.1

Fig.2.

Fig.3.

Fig.4.

Fig.5.

PAPER V.

DEMOLITION OF THE BARQUE "CAROLINA Z,"

IN THE

HARBOUR OF ST. GEORGE'S, BERMUDA, 1880-1,

By LIEUT. C. PENROSE, R.E.

(Communicated by the Commanding Royal Engineer, Bermuda.)

THE barque "Carolina Z " was of the following dimensions :—

Length (over all)	...	154 feet.
Breadth... ...	...	32 „
Depth of hold ...	...	24 „

She had been scuttled, when on fire, and run aground on a clean hard bottom, out of the channel and anchorage of St. George's Harbour.

The following were the depths (at high water) :—

At her bow	... ...	29 feet.
Amidships		32 „
Astern ...	... ...	35 „

The bowsprit, catheads, and a small portion of the forecastle showed above water at low tide. The vessel was laden with Indian· corn, in bulk, of which she contained from four hundred to five hundred tons at the time of her destruction.

The vessel was in good condition, very strongly built, and little injured by the fire which caused her to be scuttled.

She had been lying at the bottom for over a year. On the 2nd November, 1880, the military authorities were requested to destroy the vessel in accordance with the decision arrived at by the General

Board of Health. All expenses connected with the operations to be borne by the Colonial Government.

On the 4th November, the C.R.E., by the request of His Excellency the Major-General Commanding, undertook the work, and ordered a detachment of the 28th Submarine Mining Company, R.E., to proceed forthwith.

The services of a civilian diver having been engaged, owing to the R.E. divers being employed on the operations at Timlin's Narrows, on the 15th November an examination and survey of the vessel were made. In making this examination it was found necessary to blow in the after-hatch with a small charge, the explosion of which liberated a very large quantity of foul gas from all parts of the vessel, but chiefly from the forecastle, from which gas escaped for about ten minutes.

It was decided to destroy the sides of the vessel throughout those portions which enclosed the grain, endeavouring at the same time to disturb and blow away as much of the corn as possible. With this object, on the 30th November, 1880, two mines, each consisting of 270 lbs. of guncotton, in service mine cases, were placed, with the assistance of a diver, one in the main-hold (b), the other in the after-hold (a). (See Figs. 1, 2, 3, in accompanying sketches.)

These charges were 35 feet apart, this distance being regulated by the distance apart of the hatches, the depth of water, and the estimated effect of the above mentioned amount of guncotton. The centre of each charge was 27 feet below high water.

A third charge of 270 lbs., which would otherwise have been similarly placed in the fore-hold (see c, Figs. 1 and 3), was omitted on account of the liability of damaging houses and vessels in the neighbourhood.

The explosion was postponed until the wind should blow from the N. or N.E., and this delayed it until the 7th January, when it was decided to wait no longer.

The result of the simultaneous explosion of these two charges was to blow out the centre portion of the sides of the vessel and of the main and upper decks. The main and mizzen masts were brought down, the lanyards of the rigging having been cut away previously by the diver.

The diver reported that the corn was blown out of the vessel, and that she was opened right through from side to side for about 60 feet amidships. (See Fig. 4.)

The forepart of the vessel and part of the stern stood, although much shaken, the decks, up to the foremast, being heaved up.

The forepart of the vessel being now so much blocked up with wreckage it was impossible to place the next charges inside, so that two charges, each of 130 lbs., were, on the 13th January, placed under the bilge with a view of destroying that portion of the vessel which still contained a good deal of the rotting grain. These two charges (see *Fig.* 4) were at a depth of 30 feet, and 20 feet apart.

This explosion (14th January) carried the destruction of the sides and bottom as far as the bitts—20 feet from the stem, and brought down the foremast. (*Fig.* 5.)

On the 18th January, a charge of 100 lbs. guncotton (*Fig.* 4) was placed in the stern of the vessel, at a depth of 18 feet, and 15 feet from the stern-post, in order to complete the destruction of the after-run of the vessel.

This charge, which was fired the same day, destroyed the after-run and cleared away the decks right aft, only a small portion of the rail and bulwarks being left.

The foregoing explosions effectually destroyed the vessel as a focus of foul and unhealthy gases, but the forecastle and a small portion of the stern, as well as some loose detached pieces of wreckage, still remained to block the water-way.

Instructions having been received to clear away these portions of the vessel, on the 3rd February, one charge of 200 lbs., was placed in 20 feet of water just aft of the bitts, 20 feet from the stem, room for the placing of this charge having been cleared by the explosion of a small charge of 25 lbs. (*Fig.* 5.)

The explosion of the 200 lb. charge, together with that of a second small charge of 25 lbs. placed close to the stem in the strongest part of the ship, effectually cleared away the bows of the vessel, as well as a large quantity of wreckage which had collected there,—the results of former explosions.

On the 15th February, five small charges, amounting to 90 lbs. guncotton, were fired with a view of clearing away the wreckage of the three masts which had sunk head downwards and become entangled in the wreckage, and also to blow away some loose pieces of wreckage which were visible 6 feet or 8 feet below the water.

The stump of the main-mast anchored by the wire rigging was left to buoy the site of the vessel. (*Fig.* 6.)

The foregoing explosions completed the work asked for by the Colonial Government. The work was much delayed through having to wait for wind from certain quarters as well as on account of bad weather.

COOPER PENROSE,

18th April, 1881.　　　　　　　　　　　　　　　　　LIEUT., R.E.

APPENDIX I.

NOTES ON THE OPERATIONS CONNECTED WITH THE DESTRUCTION OF THE BARQUE " CAROLINA Z."

The first two charges were contained in the service 250-lb. mine cases. 270 lbs. were placed in each case, the loading-hole end of the case not being concreted as on service. The primers were contained in primer envelopes, service pattern. The two 130-lb. charges used in the second explosion were made up in the service 100-lb. waterproof bags, the primers being enclosed in the now obsolete waterproof primer bags.

All the remaining charges were made up on the following plan, which has the recommendation of being extremely cheap. The charges moreover take a very short time to make up, and their effect seemed to be just as great as if they had been enclosed in more costly cases. The discs are made up in strings of from 8 to 14 in each string, according to the size of the charge (25 lbs. to 200 lbs.) required. These cylinders of discs are then arranged round the dry priming charge, which is enclosed in a water-tight case. This waterproof envelope was composed of two of the old water-proof priming bags well rendered with pitch, the unpitched bags being found to leak at any considerable depth. The charge takes the form of an hexagonal prism when built up in the manner just described. This prism stands on a small square platform of wood, and a similar platform is placed on the other end. Four iron bolts with nuts and washers hold the charge together in a compact mass, enough pressure being applied by means of the screw nuts to squeeze some of the moisture out of the wet guncotton. The discs cannot now absorb any more water when placed in the sea, and the charge remains effective as long as the primer remains dry. The detonators used were those supplied for submarine mining service—No. 12, Low Tension.

The large charges were fired from a distance of 400 yards, a piece of cable being laid just before the explosion. Short ends were connected to the mines when laid, and these were brought up to the surface and fastened to the rigging. An earth-plate was also connected to the forward 270-lb. mine, so that we were able to test each mine separately for conductivity and insulation. This testing was carried out twice a week during the six weeks that elapsed between the laying and firing of the charges. The smaller charges were not tested, as they were fired as soon as laid. The effect of the charges of 270 lbs. was very great. These charges were place t just a little deeper (27 feet) than the most favourable depth for ateral effect, as obtained from Capt. Abney's formula:—

$$D = 6\cdot 7 \text{ lbs. (charge in lbs.)} ^{\frac{2}{9}},$$

in this case, $23\frac{1}{2}$ feet.

It may be assumed from these operations, that a 270-lb. charge in 27 feet of water will destroy the side of a wooden ship at 23 feet distance horizontal, besides shaking the vessel's timbers within a radius of 35 feet.

The mines were fired with a battery of Firing Leclanché cells, 20 being used with long cables and 10 with the short ones (small charges).

APPENDIX II.

STATEMENT SHOWING NUMBER OF MEN EMPLOYED, AND GUNCOTTON AND MONEY EXPENDED ON THE DESTRUCTION OF THE "CAROLINA Z."

The work was commenced on the 4th November, 1880.
The work was completed on the 15th February, 1881.

Total number of working days—25.

Strength of working party averaged daily ... ... $\left\{ \begin{array}{l} \text{1 Officer,} \\ \text{7 N.-C. Officers and men,} \\ \text{1 civilian diver employed on four} \\ \quad \text{occasions.} \end{array} \right.$

Amount of gun-cotton used—1320 lbs.

Cost of operations:—

	£	s.	d.	£	s.	d.
Working pay—						
Officer	12	10	0			
Military working party... ...	19	2	1½			
*Civilian diver	9	18	0			
				41	10	1½
Value of Ordnance stores	219	1	11			
,, Local stores ..	6	5	10			
				225	7	9

Total...£266 17 10½

---

* The civilian diver was a remarkably good one, and as he had already been employed in some attempts to raise this vessel he was well acquainted with her state inside, so that much time was saved at the preliminary examination.

PLAN OF VESSEL.

FIG. 1.

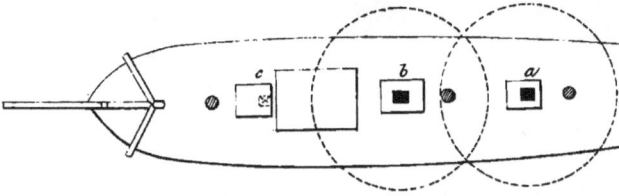

SKETCH OF VESSEL BEFORE 1ST EXPLOSION.

FIG. 3.

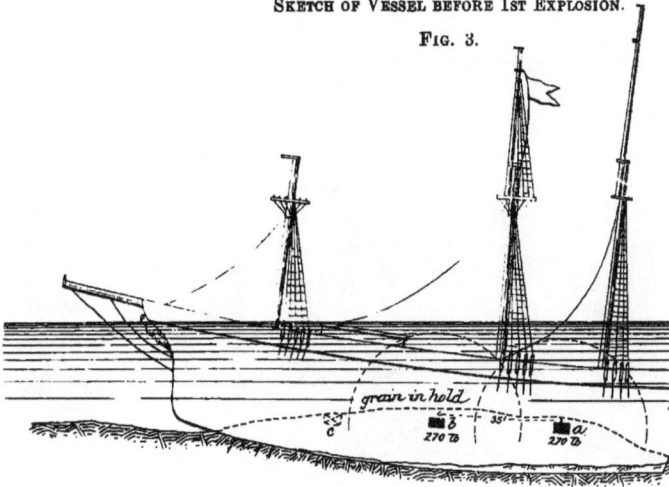

AFTER 1ST EXPLOSION, BEFORE 2N

FIG. 4.

PLAN OF VESSEL.
FIG. 1.

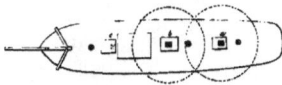

SECTION
FIG. 2.

DEMOLITION OF BARQUE
"CAROLINA Z,"
Bermuda, 1880.

SKETCH OF VESSEL BEFORE 1ST EXPLOSION.
FIG. 3.

AFTER 2ND. EXPLOSION (HULL OF VESSEL DESTROYED)
FIG. 5.

AFTER 1ST EXPLOSION, BEFORE 2ND.
FIG. 4.

FINAL CONDITION OF VESSEL.
FIG. 6.

Scale

ACCOUNT OF THE CONSTRUCTION OF

BRIDGES OVER THE KABUL RIVER,

NEAR JALALABAD,

DURING THE OPERATIONS IN AFGHANISTAN, 1880,

By Captain R. H. Brown, R.E.

Object of the bridge.—During the operations in Afghanistan, of 1879-80, it was considered desirable to construct a bridge over the Kabul River at Jalalabad, for the purpose of facilitating the collection of supplies, and for certain political reasons.

Description of river at site of bridge.—The site chosen for the Bridge was the same as that of the preceding year,* where the Kabul River is made up of three channels, and divided by sandy islands more or less covered with boulders. (*Plate* I.).

The channel under the right bank was 167 feet wide, with a greatest depth of 3 ft. 9 in., and a current of nearly 5 feet a second, surface velocity. (*Plate* II., *Fig.* 1).

The centre channel was 70 feet wide, 2 ft 9 in. deep at the centre, with a sluggish current of about 1 foot a second. (*Plate* II., *Fig.* 2).

The third and most considerable channel, under the left bank, was 263 feet wide, with a greatest depth of 6 feet, and a current of rather more than 4 feet a second, surface velocity, in the deepest part of the channel at the site of the bridge. (*Plate* III.).

The bed of each channel was covered with boulders, the largest being above the size of a man's head.

State of bridge on 28th January.—Previous to the 28th January, 1880 (the date on which I received orders to carry on the construc-

---

* See Paper VIII., Vol. IV., *R.E. Professional Papers* (Occasional Series).

tion of the bridge), the first channel had been bridged by the late Lieutenant Dobson, R.E., with the aid of his Company of Madras Sappers and Miners, four-legged trestles being used for the piers; but for want of sufficient and suitable timber (all of which had to be arranged for locally, no assistance having been asked from the Attock workshops) roadbearers were wanting in some bays, and a temporary roadway only, of any planks that were available, had been laid to pass the Sappers across for work on the second channel, where two abutments had, by the 28th January, been nearly completed with boulders. The steep ramp of the preceding year, leading on to the bridge, had been made much less steep by a heavy bit of excavation executed by the Sappers, assisted by local labour.

During the construction of the first portion of the bridge, an attempt was made to form the pier, of the deepest part, of a cage, to be filled with boulders similar to those described below, but strength was sacrificed to lightness, and in the operation of moving the cage into position, it proved too weak to resist the force of the current and was swept away in small pieces. A four-legged trestle was then substituted for the cage.

Lieutenant Dobson, R.E., with half of his Company of Queens' Own Sappers and Miners, being ordered to join the expedition into the Lughman Valley, the bridge came to a standstill till orders were sent to me on the 28th January to go on with it.

Timber supply.—Meanwhile a raft of 130 timbers, averaging 22 feet long, and of sections varying from a mean breadth of 1 ft. 3 in., by a depth of 1 foot, to a mean breadth of 8 inches, by a depth of 7 inches, had been discovered stranded about two miles down the river. This raft was forthwith broken up and the pieces towed up the river, singly, by natives of an adjoining village, who contracted to bring the wood to site at so much a log.

Nature of pier adopted.—After making an examination of the two branches of the river to be bridged, and taking sections of the channels, it was decided to form the piers of cages filled with boulders.

Width of roadway.—As the planking available for the roadway was barely 10 feet long, the width of the bridge was now fixed at 9 feet in the clear between the ribands, this width being sufficient for the requirements, though the first part of the bridge had been designed to allow of a greater width of roadway.

Number of roadbearers.—The thickness of the available planking (half trees roughly squared) determined the number of roadbearers necessary to support the planks at the proper intervals to enable them to carry a 12-pounder gun and wagon. It was found, by the rough calculations following, that, allowing 21 feet from centre to centre of pier, or 17 feet span in the clear, five roadbearers of the timber brought from down the river would be amply strong enough to support a disorganized unarmed crowd.

Calculations.—The planking available being 7 inches broad, and $2\frac{1}{2}$ inches thick, it was required to find at what intervals it must be supported to enable it to carry a 12-pounder B.L.R. ammunition wagon.

Weight on hind wheels of ammunition wagon = 26 cwt, or 13 cwt. on one wheel.

Hence the weight to be supported by the planking was a live load of 13 cwt., acting at the centre.

Allowing a factor of safety of 4,

We have $lCw = \dfrac{f_0}{4} - \dfrac{I}{y_0}$ where l is to be found.

$C = \frac{1}{4}$ when loaded at the centre.

$f_0 = 6600$: for fir.

$\dfrac{I}{y_0} = \dfrac{b\,d^2}{6} = \dfrac{7 \times \frac{2.5}{4}}{6} = \dfrac{175}{24}$

$w = 13 \times 112 \times 2 = 2912$ lbs.

Substituting in the equation —

$lCw = \dfrac{f_0}{4} - \dfrac{I}{y_0}$

We get $l \times \frac{1}{4} \times 2912 = 1650 \times \dfrac{175}{24}$

Whence $l = 16\frac{1}{2}$ inches, or 1 ft. $4\frac{1}{2}$ in.

Therefore, with a 9-ft. roadway, and a bearing surface of roadbearer of 8 inches, it would be necessary to have five roadbearers, 2 feet apart from centre to centre, to obtain 1 ft. 4 in. between the roadbearers in the clear.

Hence, assuming five roadbearers $8\frac{1}{2}$ inches broad, 17 feet span, and 9 feet roadway in the clear, we have

Weight of bridge = 17 × 100 = 1700 lbs.

Disorganized unarmed crowd = 133 × 17 × 9 = 20349 „

Total.. 22049 lbs.

Or say 200 cwts.

Then $\dfrac{bd^2}{l} = \dfrac{200}{4} = 50$

$\dfrac{8\frac{1}{2}d^2}{17} = 50$

Whence $d = 10$ inches.

Therefore beams $8\frac{1}{2}$ inches wide, and 10 inches deep, will suit for the inner roadbearers.

Assume for the outer beams (which take only half the weight of the inner) also a width of $8\frac{1}{2}$ inches.

Then $\dfrac{8\frac{1}{2} \times d^2}{17} = 25$ Whence $d = 7$ inches.

The arrangement of roadbearers, shewn on *Plate* VI., *Fig.* 3, being suitable to the material at hand, was therefore adopted, the roadbearers actually used exceeding in almost all cases the sectional dimensions given in the drawing.

Height of roadway.—The height of the underside of the road-bearers above water level was fixed at 4 feet, that being the height of roadway in the trestle bridge.

Description of cages.—The cages for the centre channel were made 3 feet wide at the top, and 4 feet at the bottom, with a cutwater up-stream, and a batter of 1 foot in the down-stream face, and of varying heights to suit the different depths of water. The main or side frames, A B C D, *Plate* IV., *Fig.* 1, were composed of timbers of section about 7 inches by $2\frac{1}{2}$ inches, secured to one another by two iron spikes at each joint. The dotted lines in the drawings on *Plate* IV., represent light pieces of wood, about 3 inches by 3 inches section, nailed inside the main frames to subdivide the spaces and confine the stones in the cage. Where necessary, the spaces were further reduced by lathes placed vertically, or in any position required.

The two side frames were held together and kept apart by notched cross pieces *a a*, two to each upright, passing from side to side, projecting 9 inches outside the frames, and kept in place against the uprights by an iron spike. The 9-inch projections were most useful helps in lifting the cages, and were further convenient for fastening on ropes, serving also as steps on which to stand in the course of the construction of the bridge.

The nose piece of the cutwater was held back by pieces of wood *b b* (*Plate* IV., *Figs.* 1 and 3), fastened to it and to the cross pieces *a* of the up-stream uprights.

Gages of left channel.—The width of the cages of the left channel were increased by 4 feet at the top, the bottom width varying from 5 feet in the shortest to 6 feet in the tallest cage, and the base of the batter of the down-stream face being increased up to a maximum of 2 feet. (*Plate* V.).

The smaller cages were not braced diagonally from side to side, as the structure proved to be sufficiently stiff without doing so, and it was supposed that if the cages were made too rigid in all directions the footings would be less likely to take a firm bearing on the bed of the river. In the larger cages, however, there was added diagonal bracing vertically, horizontally, and from the bottom corners of the cages to the opposite top corner, making the last of rope that would give to a certain extent, and thereby allow the footings to take a bearing. (See *Plate* V.). The number of cross pieces *a* were also increased to three to each pair of uprights, and were doubled in the case of the centre uprights, one on each side, and clamped together by hoop-iron. (See *Plate* V., *Fig.* 3).

In the larger frames, in order to reduce the weight of the cage, the intermediate pieces added to lessen the spaces, with a view to confining the stones, were at first fixed on only up to the height to which the water level would come, those above water level being fixed after the cage had been got into position and weighted.

Number of spans.—The centre channel bridge was built in four spans, and that of the left channel in thirteen spans (See *Plates* II. and III.). I should have stated above that the reason for adopting cage piers instead of trestles, in the centre bridge, was to practice the workmen (who were natives either of Peshawur or or Jalalabad) in the construction and handling of the cages, and also to ascertain what was the best form of cage to be made out of the materials at hand, before commencing work on the most formidable portion of the bridge in the left channel, which was considered to have too great a depth and current to allow of the adoption of wooden trestles with timber of inconvenient dimensions for their formation.

Method adopted of getting cages into position.—As the depth of water in the centre channel originally did not exceed 3 feet, and as this had moreover been reduced nearly a foot by diverting, into the right and left channels, some of the smaller channels feeding it, there was no difficulty experienced in getting in the piers of this portion. About 30 coolies carried each cage in by hand and placed it in correct position. The cages were then filled with stones, a bearing for the five roadbearers constructed and bedded on each pier in a top layer of pebbles, and the roadbearers hauled into place, and sawn to correct lengths to butt against each other, their cross sectional dimensions being too great to allow of their overlapping and lying alongside of each other. (*Plate* VI., *Figs*. 1 and 2).

Placing cages in left channel.—In the left channel 9 out of the 12 piers were carried by hand into position. Numbering from the right bank (*Plate* III.), Nos. 1, 2, and 3 piers were built on the bank and carried in direct by a gang of coolies. The side frames of the cages for Nos. 11 and 12 piers were formed on the right bank, floated across the river, fitted together on the left bank, and carried into position by hand.

As considerable delay was caused in passing the carpenters and materials across the river in the leaky old ferry punt, which was the only boat available, and as it was not safe to leave materials on the left bank at night, it was thought better to completely form Nos. 7, 8, 9, and 10 cages on the right bank, and float them into place by fastening them to two roadbearers, and having them hauled across by coolies on the opposite bank. This end was attained in a more or less satisfactory manner in each case, the cage grounding in the shallow water on the other side of the deep channel. The roadbearers were then untied and drawn away, and the cage put into correct position by hand. In this operation "mussucks" (inflated hides) should have been used instead of beams to float the cages, which would then have been subjected to less straining and knocking about on arriving at the shallow water.

Cages Nos. 4, 5, and 6 could not be placed by hand as the depth of water was too great where they had to go.

Pier No. 4.—The roadbearers having been laid as far as pier No. 3, the cage for pier No. 4 was drawn along them till it was over No. 3 pier. It was then laid on its side and slid down two baulks into the water, after first fastening on to it fore and aft guys, to be hauled on from either bank, and also ropes of the proper lengths, to show, by their becoming taut, when the cage should be in proper position with respect to No. 3 pier (*Plate* VI., *Fig*. 4). This method succeeded tolerably well, but on account of the weight and size of the cage, and the contracted space to work in, there was some difficulty in getting it into the water, and it was subjected to a considerable test of strength in the process.

It was, therefore, necessary to adopt a different method with piers Nos. 5 and 6, which were still larger.

Pier No. 5.—The cage of No. 5 pier, which was 10 feet high, had to be placed in position in 6 feet of water, running at 4 feet a second above and below, but more at the site of the bridge, on account of the now contracted water-way. In order to be able to provide ballast for the cage, when floating vertically, string netting of country rope was fastened across the base of the cage, strong enough to support a small number of boulders, but not strong enough to resist the increased weight when the cage was further loaded. The cage was formed close to the water's edge on the right shore, but with a shallow between it and the deep channel.

A raft of timbers, *a b, c d, e f,* tied together by cross pieces *g, g, g, a c* and *a e,* on which to float the cage, was constructed (*Plate* VII., *Fig.* 1.) Ropes were fastened from *a* to *d* and *a* to *f,* to act as ties. Four ropes, A, B, C, and D, were fixed to the beam *a b,* two up-stream and two down-stream, one pair for either bank. The cage was then laid on its side on the raft (which had been formed in a convenient position for so doing), and lashed to it, being hinged by strong ropes at *h h* to *a b,* at the height to which the water would reach when the cage should be in position (*Plate* VII., *Fig.* 2). The rope A was then hauled on, and the raft and cage drawn into the shallow water, where the buoyancy of the raft was further increased by eight inflated skins, four fastened under *c d* and four under *e f.* The ropes A and C were then hauled on, and B and D paid out till the raft was drawn into deep water. By paying out and hauling on the four ropes as required, the cage was floated down into its proper position. A man was then sent on to the raft to cast off the lashings of *g g g* to *e f,* and those at *c* and *e.* This operation was facilitated by means of a boat, which travelled on a rope fastened round the noses of the two nearest piers, with sufficient slack to let the boat travel backwards and forwards just clear and down-stream of the position of pier No. 5.

After untying the lashings uniting *g g g* to *e f,* and the skins tied to *e f,* the beam *e f* was drawn away and the cage came part of the way up towards a vertical position. The opposite beam *c d* and skins were then unlashed and removed, and an attempt was made to draw out *g g g,* but their lower ends had got jammed against the bed of the river. It was intended when these should have been got out to haul the cage into a vertical position by ropes fastened to the top of it and hauled on from the adjacent piers. But as the pieces *g g g* appeared to be fast, it was decided to haul the cage up as it was and take the chance of the timbers g g g clearing themselves. R >pes were accordingly fastened to the top of the cage and hauled on, the result being that the hinges at h h gave, and the cage was swept away down stream clear of the beam a b, wh'ch was still kept in position by the ropes A, B, C, and D. The failure was due to the jamming of the pieces g g g, and to the hinges h h not being strong enough to stand the extra strain which was thereby brought upon them. It would undoubtedly have been better to have had no portion of the raft projecting beyond the footings of the cage, but to have given the necessary buoyancy to this side by an extra number of inflated skins; the pieces g could then have been easily removed as they would not have got jammed.

The cage was caught by the rope on which the boat travelled, and was then hauled on its side into the shallower and comparatively still water below pier No. 4, in which situation ropes were fastened on to the top of the cages by coolies, wading in the water, and the cage hauled into a vertical position. This done, the ropes A, B C-and D, which were before tied to the beam a b, were now fastened to the cage at its four corners about half-way down. Eight partially inflated skins were then fastened round the cage just below the water-level, but as it was too late in the day to attempt to get the cage into position and load it, it was left in this state till the next morning, when by inflating the skins, and hauling on and paying off the ropes, the cage came without any difficulty into position. The skins were untied or spiked to empty them of air, stones were passed across in the boat and the cage partially weighted with them. The cage having slipped a little out of its proper alignment with the other piers, its position was corrected by rocking the cage by means of the side-ropes, and hauling on the up-stream shore ropes. Temporary baulks were then run across from the adjacent piers, and stones passed over from hand to hand by lines of coolies seated on the baulks.

Cage No. 6.—In consequence of the experience gained with cage No. 5, it was decided to endeavour to get cage No. 6 into position by floating it erect, with inflated skins tied round it to give it sufficient buoyancy. Three large skins were tied on each side, a seventh at the back outside the cage, and an eighth was jammed under the lower front cross-piece inside the cage. As many coolies bans) as could find holding room, then attempted to carry the cage in a vertical position to the edge of the deep water, but it was too heavy to be so moved. Ropes had already been fixed to the four corners of the cage and two of them passed across the river. Two shorter ropes, fastened to either side, and coiled on the top of the cage, were intended for hauling on from the adjacent piers (after getting the cage approximately into position), with a view to bringing it erect should it not come so of itself. As the cage could not be carried erect, protecting pieces to protect the inflated skins were nailed to the ends of the cross pieces on one side, and the cage was laid on that side on baulks, and hauled and pushed into the deep water where it righted itself, coming into a nearly vertical position, and floated away down stream with two carpenters (either confiding or taken by surprise) till brought up by the shore ropes being hauled taut. As in No. 5 cage, string netting had been fastened across the base of No. 6 cage, and a few stones as ballast had been thrown in. These got to one side—when the cage was laid on its side—which accounted for the cage not floating properly vertical. This, however, mattered little; the cage was quietly floated down into its proper position and worked by the ropes into place, the skins untied, baulks run across, a line of coolies formed on them, and the cage loaded with boulders.

Duration of work.—This last pier was placed on the 17th February, 19 days after the commencement of work, on the centre channel. The roadbearers were all in place on the 20th February, and the planking finished throughout the centre and left bridges on the 21st February. On the 22nd February small fascines made of long rushes were laid over both bridges (centre and left channel) and secured by ribands.

The work was delayed, as the local labourers, on whom I was dependent, took holidays on all their saints' days and whenever they considered it too windy or cold, besides coming late to work on the days that they came at all. As coercion was not the order of the day this state of things had to be put up with, no military labour being made available for the work.

Roadbearers.—The roadbearers of a few bays were got into place by floating them above the piers on which they were to rest, and then hauling up first one end on to the pier and then the other end on to the adjacent pier, and moving the bearer into position across the piers; but the majority of the roadbearers were drawn obliquely along the roadbearers of the previously laid bay, till they reached the bay for which they were intended, over which the leading end of the first roadbearer was slid along on the temporary baulks previously laid to enable the cage to be loaded.

Planking.—Every 7 feet a plank was spiked to the roadbearers, but the rest of the planking was laid loose and secured by a riband spiked to the fixed plank and to the loose planks, at 4 or 5 feet intervals.

Bridge over right channel.—On the 23rd February work was recommenced on the right channel bridge. The trestles were strengthened to support a heavier roadway than was apparently at first intended; additional roadbearers were added, the original ones re-arranged and planking laid over them.

Causeways.—During the construction of the bridges, the causeways and ramps connecting the three bridges were constructed from the adjacent sand and boulders, and covered with fascines of rushes laid across the direction of the roadway, continuous to one another. This was subsequently covered with the litter from the cattle lines and became a good road.

Date of final completion.—On the 27th February the bridge was reported complete and fit for traffic throughout.

Suggestions.—From the experience gained in the construction of this bridge, I would, in a similar case, be inclined to proceed as follows :—

The form of cage adopted seems to have been suitable, as the cages were in many instances subjected to very severe strains, and underwent a good deal of hauling and tumbling about without any of them giving way.

Those cages which could be carried in by hand, it would, of course, be best to build as near to the position for which they are intended as possible.

Those which have to be floated would be best built on a temporary platform, formed in the most convenient position for getting the cages into deep water. In the case of this bridge, the platform might have been made of boulders, with rough planks on the top, on the edge of the deep water, and a pathway of boulders thrown up to connect the platform with the shore, or a small foot bridge of any description might have been made for the workmen to cross by. (See *Plate* VII., *Fig.* 3.) Slides should be arranged, and the cage so built over them that it could be run down them into deep water in an erect position, inflated skins having first been tied on round the cage at the height most suitable to the depth of water in which it is intended the cage should float. Before entering the deep water, stones for ballast should be thrown into the cages, being held in by string netting across the base. It would be best to divide the base into four compartments by the addition of vertical netting down the centre, longitudinally, and across the centre from side to side, so that if the cage tilted it could be made to float vertically by throwing stones into the proper compartment. There should be ropes fastened to each corner of the cage, one for either side of the river up-stream, and one for either side down-stream, by which the cage would be guided into correct position and kept there until the skins were untied, or spiked, and the cage loaded, when the ropes could be untied. These ropes must be tied at, or above, what will be the water line on the cage when in position, otherwise it will be found difficult to untie them afterwards; but, in order to bring the pull lower down on the cage, the ropes can be passed round a part of the frames below, and fastened at some place above water line, as shewn in *Plate* VII., *Fig.* 4. They could then be afterwards untied and drawn away, The ropes must not, of course, be cast off or slackened at all till the cage is sufficiently weighted to ensure no further movement, but they must be cast off before the part of the rope below water gets jammed by the stones thrown in.

Labour employed.—The carpenters employed were Peshawur men for the most part, a few of them only being natives of Jalalabad. The rest of the labour, which was plentiful, but of very inferior quality, was collected from Jalalabad itself and surrounding villages. Lieutenant Langley, R.E., with half a company of Madras Sappers, assisted for a short time only, during which half of the centre bridge was planked by the Sappers, and planks prepared for the other half, at which stage they were ordered away to other work. Sergeant M'Dowell (Overseer, D. P. Works) was put under my orders after the left channel bridge had been commenced, and assisted in the superintendence of the labour.

Subsequent history of the bridge.—From the date of the completion of the bridge up to the 22nd March the river rose from 4 to 6 inches. From 22nd March gauge readings were taken daily.

Nothing reliable could be ascertained concerning the height to which the floods rose, but it was not contemplated that the bridge should withstand the river in high flood, and it was therefore necessary to watch the rise of the river in order to ascertain whether it would be necessary to dismantle the bridge.

During the last week in March the river rose 2 inches. On the 1st and 2nd April the rise was 7 inches, and, on the 3rd April, No. 6 pier of the left channel bridge was observed to have sunk 1 foot at the nose and something less at the tail of the pier, due, no doubt, to the bed being scoured away in the contracted waterway, a small rise in a river, with a bed as steep as that of the Kabul River, producing a great increase of velocity and discharge.

The river, after remaining at the same level for four days, fell 6 inches between the 6th and 13th April. On the 11th April, as pier No. 6 shewed no signs of further subsidence, the roadway was brought level by packing up the roadbearers over the pier, the cage being further weighted with stones packed in up to and between the roadbearers.

There was no further rise in the river till the 29th April, when it rose 6 inches, and again 6 inches on the 30th April.

Meanwhile it had become evident that to prolong the life of the bridge it would be necessary to provide more waterway in the centre channel, as a rise in the river produced most effect in this channel on account of the small waterway and the low level of the channel itself, compared with the right channel, which was higher than either of the other two. Another bridge of four spans, in continuation of the centre bridge, was put in hand. The work consisted of sinking in the sand three cage piers, and cutting a channel between them to carry off some of the water of the centre channel. The cages were in position and partly sunk on the 1st May, but in consequence of the rapid rise of the river the right pier of the centre channel subsided at 7.30 a.m., and half-an-hour afterwards was carried away. Communication was kept up between the two sides of the river by means of a ford higher up across the centre channel, and so connecting the two side bridges.

The river kept nearly steady at the level it reached on the 1st May till the 4th. On the latter date it was noticed that pier No. 7 of the left channel had sunk about a foot at the nose, and pier No. 6 about 3 inches at the tail. The up-stream roadbearers on pier No. 7 were thus brought down to nearly a level with the water above the pier.

On the 5th May the river again rose, and I ordered the dismantling of the centre and left channel bridges, which were more
effected by any rise than the right channel, for the reason given
above, viz.:—that these channels were on a lower level than the
right channel.

By the evening of the 6th May the roadway of the centre and
about half of the left bridge had been collected on the island
between the two bridges, but on account of the rise in the river
the ford had become impracticable, and work on the left bridge had
to be suspended.

By the 7th May water was flowing over the whole length of the
raised roadway between the right and centre bridges, at the place
where the additional waterway was to have been provided, and was
finding its way along high level channels into the deeper ones.
The water was flowing over the two remaining piers of the centre
channel bridge, so that their position was only marked by the
backing up of the water. The three new cages which had been
placed in position had been filled with boulders and left, more
cages having been formed ready to restore the centre portion if
such should become practicable through the subsidence of the flood.
I had been in hopes on the 3rd May that the flood had reached its
highest, and that the bridges might be restored, but the rise on the
night of the 4th decided me to dismantle the roadways of the centre
and left bridges, and to stop the preparations for restoration.

On the 6th May the water could be seen flowing over the centre
bays of the left bridge, where the piers had subsided, the roadway
of which part had not been dismantled. On the 7th, 8th, and 9th
May rafts of inflated skins were formed, and the remaining portion
of the left bridge dismantled and the materials conveyed across to
a place of safety near the right bridge, as were also all the new
cages and other timber dismantled before. Eight beams only in
the left bridge, over which the water was flowing, could not be
moved and had to be abandoned.

At 7 a.m. on the 10th May the centre pier of the centre bridge
was carried away, and the right side trestle of the right bridge sank
about 4 inches at the nose.

On the 11th May it was noticed that the 7th and 8th piers of the
left bridge had disappeared.

The river continued to rise till the 12th May. The total rise
since the construction of the bridge in the right channel was 2 feet

8 inches as shown by the gauge readings; while in the centre and left channels the rise must have been over 4 feet, as was shown by the piers being completely under water.

It was remarked from the gauge readings that the river, as a rule, rose at night and commenced falling after noon, a fact probably due to the melting of the snows during the day-time higher up the river.

The river fell again from the 12th to 15th May, and rose again from the 15th to the 22nd May, when it was found that No. 12 pier of the left bridge was missing. At 8 a.m. on the 22nd pier No. 9 was also seen to float away. The first trestle of the right bridge had still further slightly subsided, and the water was flowing over the top of the trestle cutwaters. Some of the troops who had taken part in the Besud expedition being still across the river, the Brigadier-General requested me to leave this portion of the bridge standing till the last moment, and the dismantling was accordingly put off, but on the 23rd May, as the river continued to rise, and the abutment on the right bank had washed away, the dismantling was commenced. About 11 a.m, while the men were at work on the bridge, and three bays had been dismantled, the river rose suddenly to the underside of the planking and carried away the complete structure, workmen and all, leaving nothing to mark the site of the last bridge. The workmen were all got out safely and most of the timber recovered lower down the river.

The river remained steadily high (about 6 inches below the mark of the wave which carried away the right bridge) till the middle of June, when it began to fall. On the 25th July the river appeared to be lower than it had been during the preceding cold weather.

When I left Jalalabad, in the middle of August, 1880, one pier in the centre channel, the three new piers for the additional water-way, and seven piers in the left channel, were still in their original positions, though two of the latter were tilted to one side.

R. H. B.

SCALE $\frac{1}{160}$

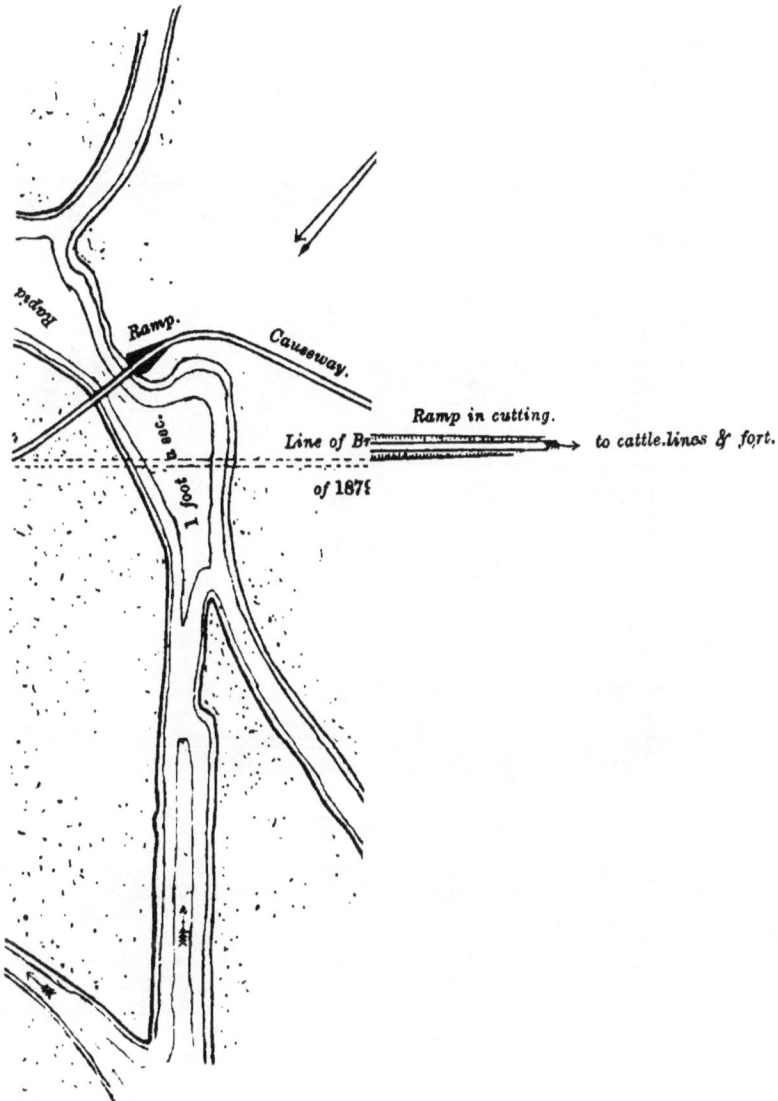

Ramp.

Causeway.

Ramp in cutting.

Line of Br ——— *to cattle.lines & fort.*

of 1878

1 foot h sec.

Scale ₁₀₀₀₀.

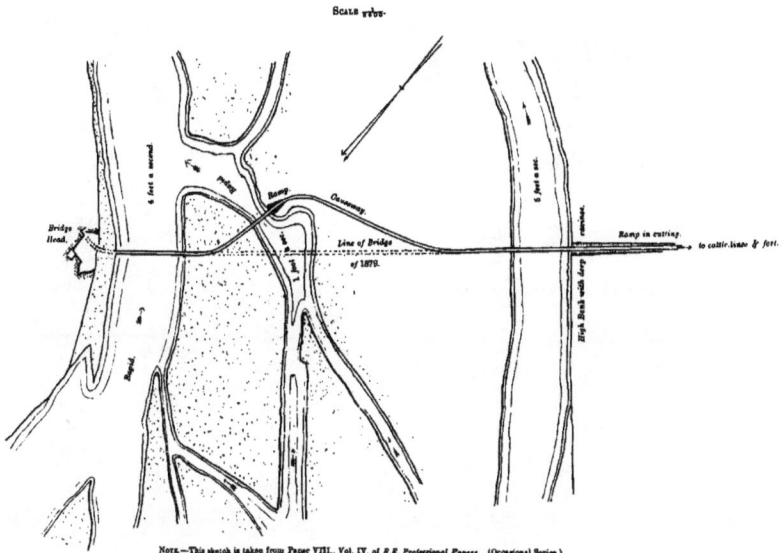

Note.—This sketch is taken from Paper VIII., Vol. IV. of *R.E. Professional Papers.* (Occasional Series.)

Fig. 1.

ON OF RIGHT CHANNEL (BRLES).

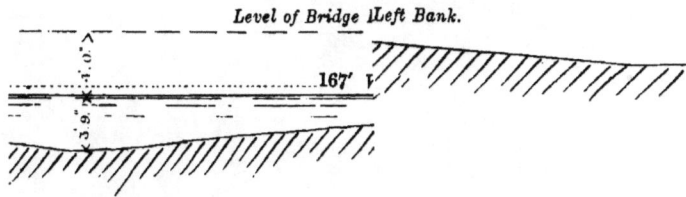

Level of Bridge l*Left Bank.*

167' V

Fig. 2.

F CENTRE CHANNEL (BRIDGE

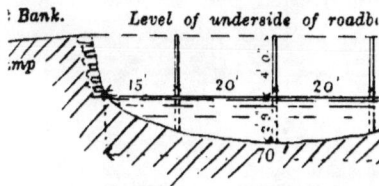

; *Bank.*   *Level of underside of roadb(*

.mvp

15'   20'   20'

70

SCALES.

HORIZONTALS $\frac{1}{30}$

VERTICALS $\frac{1}{100}$.

Fig. 1.

SECTION OF RIGHT CHANNEL (BRIDGED WITH FOUR-LEGGED TRESTLES).

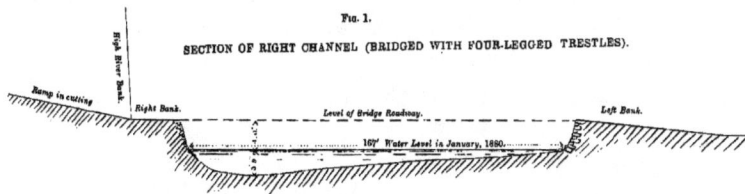

Fig. 2.

SECTION OF CENTRE CHANNEL (BRIDGED WITH CAGE PIERS).

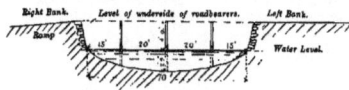

SCALES.

HORIZONTALS $\frac{1}{700}$.

VERTICALS $\frac{1}{100}$.

SECTION OF LEFT CHANN

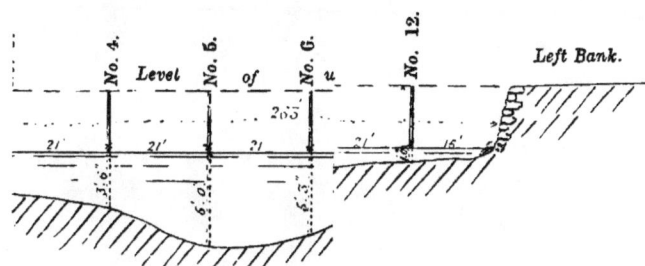

No. 4. No. 5. No. 6. No. 12.

Level   of   u   Left Bank.

205

21'   21'   21'   21'   16'

3.0'   6.0'   6.3'

SCALE!

HORIZON

VERTICA

ne of the dimensions of minor import
entered from memory, the book con

SECTION OF LEFT CHANNEL (BRIDGED WITH CAGE PIERS).

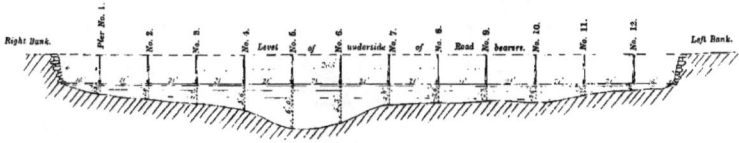

SCALES.

HORIZONTALS $\frac{1}{720}$.

VERTICALS $\frac{1}{120}$.

NOTE.—Some of the dimensions of minor importance in the above section are approximate only, being entered from memory, the book containing the actual measurements having been mislaid.

Plate IV.

Fig. 1.

DE ELEVATION OF CAGE
IN 3' OF WATER.

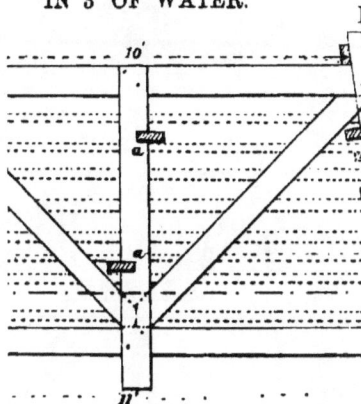

Fig. 2.

STREAM END ELEVATION.

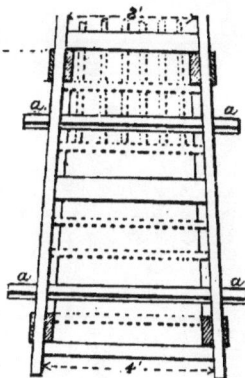

Fig. 3.

ING ATTACHMENT OF NOSEI

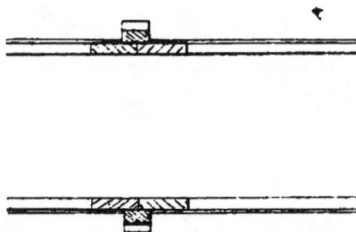

Scale $\frac{1}{40}$.

Fig. 1.

SIDE ELEVATION OF CAGE
IN 3' OF WATER.

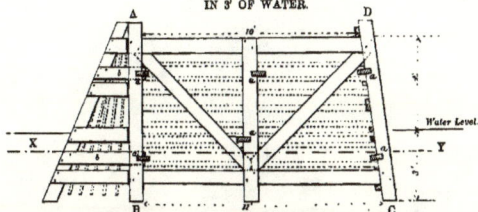

Fig. 2.

DOWN-STREAM END ELEVATION.

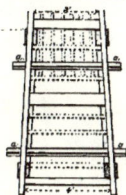

Fig. 3.

PLAN AT X Y, SHEWING ATTACHMENT OF NOSEPIECE.

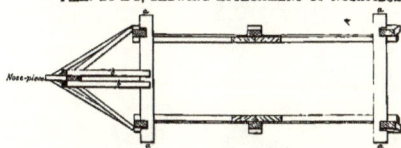

SCALE $\frac{1}{48}$.

CAGE

Fig. 1.   Fig. 2.

ELEVATION.   -STREAM END ELEVATION.

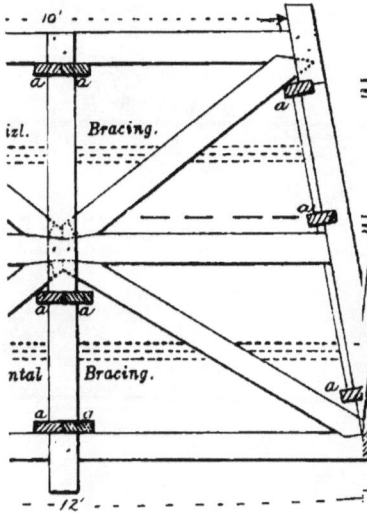

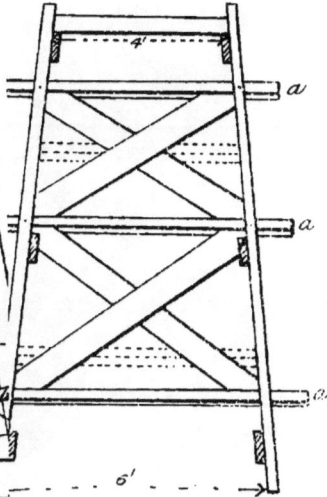

Fig. 3

PLAN AT LI

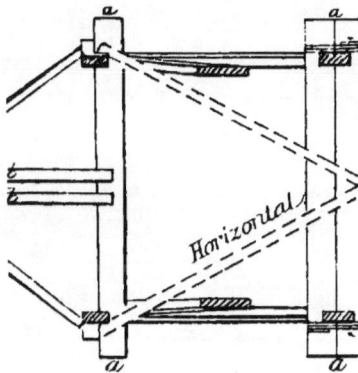

CAGE OF PIER No. 5.

Scale ₁/₂₀.

Fig. 1.
SIDE ELEVATION.

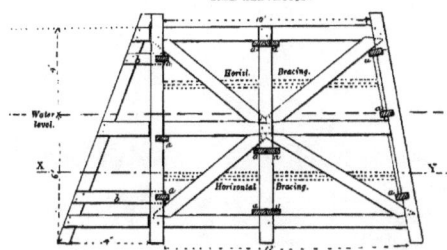

Fig. 2.
DOWN-STREAM END ELEVATION.

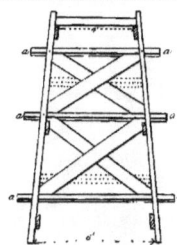

Fig. 3.
PLAN AT LEVEL X Y

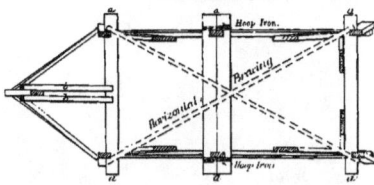

SCALE FOR FIGURES 1,2,AND
$\frac{1}{40}$.

3. 4.

WING BEARING
RERS.

LE $\frac{1}{60}$.

'ope.

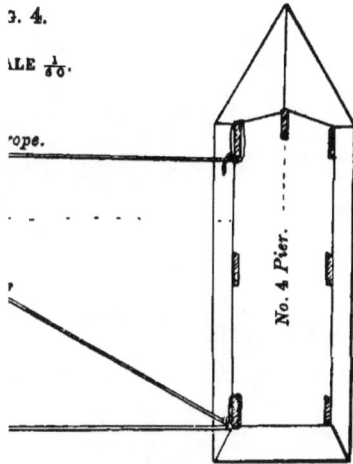

ribund §

Scale for Figures 1. 2. and 3.

Fig. 1.

SECTION OF PIER, SHEWING BEARING
FOR ROADBEARERS.

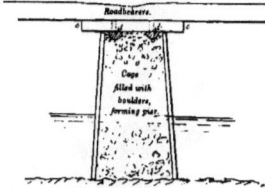

Roadbearers.

Cope
filled with
boulders,
forming pier.

Fig. 4.

Scale

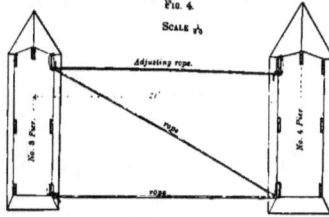

Adjusting rope.

No. 3 Pier.

No. 4 Pier.

Fig. 2.

PLAN
OF
BEARING
FOR
ROADBEARERS.

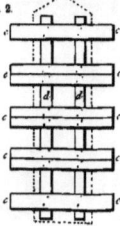

Fig. 3.

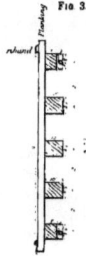

CALCULATED
SECTIONS
OF
ROADBEARERS.

"pp": packing between
outer Roadbearers and
Bearing over Pier.

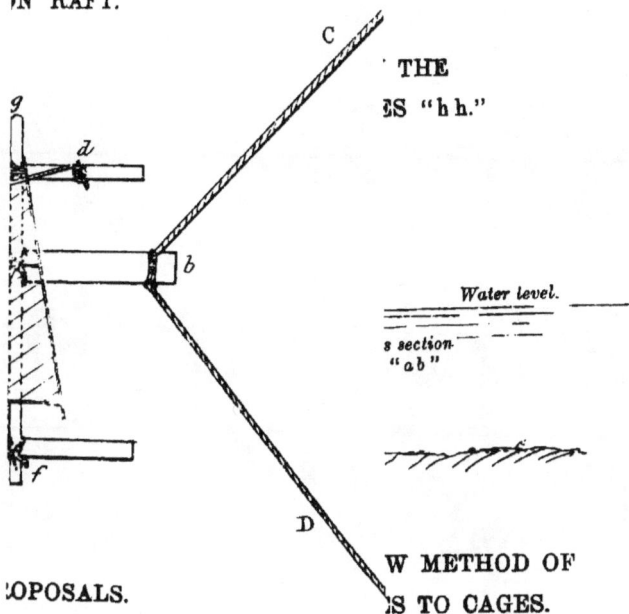

N RAFT.

C

THE
ES "h h."

g

d

b

Water level.

s section
"a b"

f

D

W METHOD OF
OPOSALS.   S TO CAGES.

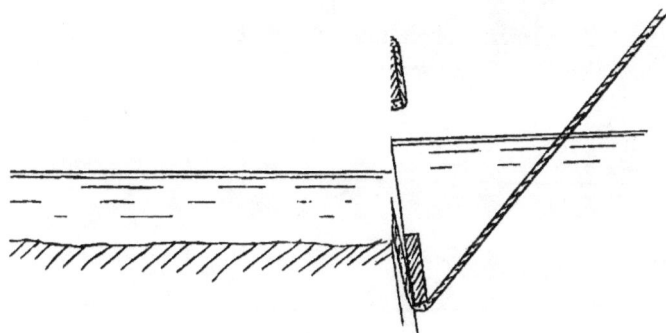

FIG. 1.

CAGE OF PIER No. 5 ON RAFT.

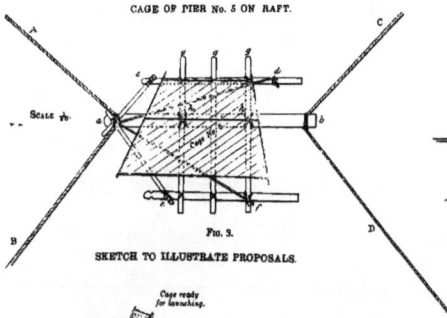

FIG. 2.

SKETCH TO SHOW THE
INTENTION OF HINGES "h h."

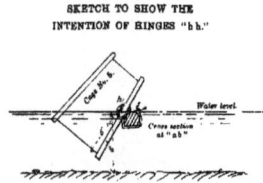

FIG. 3.

SKETCH TO ILLUSTRATE PROPOSALS.

FIG. 4.

SKETCH TO SHOW METHOD OF
FIXING ROPES TO CAGES.

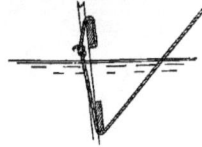

RAILWAY CURVES.

BY THE LATE CAPTAIN W. H. JOHNSTONE, R.E.

Communicated by Major H. Wilberforce Clarke, R.E.

STAKING OUT CURVES.

RAILWAY curves are generally set out by the method of tangential angles, with a theodolite.

Let TAt be a tangent to the curve at the point A; O be the centre of the circle of which the curve forms part; and AB, BC, CD, DE, &c., a number of equal chords. Join OA, OB, OCT, &c., and AC, AD, AE, &c. Draw OF, perpendicular to and bisecting AB. Let AOF $= a =$ half the angle subtended at the centre of the circle by each of the equal chords.

By Euclid III. 32 and III. 20.

Tangential angle tAB = angle in alternate segment.

$\qquad$ = half the angle at the centre BOA.

$\qquad$ = AOF.

$\qquad$ = a

„ $\qquad$ „ $\quad t$AC = half the angle COA.

$\qquad$ = BOA.

$\qquad$ = 2 a.

„ $\qquad$ „ $\quad t$AD = half the angle DOA.

$\qquad$ = 3 a.

„ $\qquad$ „ $\quad t$AE = half the angle AOE.

$\qquad$ = 4 a.

By measuring successive chords AB, BC, CD, &c., and by setting out successive tangential angles with a theodolite at A, the position of the points BCD, &c., is fixed. As it is seldom possible to set out more than a few chains from one point, it becomes necessary to shift the theodolite. Suppose the theodolite to be removed from A and set up at C. Produce the chord BC to b.

Then the angle $bCD = 180 - BCD$.

$$= 180 - (BCO + DCO).$$
$$= 180 - (BCO + CBO).$$
$$= BOC.$$
$$= 2\,a.$$

Sight back on the last peg B, turn the telescope over in altitude, and set off twice the primary tangential angle. This will determine the forward peg D.

If the sight had been directed back upon A, it would have been necessary to set off 3 a to obtain the direction of the forward peg D.

If with the theodolite at C, we sight back on B and set off a, or sight back on A and set off 2 a, the telescope of the instrument will point in the direction of the tangent to the curve at the point C, hence it is easy to set out a compound or a reverse curve by changing the tangential angle, or the direction of setting out, or both.

The tangential angle in any particular case depends upon the radius of the curve and the length of the chord which it is desired to set out. In England, curves are classified according to their radii of curvature; in America, according to the angle which each chord subtends at the centre of the circle of which the curve forms part. This angle has been already shown to be double the tangential angle. Thus, in England, we speak of a curve of 2,000 feet radius, and we calculate its tangential angle for chords of 100 feet to be $1° - 25' - 57''\cdot16$. In America, they would use a $2° - 52'$ curve, and would calculate its radius to be about 1,999 feet.

To calculate the tangential angle for any particular radius and chord is very simple. Referring to *Fig.* (1).

$$\text{Sin A O F} = \frac{A F}{A O}$$

$$\text{Sin } a = \frac{\frac{1}{2}\,\text{chord}}{\text{radius}} = \frac{\text{chord}}{2 \times \text{radius}} \quad \dots \text{ (1)}.$$

The following table gives the tangential angles of 100 and 50 feet chords to the radii most likely to be used. The necessity for maintaining the chainage of a railway unbroken causes an odd distance, or a chord less than 100 feet, at the beginning and at the end of every curve. To avoid the labour of calculating the tangential angles of these odd chords by formula (1) it will be sufficiently accurate to interpolate them from the table. Thus we may assume the angle for a 25 feet chord to be half that for a 50 feet chord, and 11 feet chord to be $\frac{11}{50}$ths of the tabulated angle for 50 feet and so on in proportion.

159

To facilitate these calculations, the value of the tangential angle has also been given in minutes. This will be found much the most convenient method of staking out curves, as it reduces to a minimum the calculations in the field, while it is absolutely rigorous except as regards the two odd chords. The error arising from assuming the tangential angles of these odd chords to vary as the length of the chords is not carried on, and can never be appreciable in practice.

The American system is very much the best. It shortens and simplifies the calculations to have no odd seconds in the tangential angle, while in cases where it is not necessary to measure the tangents, no calculations whatever is required beyond adding together the tangential angles, and interpolating those for the odd chords. English engineers, however, are very conservative, and it is improbable that the present practice of reckoning curves according to their radii will be changed.

Radius of curve, feet.	100 feet chords.			50 feet chords.		
	Tangential angle.	ditto. in minutes.	Difference between chord and arc.	Tangential angle.	ditto. in minutes.	Difference between chord and arc.
	o ' "			o ' "		
400	7 10 50·86	430·848		3 34 59·97	214·999	
450	6 22 45·81	382·763		3 11 5·06	191·084	
500	5 44 21·06	344·351		2 51 57·54	171·959	
550	5 12 57·30	312·955		2 36 18·90	156·315	
600	4 46 49·71	286·812		2 23 16 86	143·281	
650	4 24 42·22	264·704		2 12 15·22	132·254	
700	4 5 45 76	245·763		2 2 48·17	122·803	
750	3 49 21·20	229·353		1 54 36·77	114·613	
800	3 34 59·97	214·999		1 47 26·83	107·447	
850	3 22 20·24	202·337		1 41 7·35	101·122	
900	3 11 5·06	191·084	•	1 35 30·31	95·505	
950	3 1 1·06	181·018		1 30 28·65	90·477	
1000	2 51 57·54	171·959		1 25 57·16	85·953	
1100	2 36 18·90	156·315		1 18 8·24	78·137	
1200	2 23 16·86	143 281		1 11 37·49	71·625	
1300	2 12 15·22	132·254		1 6 6·88	66·115	
1400	2 2 48·17	122·803		1 1 23·50	61·392	
1500	1 54 36·77	114·613		0 57 17·90	57·298	
1600	1 47 26·83	107·447				
1700	1 41 7·35	101·122				
1800	1 35 30·31	95·505				
1900	1 30 ‚28·65	90·447				
2000	1 25 57·16	85·953				
2500	1 8 45·57	68·759				
3000	0 57 17·90	57·298				
4000	0 42 58·38	42·973				
5000	0 34 22·68	34·378				
6000	0 28 38·89	28·648				
7000	0 24 33·33	24·555				
8000	0 21 29·16	21·486				
9000	0 19 5·93	19·099				
10,000	0 17 11·23	17·189				

Railways are first laid out in straight lines, and curves are afterwards inserted. Thus the case which most frequently occurs in
practice is that of a curve that has to be put in to connect two
straight lines inclined to one another at a certain angle, called the
intersection angle.

Let AT, BT, be two straight portions of the centre line of railway
meeting in T, then it is manifest that any number of curves will
connect AT, and BT, since any number of circles can be drawn
touching these two lines.

Various considerations determine the proper curve to employ in
any particular instance.

(1.) A minimum radius is generally laid down for each particular railway,
depending upon the nature of the ground, on the nature and on the gauge of the
railway.

(2.) Cæteris paribus, the larger the radius of the curve the better.

(3.) The nature of the ground and the buildings or the obstacles upon it may
necessitate the curve passing through certain points, or avoiding certain
localities.

Let R be the radius of the curve.

„ θ be half the angle of intersection.

„ TA $=$ TB $=$ T, the tangent.

„ DC $=$ V, the versed sine.

„ TD $=$ S.

Then OA $=$ AT, tan ATO.

R $=$ T, tan θ.

$\therefore$ T $=$ R, cot θ ...   ..., ... (2).

Again OT $=$ OD $+$ DT.

R cosec $\theta =$ R $+$ S.

$\therefore$ S $=$ R (cosec $\theta - 1$)   ... (3).

Also the angle OAC $=$ 90 $-$ CAT.

$=$ ATC.

$= \theta$.

$\therefore$ DC $=$ OD $-$ OC.

V $=$ R $-$ R sin OAC.

$=$ R (1 $-$ sin θ)   ...   ... (4).

From *Fig.* 1 it is manifest that the angle subtended at the
centre by each chord is double the primary tangential angle.

Hence Fig. 3 the number of chords in the entire curve—

$$= \frac{\text{Angle AOB}}{2a}$$

$$= \frac{\dfrac{\text{AOB}}{2}}{a}$$

$$= \frac{\text{AOT}}{a}$$

$$= \frac{90 - \theta}{a} \quad \dots \quad \dots \quad \dots \quad \dots \quad (5).$$

If θ and a be expressed in minutes this formula will become

$$\text{number of chords} = \frac{5,400 - \theta}{a} \quad \dots \quad \dots \quad \dots \quad (6).$$

From Fig. 3 we have

$$\frac{\text{Length of curve}}{2 \pi \text{R}} = \frac{\text{AOB}}{360}$$

$$= \frac{180 - 2\theta}{360}$$

$$= \frac{90 - \theta}{180}$$

$$\therefore \text{length of curve} = \pi \text{R} \left(\frac{90 - \theta}{90} \right) \quad \dots \quad \dots \quad (7).$$

If θ and a be expressed in minutes this formula will become:—
length of curve = ·0005817 R (5,400 — θ) ... ... (8).

These eight equations and the table of tangential angles suffice to meet all ordinary cases of staking out. One of the following three methods may be adopted, according to circumstances.

1st. Method.

Measure the intersection angle carefully; determine on the radius of the curve; calculate the length of the tangents by equation (2); measure off these tangents; set up the theodolite over one tangent point, and strike out the curve till it joins in with the other tangent point. Where the curve is tolerably short, this method will generally suffice.

2nd. Method.

Do the same; but stake out from both tangent points and join in the middle of the curve.

3rd. Method.

Calculate the tangents as before, the length of the curve by equation (8), the number of chords by equation (6), and the distance S by equation (3); set out TD = S bisecting the angle of intersection, and from the middle point of the curve thus found set out the odd distances to the whole chain, pegs on each side. Stake out the rest of the curve, working from the centre of the curve to the tangent points at each end. Half the length of the curve added to the chainage of the first tangent point gives the chainage of the middle point of the curve. The odd number of feet in this chainage must be set back and its defect from 100 feet set forward to obtain the two whole chain-pegs nearest to the middle point of the curve. The tangent to the curve at D is of course perpendicular to TD.

OBSTACLES, &c.

If obstacles occur which render part of the curve inaccessible any number of pegs may be left out, and the remainder proceeded with by measuring long chords.

In Fig. 1, suppose that B and C are inaccessible. Set out the tangential angle AD = 3a° and measure the chord AD = 2R sin 3a (equation 1).

If the intersection point be inaccessible make use of one or more *transversals.*

Let BA, CA (Fig. 4) be two straight portions of the centre line of a railway, meeting in the intersection point A, which is inaccessible.

Take any convenient points D and E in AB and AC; measure DE, and the angles at D and E.*

$$\text{then } A = 180 - (D + E) \quad \dots \quad \dots \quad \dots \quad (9).$$

Compute the length of the tangents by equation (2).

In the triangle ADE,

$$AD = \frac{DE \sin E}{\sin A} \quad \dots \quad \dots \quad \dots \quad \dots \quad (10).$$

$$\text{and } AE = \frac{DE \sin D}{\sin A} \quad \dots \quad \dots \quad \dots \quad \dots \quad (11).$$

The difference between AD and AB gives the position of the tangent point B, and that between AC and AE gives the position of the other tangent point C. We can now stake out the curve by the first or by the second method. To employ the third method we must find the middle point of the curve. Suppose AF to be a line from the intersection point to the centre of the circle of which the curve forms part, then the angle AFD = 180 − (θ + D) and AFE = 180 − (θ + E).†

---

* Unless anything to the contrary is stated, "the angle D" means the acute angle at the point D.

† θ = half the intersection angle.

In the triangle AFD,

$$DF = \frac{AD \sin \theta}{\sin AFD} \qquad \ldots \qquad \ldots \text{(12)}.$$

$$AF = \frac{AD \sin D}{\sin AFD} \qquad \ldots \qquad \ldots \text{(13)}.$$

Compute AG by equation (3).

The difference between AF and AG gives FG.

Measure DF (already found), set up the theodolite on F, lay off the angle DFA, and measure the distance FG. The centre of the curve being G the third method of staking out can now be proceeded with.

The *transversal* may cut the curve (as in the figure), touch it, or fail to meet it. It may be on the opposite side of the tangent points from the intersection point, and the AD and AE will be greater than AB and AC. If the *transversal* does not meet the curve, but lies between the tangent points and the intersection point, AG will be greater than AF.

With two transversals (Fig. 5) the procedure is the same. Measure DE and EL, and the angles D, E, and L; calculate GE and EF, then DF and LG are known. The angles at E and L having been measured, the angles at F may be inferred, and DF having been found the case becomes that of a single transversal already described.

Any number of transversals may be used, and the case reduced to that of a single one in the manner above described. The angles at the points of intersection of the transversals should be measured accumulatively, in the same direction as is done in traversing. The defect of their sum, thus obtained, from 360 degrees, will be equal to the intersection angle.

COMPOUND CURVES.

Let BT and CT(Fig. 6) be two straight portions of the centre line of a railway intersecting at T, and let O be the centre of a circle touching BT in A. It is required to find the radius of a second curve, which shall connect the curve AFE with the straight line CT and be tangential to both.

Where the curve AFE falls short of the second tangent CT.

Draw the radius OA and OD perpendicular to CT cutting the curve in E.

It is manifest that a tangent to the curve at any point between A and E will, if produced, cut CT. Hence the required curve must leave AFE somewhere between these points.

From A, a curve might be drawn to touch CT; but this would dispense altogether with the curve AFE, and would simply amount to increasing the radius AO. At E, a tangent to the curve AFE would be parallel to CT, that is to say a curve, even of infinite radius, would never meet CT.

On the curve AFE, between the points A and E, select any point F from which it is convenient for the second curve to commence. The nearer F is to A the smaller will be the radius of the required auxiliary curve; and the nearer to E, the greater will this radius be.

Let the angle BTC be 2θ.
,, ,, AOF ,, 2ϕ.
,, T be the length of the tangent AT.
,, r be the radius of the given curve.
,, R ,, ,, auxiliary curve.

Draw a tangent to the curve at the point F, intersecting BT and CT in G and H. Make HK = HF, and through K draw KQ, perpendicular to CT, cutting FO produced in Q. Then, since the angles at K and F are right angles, and FH equal to HK, it follows that FQ = KQ. Hence a curve drawn with centre Q and radius QK or QF will touch CT in K, and have the same tangent and the same normal as the curve AFE at the point F.

The angle TGH = 180−AGH.
$$= 2\phi.$$
also THG = 180−GTD−TGH.
$$= 180−2(\theta+\phi).$$
and TG = AT−AG.
$$= T−r\tan\phi.$$
Therefore in the triangle TGH.
$$GH = \frac{TG\sin 2\theta}{\sin 2(\theta+\phi)}$$
$$= \frac{(T−r\tan\phi)\sin 2\theta}{\sin 2(\theta+\phi)}$$
$$\therefore FH = GH−GF = \frac{(T−r\tan\phi)\sin 2\theta}{\sin 2(\theta+\phi)}−r\tan\phi \quad\ldots(14).$$

Now the angle $AOD = 180 - ATD$

$$= 180 - 2\,\theta$$

$$\therefore FQK = FOD$$

$$= 180 - 2\,\theta - 2\,\phi$$

$$= 180 - 2\,(\theta + \phi) \quad \ldots \quad \ldots \quad (15).$$

Hence $FH = R \tan\dfrac{FQK}{2}$

$$= R \cot (\theta + \phi) = \frac{\sin 2\,\theta(T - r \tan \phi)}{\sin 2\,(\theta + \phi)} - r \tan \phi$$

$$\therefore R = \frac{\sin 2\,\theta\,(T - r \tan \phi)}{\cot (\theta + \phi) \sin 2\,(\theta + \phi)} - \frac{r \tan \phi}{\cot (\theta + \phi)} \quad (16).$$

WHEN THE CURVE AFE PASSES BEYOND THE TANGENT CT AND CUTS IT IN THE POINTS L AND M.

In this case (*Fig.* 7) the construction is the same and the value of R is the same.

The tangent point F of the two curves must be between A and L. The nearer F is to A the greater will be the radius of the auxiliary curve; and the nearer to L the smaller will this radius be. Comparing figures (3), (6) and (7), it is manifest that the primary curve will intersect the second tangent or not according as r is either greater or less than $T \tan \theta$.

If the two branches of a curve, for any reason, do not meet correctly they may be connected by an auxiliary curve of smaller radius. This is equivalent to finding a circle which shall touch two given equal circles internally. The arcs, (*Fig.* 8) of equal radius, GBD, HBA, having been found to intersect in B, instead of coinciding their tangent at the point B are inclined to one another at a certain angle.

Let O and P be the centres of the two circles.

„ $OB = PB = R$, the radius of the given curves.

Join OP, OB, BP. The inclination of the normals OB and BP is equal to the inclination of the tangents; hence the angle $OBP = a$. Bisect the angle OBP by the straight line BF.

It is manifest that the centre of the required auxillary circle must lie in the straight line BF.

Now $OF = FP = R \sin \dfrac{a}{2}$ $\quad \ldots \quad \ldots \quad \ldots \quad \ldots \quad (17).$

Therefore the radius of the required circle must lie between zero at the point B and $R\left(1-\sin\frac{a}{2}\right)$ at the point F. Take any convenient radius r for the auxiliary curve; and from O and P as centres describe arcs intersecting one another, and the line BF, in E such that $OE = EP = (R-r)$. Join PE, OE and produce them to meet the branches of the primary curve A and D. Then $E A = ED = r$; and E is the centre of curvature of the required auxiliary arc.

$$\sin OEF = \sin BED = \frac{OF}{OE} = \frac{R \sin\frac{a}{2}}{R-r} \quad \dots \quad \dots \quad (18)$$

$$\text{Length of arc } BD = BA = \frac{\pi R (BOD)}{180}$$

$$= \frac{\pi R \left(BED-\frac{a}{2}\right)}{180} \quad \dots \quad \dots \quad (19).$$

Measure BA and BD, to find the points of departure of the new curve. To find the length of the auxiliary arc AD we have—

$$\text{Length of arc } AD = 2 \times \frac{\pi r(BED)}{180}$$

$$= \frac{\pi r (BED)}{90} \dots \qquad \dots \quad \dots \quad (20).$$

When the ground is difficult and the surveys have been made hurriedly, it may happen that in re-staking out the centre line, after the earthwork is finished, some of the curves do not fit the straight portions correctly. When this is the case it is too late to alter the radius of the curve, as the latter would leave the centre line of the banks and cuttings; the proper procedure is to employ an auxiliary curve in the manner just described.

Compound curves should never be used to patch up incorrect work which can be rectified. At any time before the earth work is far advanced, or in any situation where it is possible to do so, if any thing wrong is discovered in a curve, carefully measure the intersection angle and tangents, and try it over again.

Reverse curves, called S or surpentine curves, should never be permitted in the main line of a railway, as they involve a sudden change of cant from one side to the other. Curves in opposite directions should always have a piece of straight between them.

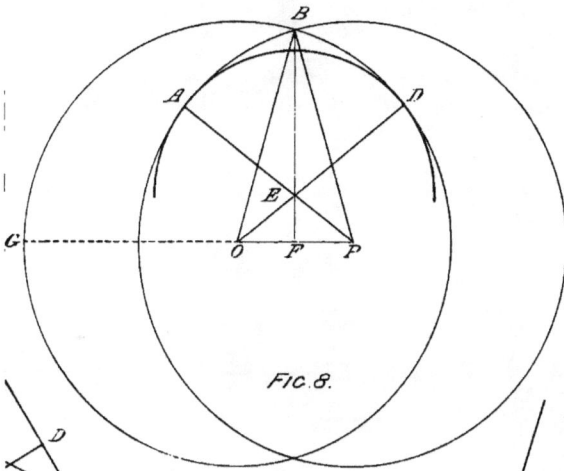

FIG. 8.

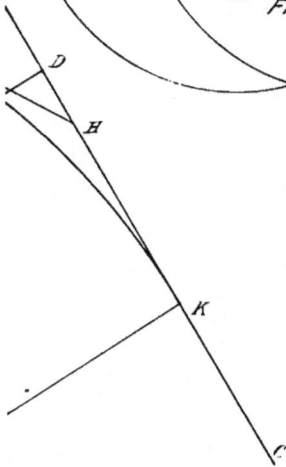

IC.6.

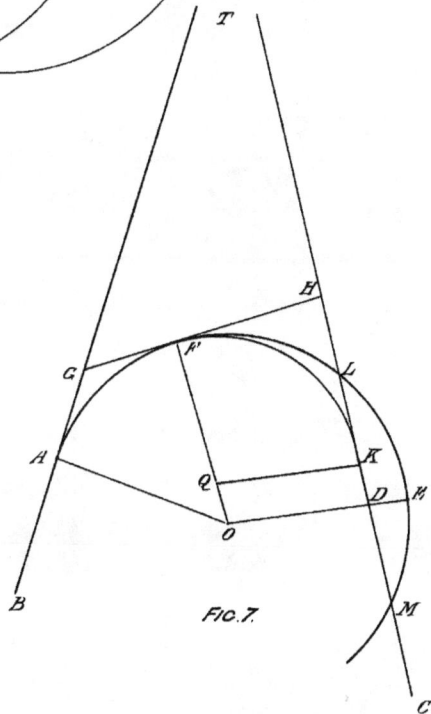

FIG. 7.

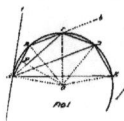

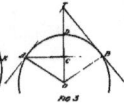

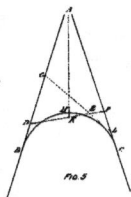

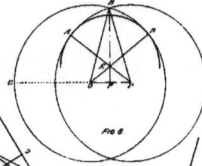

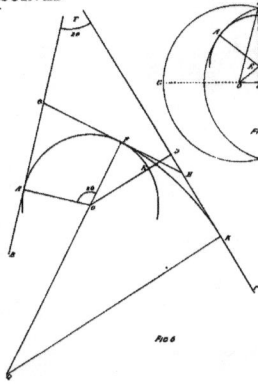

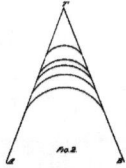

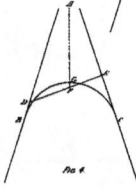

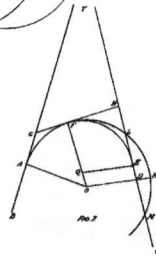

PAPER VIII.

EXTRACTS FROM A REPORT TO THE SURVEYOR-GENERAL OF INDIA

ON THE

TRIANGULATION OF NORTHERN AFGHANISTAN.

By Major T. H. Holdich, R.E.

Throughout Northern Afghanistan, the triangulation has been based on points (consisting entirely of mountain peaks) fixed from within the limits of the frontier of India, by observations taken at long distances from the ends of short bases. These bases had in many instances been purposely selected, so as to be short enough to render the identification of the trans-frontier peaks more certain. Hitherto these points had served the purposes of geography sufficiently well by defining the backbone and direction of some of the principal Afghan mountain ranges, but from the commencement of the last war they became the initial points of a system of triangulation, which gradually developed into two or three fairly distinct series, extending from east to west into the heart of the country. It was due to these points that anything like exact surveying became possible during the early phases of the first campaign of 1878–79, as surveyors could take immediate advantage of the opportunities offered by the opening of the campaign to carry on plane tabling and triangulation hand in hand, without the measurement of bases or the labour of preliminary computations.

The great majority of these points had been fixed by Lieutenant Walker, R.E. (now Surveyor-General of India), about 30 years ago, when the frontier was in a far more unsettled condition than it is at present, and when every observation involved much personal risk and great labour. Some of his observations were taken across distances of upwards of 100 miles, with an instrument of no better class than an old pattern 3½-in. theodolite ; so it was not a matter of much surprise that they were of somewhat unequal value for a trigonometrical basis, although sufficiently good for geographical data ; nor was it until the final reduction of all observations was undertaken, that it was possible to define exactly which could be accepted for the purposes of initial data, and which should be refixed for the basis of topography.

I do not think that at the commencement of the campaign triangulating officers started with a full appreciation of what might be effected with the 6-ft. subtense theodolites, which proved to be specially adapted to the rough work of military surveys, not only as triangulating instruments of a very high class, but for traversing purposes when used with a subtense pole under such conditions as precluded the possibility of carrying on triangulation. Certainly the opportunity of using those instruments was at first far more restricted in North Afghanistan than it was in the south, where there was always a fair chance for survey enterprise. The use of heliotrope signals was almost an impossibility, partly owing to the introduction of heliography for army-signalling purposes, and partly to the risk of detaching signallers ; the hills were peculiarly rough and difficult of access, while they rarely offered any special mark or prominent peak for observation, and the operations of surveyors were of course limited by military exigencies which pressed upon them particularly hardly at first, in the preliminary steps of the triangulation, where it was all-important that they should work on a wide front. Under these circumstances it is hardly surprising that a well-connected series of triangles connecting Kabul with India was hardly thought of either along the line of the Khyber or the Kuram. And yet the final results have resolved themselves into such a series along the line of the Kuram, and (with a weak link or two in the chain) along the line of the Khyber also ; and in spite of the absence of definite survey markstones or poles the general triangulation is not far inferior to the ordinary tertiary work of Indian topographical surveys.

When the triangulating officer was working from peak to peak, with only an approximate idea of the final direction of his work, bound all the time by the necessity of remaining close to one line of route, which prevented the lateral extension necessary to form a series, it was not easy for him to foresee the exact value of the work he had in hand, or into what shape it might resolve itself when taken in conjunction with that of other officers working far away on totally distinct lines.

This has been peculiarly the case with regard to the work along the two routes to Kabul, viz., the Khyber and the Kuram. On the more northern route the triangulation, which was commenced by Lieut.-Colonel Tanner, and completed by Major C. Strahan, R.E., was based entirely on trans-frontier peaks fixed from the great Indus series. No continued chain of triangulation was kept up, and no bases were measured. The western extremity of this branch terminates in three or four conspicuous peaks, fixed by intersection, overlooking the plain of Kabul, which peaks Major Strahan had determined to convert into trigonometrical stations as the Khyber column progressed towards Kabul. But the work was suddenly suspended by the treaty of Gandamuk, and on the second outbreak of the war, Major Strahan was unable to resume it. The positions of these final peaks were still uncomputed, owing to the dangerous illness of Major Strahan after his return to India, when the thread of the work was again taken up, in October 1879, and although his triangulation was connected with Kabul by myself when the Khyber route was opened up, and sufficient points for topography were laid down, yet, as I did not happen to utilize the exact peaks he had fixed on as trigonometrical stations, the junction was better effected subsequently when Lieut.-Colonel Woodthorpe brought the Kuram series round to close on those peaks.

The Kuram triangulation was also based on trans-frontier peaks; but not by interpolation from three or more of them (as was the case with the Khyber series), but by direct extension from two, of which the values were given in the Indus Series Volume. The two points were "Sangar" and "Khadimakt," both of which had been fixed by intersection from stations in the Kohat Minor Series. Last season's triangulation in the Kohat district, however, led to these points being visited and well fixed as trigonometrical stations, when it was found that the G. T. value of Khadimakt needed revision, and a fresh computation of the entire series became necessary. From the initial base for a distance of about 100 miles, the series is carried pretty regularly to the north-west, and includes as one of its northerly stations the peak of Sikaram, on the Sufed Koh range of mountains. Sikaram being about the most strongly fixed of all the G. T. trans-frontier peaks in this neighbourhood, and being common both to the Khyber and the Kuram series, has been of great importance in connecting the two systems, and in furnishing to a certain extent a fresh point of departure for the Kuram triangulation. Unfortunately the Kuram series narrows to a single point on the Shutargardan pass. No permission could be obtained from the military authorities to visit peaks either to the right or left, and consequently the Kuram series from this point depends on its extension from one or two unvisited lateral points, furnishing triangles of which two angles only have been observed, and they are all of them apparently peaks of an indifferent class for recognition. In each case there is room for doubt whether the points observed north and south from Shutargardan are absolutely identical with the points on the same hills observed east and west before and after reaching Shutargardan. It is probably due to the shape and direction of the ridges (which apparently run east and west) that this slight difference in the point observed introduces no appreciable error in the linear values of the common sides, computed both by the points north and those south of Shutargardan. The agreement between the two values is fairly good, but the triangles being comparatively small, and the sides short, the non-identification of the exact point probably introduces an error in azimuth, which here becomes apparent for the first time, and which it is difficult to account for in any other way. After passing the Shutargardan the series emerges into the open plains again at Kushi, and from there to Kabul there exists a strong net-work of triangles, based on peaks of great altitude, which is as good as any minor series in ordinary topographical work. From Kabul the triangulation extends eastwards till it joins on to the Khyber series, Lieut.-Colonel Woodthorpe having succeeded in reaching one of those peaks overlooking the Kabul plain which Major Strahan had observed and fixed as a forward station, but which, of course, he never himself reached. Here, then, a strong junction could have been effected, which would have turned the difficulty at Shutargardan, had Lieut.-Colonel Woodthorpe been able to identify Major Strahan's Khyber stations. But the means were wanting; no chart of Major Strahan's triangulation which would at once have indicated the peaks in question was then forthcoming, and the opportunity never occurred again. Such is the nature of the Afghan hills, that prominent peaks are most difficult to find. Indeed, there is no one peak throughout the country that offers a point for trigonometrical observation such as can always be recognised. Lieut.-Colonel Woodthorpe multiplied his observations to the greatest extent that time would allow, sparing no pains to hit off the exact spot (unmarked in the distance) on which he had stood before, or which might be another surveyor's station. It is indeed owing to the multiplicity of his observations, and their careful minuteness, that such results have been obtained as are now included in the general report; but yet, where he had no plane table chart to narrow down the limit of his observations, he sometimes failed (as in this instance he failed) to recognise the exact position of Major Strahan's stations; and unfortunately at the same time he was prevented by clouds from identifying Sikaram. Thus the junction with the Khyber series was considerably weakened. The triangulation that I carried through between Major Strahan's stations near Gandamak and Kabul was insufficient for the main purpose of connecting the two systems; for exactly the same reason I failed to identify Major Strahan's stations. This difficulty in triangulation of this nature is one which must be specially noted in future. With the assistance of a chart there is no great difficulty; without it, the whole experience of these surveys shows that it is only by a rare chance that any surveyor picks up another surveyor's station from mere description only in such a monotony of mountains as exists in Afghanistan.

The computation of the Kuram series (accepting the values of the Khyber triangulation as final) from Kohat to its junction with the Khyber line has occupied much care and time, many tentative computations having been made with a view to test values of initial azimuths and bases by the results given on closing with a fixed G.T. point. With a series of irregular triangles, where in nearly all cases a triangular error can be traced with far more probability to one angle than to a general error between the three, any exact and rigid method of apportioning final error seems out of place. The adjustment in this case has consisted rather of a careful examination of angle books, and of the balancing of possible influences of time, opportunity, atmosphere, and position, than of the adjustment of errors in graduation and level. The final results are fairly satisfactory, more exact, indeed, than anything that was contemplated at the outset of the survey. The Kuram series was computed up to a long side between Kurd-Kabul and Korogh stations, and the Khyber series was extended from Major Strahan's bases so as to close on the same side. The agreement of the common side (which was to a single foot) was closer than the nature of the survey could warrant, but it was a fairly satisfactory check on the coincidence of linear values in the two series.

But although the linear agreement was satisfactory, the computation of latitudes and longitudes of the final points of each series did not lead to quite such accordant results. This, of course, was due either to the accumulation of small angular errors affecting the value in azimuth of the sides of triangles composing one or both of the series; or, more probably, to one considerable error of two or three minutes, so applied in the course of computation as to have little or no effect on linear values, while its own weight was perceptible in azimuth. Major Strahan's final values in azimuth were implicitly to be trusted, as he had taken a most elaborately careful series of observations for azimuth so near to the end of his work as to leave no room for errors to creep in. If similar observations could have been taken anywhere between Shutargardan and Charasia, the adjustment of the difficulty would have been easy enough; but the opportunity for such observations was wanting, and the position of the error can only be surmised.

The linear values of the two series being in accord, and the points Sikaram and Kurd-Kabul being common to both of them, and furnishing the means of proving that azimuthal values agreed on both sides up to that point, angular values for determining all azimuths west of Sikaram were obtained by means of the quadrilateral formed by Kurd-Kabul, Sikaram, Shutargardan, and a well-defined peak in the heart of the Logar country, called Logar Hisarak. In this quadrilateral the linear values of all four sides, with the two angles observed at Sikaram and Logar Hisarak (which were of unusual strength from the repetition of observations on both faces of the instrument), were accepted as the data for determining the remaining quantities; and the value in latitude and longitude of Logar Hisarak thus obtained, with its azimuthal value from Kurd-Kabul and Shutargardan, respectively supply the data for computing out all the values of points on the Hindoo Kush, Koh-i-Baba, and Paghman ranges west of Kabul. Of course these positions are but approximations after all; but the probable error in absolute position of any one of them is not more than ten seconds, either in latitude or longitude, which, considering that the actual summit is often difficult to define within those limits, is quite near enough for all practical purposes of future topography. Relatively, of course, the error would be much less.

With the computations of the Northern Afghanistan triangulation, the reduction of the observations in Waziristan has been completed; and these have an important bearing on much of the Kuram and Khost surveys, and, to a certain extent, form a connecting link between the triangulation of the north and that of the south. The westerly peaks of Waziristan overlooked a large tract in the heart of Afghanistan, which is at present but a blank in the maps of the country. Between western Waziristan and the great high road joining Kabul and Kandahar there are no very important ranges, and the topographical features of the country generally may be described rather as hilly than as mountainous, so that there was some difficulty in fixing points of sufficient prominence to be readily recognisable, especially within the very narrow limits of time that could be allowed for the observations. The altitude of the peaks which were reached by the survey officers was either such as to leave very little time for observation when the summits were reached, or they were situated in ground occupied by the Mahsud Waziris in force, and time was lost in the necessary disposition of troops to support the survey parties.

Pirghal (11,500 feet above sea) is the highest peak in India south of the Himalayas, and Shuidar (11,000) was held by the Waziris, who attacked the survey party at the very summit of the peak. But in spite of these difficulties a certain number of points within that blank space have been laid down, and valuable observations have been taken from this southerly point of view, which check the position of many important peaks of the Northern Afghanistan triangulation, which would otherwise have been indifferently fixed. To the south-west observations were taken across the intervening space of 200 miles to the great southern peaks of Kund, the central point of the Kojak mountain system, and many bearings were recorded which will be useful checks on the traverse carried by Lieut. Gore from Kandahar to Kabul, and on the exploration line of the Bozdar, along the Zhob and Gomul to Lake Abistada.

This combination of the work of different surveyors working over a vast extent of territory on entirely separate lines—such as the Khyber, the Kuram, the Khaisor (Waziristan), and the Bolan, all more or less parallel to each other, and consequently bearing more or less on common points intermediate to them—has been useful in pointing to certain deductions which may serve as guides in conducting such surveys in future. The results of computations so far seem rather to point to the following conclusions:—

Although the system of starting triangulation by means of interpolation has been used with great success in Afghanistan, yet it should be noted that the value, for a series, of such a starting-point as can be gained by interpolation from intersected peaks only, is an exceedingly troublesome value to arrive at by computation. For if the same weight is to be given in the first instance to every one visible of the surrounding fixed peaks, they should be taken in combinations of three for the purpose of computation, each combination resulting in a definite but possibly fictitious result, differing from the others in proportion to the inaccurate value of one or more of the three peaks. If there were many such peaks, all the various results of these combinations would form a small figure, of which the centre of gravity would be the best approximation to the true position of the interpolator. But the position of the peaks with regard to the observer has also to be taken into account, and the angles of intersection at the point of interpolation, so that it becomes a very difficult matter to regulate the weights of each fixed peak in the computation. The final result, after all, is probably frequently no better than that joined by ordinary interpolation on a carefully-projected plane table, when the value of each peak can be readily estimated, and the final average result measured off by co-ordinates from the graticule lines. Indeed, so long as the survey is carried on only within the limits of country over which a certain number of such intersected points are laid down, the necessity for triangulation and computation almost vanishes. The plane table may be trusted for all that is necessary. It is only when it is necessary to establish the utmost possible accuracy in the linear and azimuthal values of the sides connecting several peaks, for the purpose of using those sides as bases to fix the position of far-off mountain ranges by extremely fine intersections, that systematic triangulation with good instruments is a necessity.

Each surveyor working along a line of his own in an unsurveyed country, where all information is of importance, and where his work may in future be combined with that of others, or be continued by others, should, if he can possibly manage it, carry on a plane table chart of triangulation, in combination with his observations. The assistance that this affords to the officer who succeeds him, or who has to close on his work, or who has to compute his observations, is incalculable. In the two first cases it is absolutely essential. In the last case it has been found that the plane table furnishes a most valuable record of approximate distances, leading to the identification of many points which would otherwise remain uncomputed. It is often exceedingly difficult to estimate the distance of a peak in miles from the observer, if it is a matter only of judging an abstract distance in varying conditions of atmosphere. But it is simple enough to put down an indication of the shape and nature of the peak on the approximate spot on the chart which it should occupy relative to other points already known, and which can be seen by the observer. Several points of great value thus estimated and sketched on the plane table, as well as observed with the theodolite, have been recognised without difficulty by their indicated position and shape amongst similar records by other observers, observing from other points ; and some few indeed have been fixed by the intersection of two rays only, the observations being by different observers, but the plane table record leaving no reasonable doubt as to the identity of the object of intersection.

Another point of evident importance is that observations should be taken from and to the highest point of the peak or hill. This has always, of course, been a recognised rule with trigonometrical surveyors, but it was not always recognised quite so readily by the military commanders who had to arrange for the support of the survey party. No other point can possibly be made of the same value to other observers. In fact, where it was impossible to observe from conspicuously the highest point of a hill, in a great majority of cases the station was seldom recognised again even by the same observer.

In the combination of the work of separate observers, observations for altitude have proved exceedingly useful. The computation of heights does not involve such very minute accuracy as to length of base, but that the result is generally near enough to indicate whether the point is the same as that observed by another surveyor or not. A very rough approximation to the distance will generally decide this. Consequently, the most important of the far-off geographical peaks that occur in a round of observations should be those most carefully observed for altitude. Coincidence in the value of heights is almost a better check on an intersection by two rays than coincidence in the matter of estimated distance.

With regard to astronomical observations, those for the determination of azimuth have proved by far the most important in reducing the Northern Afghanistan computations. One particular application of azimuthal observations should not be lost sight of. Two observers may take observations to the same peak from points very far distant from each other on perfectly separate systems of triangulation. There may be no doubt whatever about the identity of the point from the coincidence of estimated distances or heights, but the final value of its position may depend on computation from these two points alone. Under these circumstances there is no difficulty in getting a value to the base between the two points, and to the azimuth of either one of them from the other, by reduction from the differential values of their latitudes and longitudes as determined in each series. But if AB be the two points from which C is observed, and A and B are not intervisible, the only way of arriving at the values of the angles CAB CBA, on which the whole computation depends, is by the difference between the values of azimuth of A and C from B for the angle ABC, and of B and C from A for the angle BAC. The azimuth of B from A and of A from B has already been determined from these differential latitudes and longitudes, but the value of the azimuth of C from either of them depends entirely on the accuracy of the triangulation and the correctness of origin for the azimuths in the two series to which A and B belong. A minute or so of error in either series would not greatly affect its values, but this minute applied to the computation of a far-away peak C would affect its position in proportion to its distance and the acuteness of the intersecting rays; so that azimuthal values may be of far greater importance than would be suggested by any weaknesses discovered in the course of computing a series only.

Another matter to which it seems well to draw attention is the combination of the work of surveyors as far as possible with that of signallers. The use of the heliograph in the field to a certain extent prohibits the use of the ordinary heliotrope of the Survey department, because of the confusion that might possibly arise between the flashes of the two instruments. But it almost always happens that points suitable to a survey station are suitable also for signalling purposes ; the conditions which the surveyor hopes to find fulfilled by ascending a commanding point being just those most valuable to the signaller also. Signalling can best be carried on by means of long rays and the use of large glasses, because fewer men can thus keep up communication along any given line, the chief difficulty in maintaining signalling operations always being the necessity of guarding each post. But long rays can only be secured from the highest and most commanding peaks, just the points which the surveyor must ever be striving to reach. When two surveyors have signalling communication between them, and are observing at the same time from far distant points, the advantage of being able to define to each other what points are being observed is so great that no opportunity of combining work in this way should be lost.

The general results of the computation for altitude are such as tend very much to shake confidence in aneroidal observations. From the Indus Valley series to Kabul a double line of reciprocal trigonometrical observations was taken from peak to peak along the entire length of the Kuram series, and the finally computed result of the height of the Kabul Hill Station (on the Sher-Darwaza Hill above the Bala Hissar) differs by only two feet from that computed by Major C. Strahan. This value also agrees with those determined barometrically (with a mercurial barometer) by Lieut. Gore along the Kandahar to Kabul route, but it has the effect of lowering previous estimates considerably. Indeed, the whole face of Afghanistan about Kabul, including the peaks of the Hindu Kush, has diminished in its altitude above sea level from the values previously determined by about 500 feet. About Jalalabad the values remain much the same. The best previous values were determined with a measured barometer by Dr. Griffiths, about 40 years ago, but Dr. Griffiths, unfortunately, did not live to compute his own observations. The value of refraction was found on the whole to be somewhat greater than that usual in the plains of India. Expressed in decimal of the arc contained between any two points it amounts in Afghanistan to about ·08, thus slightly exceeding the normal $\frac{1}{15}$ or ·067, contrary to the usual rule whereby refraction diminishes with increasing altitude.

The whole season having been so far occupied in reducing all the computations of the different series and lines to common terms with those of the Great Indus series, in which all those of Southern Afghanistan are recorded, I have but little to report about the topography. This does not, of course, cover all the ground that has been covered by triangulation, and although it has all of it been worked throughout on the plane-tabling system, it cannot all be regarded as of equal value. The great mass of the topography (which roughly covers about 35,000 square miles, including Southern Afghanistan and Waziristan) in and round Kabul and Kandahar, along the lines of route, and in Waziristan, is of a class much higher than mere military reconnaissance, though not, of course, of the value of exact surveys on the same scale as usually turned out by the Indian Survey. But beyond all this, there is a good wide fringe of reconnaissance pure and simple that has yet to be compiled on the trigonometrical basis, and that may hereafter be checked and improved by further exploration.

A narrative of the exploration conducted by the Bozdar in the valleys of the Zhob and Gomul has been carefully recorded by Lieut. Hon. M. G. Talbot, R.E. Much of the information supplied by the Bozdar is of value, and the whole of his work will probably find a place in the ¼-inch map of Northern Afghanistan, which will be completed next season.

T. H. H.

PAPER IX.

ORGANIC COMPOUNDS IN THE SUN.

*A Lecture delivered at the Royal Engineers' Institute, Chatham,
December 7, 1881.*

By Capt. W. de W. Abney, R.E., F.R.S.

It is with extreme diffidence that I venture to give a lecture to my
brother officers; but still I could not resist the request made by the
Secretary of the Institute, who wrote and asked me to address you on
this subject, which he thought might have some degree of interest
for you.

The object I have in view to-night is first to show you a new
method of analysis by means of the spectroscope as applied by
Colonel Festing and myself, and also to show you the connection
between physical astronomy and physical chemistry.

It may be objected that I have called certain substances, which will
be found in the sun, 'organic' substances. What I mean by this
term 'organic' is this: that these particular substances, viz. carbon
compounds, which we find in the sun are those which on this earth are
usually derived from organic matter. Of course we cannot pretend for
an instant that this same matter which is found in the sun is due to
living matter there; first of all because it is in quantity so enormous;
and, secondly, as I need hardly point out, the transcendental temperature which exists there renders such a theory quite out of the question.

At the end of 1878 or the beginning of 1879 I had the honour of
giving a lecture here on the subject of 'the so-called thermal spectrum,'
in which I showed the means I had adopted to photograph the dark
rays which lie beyond the visible spectrum. In the diagram before
you, ' K,' is the extreme visible limit of the spectrum at the violet end;

'A' is the extreme visible limit at the red end of the spectrum; but below 'A' lie an enormous quantity of rays, which can be disintegrated out the prism, and mapped. Such a map of necessity shows the spectrum as white, marked by certain absorption lines in black. Had

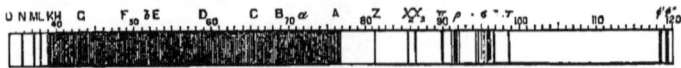

Fig. 1.

I completed that diagram of the spectrum, which, by means of photography, I have been able to investigate, I should have had to have taken a length stretching to the far end of the room. However, the part which we are chiefly interested in to-night lies between the line 'A' and the other line, about wave-length 1,200.

In the lecture to which I have referred I endeavoured to show that the so-called heat rays are miscalled. There are no such things as heat rays; there is no such thing as 'radiant heat'; but that 'radiant heat' should be called 'radiant energy,' and the effect of the 'energy' is shown either by its chemical effect or else by a heating effect on the body on which it falls.

It may not be out of place to show you a very simple example of the effect of the dark rays upon a photographic plate : it will enable you perhaps to see better how it is we are able to photograph those dark lines which lie below the 'A' line.

It may be in the recollection of you all that not very long ago Professor Graham Bell brought out an instrument called a 'photophone.' The action of the photophone briefly was this : a ray of light was caused to impinge upon a selenium cell, to which was attached a telephone; and when the impact of the ray of light was intermittent, caused by turning a rotating wheel between it and the cell, you then got a musical note higher or lower, according to the velocity with which the slits of the rotating disc passed before the ray of light. Professor Bell placed various substances between the light and the selenium cell, and amongst other things he found to his astonishment that when ebonite intervened he still heard a musical note; in other words, that through perfectly opaque matter radiation passed from the source of light to the selenium cell. This created a great *furore* in scientific circles in London, and all kinds of wonderful actions were attributed to this ebonite—that it absorbed the rays and then gave them out, and a variety of other suggestions were made regarding it. It struck me that the best way to test this property would be to see if we could photograph through a thickness of ebonite. Accordingly we arranged the electric light so as to throw the image of the points upon the focussing screen of the camera, and then interposed between the electric light and the sensitive plate a screen of ebonite. If the ebonite was transparent to the dark rays, then, of course, we ought to be able to photograph the carbon points when using a silver salt sensitive to dark radiation; and it is such a photograph that is now on the screen, which shows that ebonite is transparent to the dark rays below the line 'A.' That is a very good example of what can be done by this means of photography.

I propose now to show you the character of the solar spectrum which we get below 'A.' It is much more open and freer from absorption lines than is the visible spectrum.

Fig. 2.

Most of you are aware of the meaning of the black lines in the solar spectrum. They are due to metallic or other vapours either in the solar atmosphere or in our own atmosphere. For instance, if we vaporise calcium, the bright lines in the spectrum of the vapour are found to be coincident with certain dark lines in the solar spectrum.

I will now show you the 'iron' spectrum, in which you will see a great many coincidences given, but not so many as are obtained by photographic means. [Shown.]

When we come to photograph the spectra of different metals in the infra red region of the spectrum, we find very few which give any lines at all. At present, out of twenty metals that I have examined, I find only two which give any lines whatever below the visible part of the spectrum, viz., sodium and calcium. Potassium also has a line, but that is absolutely visible though with extreme difficulty. Sodium, potassium, and calcium have all very low fusing points, and metals which have very high fusing points have very few lines even in the red region. Therefore we may expect that only a very few metals—viz., those which have very low fusing points—will have lines corresponding with the absorption lines in the infra red of the solar spectrum.

This, then, made it probable that we should have to look to some other bodies for the explanation of these dark lines in the infra red region; and instead of elementary bodies they must probably be due to compounds. The heavier a body is, the more probable will it be that it will vibrate with long wave lengths, and at longer intervals of time.

Suppose a violin string to give a certain note : if you load that string or make it heavier, it will give a lower note. If you have a molecule which will vibrate at a certain wave-length, if you weight it, it will vibrate at a greater wave-length. On this account, then, Colonel Festing and myself thought very naturally that the dark lines we saw in the solar spectrum must be due to compound bodies rather than to elementary bodies with the spectra of which spectroscopists are so well acquainted.

I have here a table of absorptions copied from one of Professor Tyndall's works, 'Heat as a Mode of Motion.'

ABSORPTION OF RADIANT ENERGY BY LIQUIDS.

Source of heat, a platinum spiral raised to bright redness by a voltaic current.

	Thickness of Liquid in parts of an inch	
	·02	·27
Carbon disulphide . .	5·5	17·3
Chloroform . . .	16·6	44·8
Methyl-iodide . .	36·1	68·6
Ethyl-iodide . . .	38·2	71·5
Benzine	43·4	73·6
Amyline	58·3	82·3
Ether	63·3	85·2
Alcohol	67·3	89·1
Water	80·7	91·0

Professor Tyndall examined the absorption of these different compound bodies by placing a certain thickness of the liquid between a thermo-pile and the source of heat which he used to cause a deflection of the needle in the attached galvanometer ; and he found, when he used a red-hot platinum spiral, that for every ·2 parts of an inch of bi-sulphide of carbon he got 5·5 parts of the energy absorbed ; chloroform, 16·6 ; of iodide of ethyl, 36·1, and so on. Suffice it to say he found, the more complex the molecule of the liquid, the more absorption he got. This method of examining the absorption of liquids is very much as if I were to tell you that, if so much light from a candle was cut off by a coloured glass, without saying what colour it was. It is valuable as to the amount of energy absorbed, but it does not localise the place in the spectrum in which this absorption takes place.

For this reason, we determined to see whether the spectroscope would throw any light upon the locality of the absorptions shown by these different compounds which Professor Tyndall had examined. A tube, 6 inches in length, having glass ends, was filled with the liquid to be tried, and placed in front of the photo-spectroscope. .

We commenced with water, and, after the first photograph, we were astonished to find that water gave a very definite spectrum—that is to say, that it had absorption bands which I do not think anybody ever suspected before. We went on to other compound bodies—alcohol, ether, and ethyl-iodide—all belonging to the same series. I must point out these diagrams to you in order that you may understand the argument which I shall bring before you presently. Chemists consider that a molecule is made up of different atoms, and these atoms are bonded together in different ways. Carbon can take up a certain amount of hydrogen and oxygen, and they are in the habit of portraying these combinations by lines. The first substance we took was alcohol, which has a formula of $C_2 . H_6 . O$, but chemists show that one carbon is bonded with another carbon, and the other different atoms are bonded together in the following way:

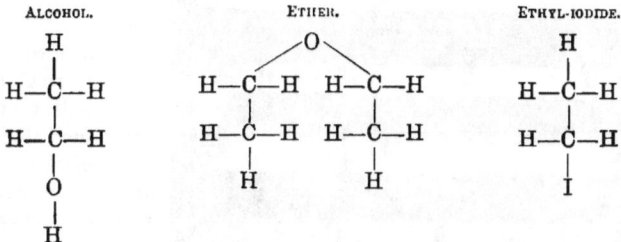

ALCOHOL.	ETHER.	ETHYL-IODIDE.

$$
\begin{array}{ccc}
\text{H} & \quad\quad \text{O} & \text{H} \\
| & \quad\nearrow \; \nwarrow & | \\
\text{H—C—H} & \text{H—C—H} \quad \text{H—C—H} & \text{H—C—H} \\
| & | \quad\quad\quad | & | \\
\text{H—C—H} & \text{H—C—H} \quad \text{H—C—H} & \text{H—C—H} \\
| & | \quad\quad\quad | & | \\
\text{O} & \text{H} \quad\quad\quad \text{H} & \text{I} \\
| & & \\
\text{H} & &
\end{array}
$$

So with ether we see here another form of molecular grouping, which I may say, until our paper was published, was really based more upon theory than knowledge, but which really from analogy turns out to be absolutely correct in the analysis we have made. Again, ethyl-iodide has two carbons, with hydrogen atoms on each side, combined with one of iodine.

So I might go on with the rest, and show the constitution of all these different bodies in the table.

On trying alcohol and ether and ethyl-iodide, we found most remarkable spectra; and I have two of the first photographs which we took, which I will show you. [Shown.]

The alcohol spectrum and the ether spectrum both show very definite bands. The ethyl-iodide shows a very fine series of sharp bands and lines.

On examining the different photographs we remarked a variety of different kinds of absorption. First we found the absorption which ran in bands with sharp edges; then absorptions which ran in bands with one edge sharp and the other slightly diffused; then we had lines, and then we had general absorption at the lower end of the spectrum, creeping up gradually. The lighter the molecule was, the more the general absorption crept up from 120 up towards 900. I will show you the character of the bands we obtained.

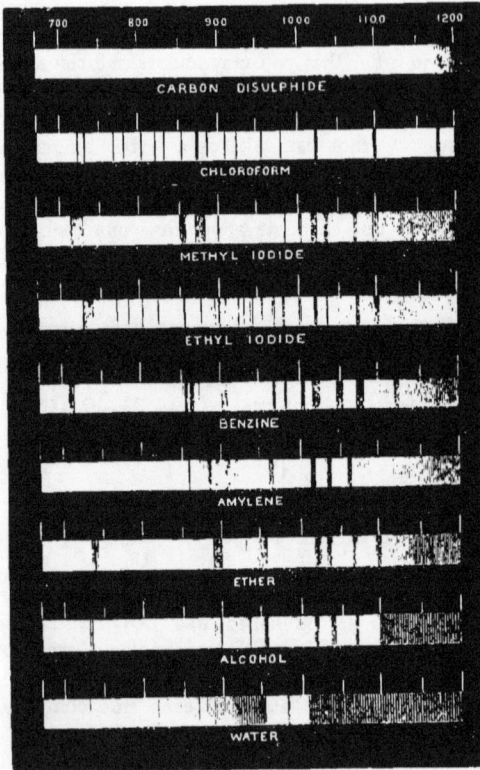

Fig. 3.

Here is methyl-alcohol—an alcohol we are not in the habit of discussing in England, though there is some of it in claret. Here we have the ordinary alcohol of commerce.

When we measured these absorption bands, we very soon found that the edges of the bands always coincided with certain lines in other spectra: thus the edge of the ethyl-iodide band coincided with certain lines in the methyl-iodide, and we also found that the edge of the ether band coincided with certain lines to be found in the ethyl-iodide, and so on. This could not be a mere matter of coincidence; there must be some law regarding it, and that law we determined to find out.

You will see by the diagram that the bodies which we have tried are excessively complicated. The next body we tried was one which had less complication about it, in which we had one carbon combined with only one hydrogen and three atoms of chlorine, which is chloroform

185

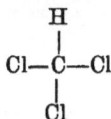

CHLOROFORM.	CARBON TETRA-CHLORIDE.	CARBON DISULPHIDE.

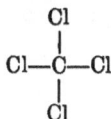

$$
\begin{array}{ccc}
\text{H} & \text{Cl} & \text{S} \\
| & | & \| \\
\text{Cl}-\text{C}-\text{Cl} & \text{Cl}-\text{C}-\text{Cl} & \text{C} \\
| & | & \| \\
\text{Cl} & \text{Cl} & \text{S}
\end{array}
$$

On putting chloroform before the slit and photographing it, we were delighted to find that all those bands had entirely vanished, and instead of bands we got nothing but a spectrum of lines. Having got rid of two hydrogens from the carbon compound, we next tried the effect of taking away the last hydrogen. This was done by spectroscoping tetra-chloride of carbon, which is one atom of carbon combined with four chlorines. On photographing that, we found that not a vestige of absorption took place: in other words, there were no lines and no bands, but only the general darkening at the lower end of the spectrum. We thus knew that it was not carbon to which these absorption bands and lines were due. To confirm this, we tried bi-sulphide of carbon—a combination between carbon and sulphur—and in this case we found no lines again; and, as you will notice in Professor Tyndall's table, there is very little absorption at all shown by bi-sulphide of carbon, and very little by chloroform. What were these bands and lines due to? It struck us they must arise from the hydrogen present, and if we could get hydrogen combined with something else without carbon, probably we might get lines also. So we took hydrochloric acid, which is hydrogen and chlorine, placed that in front of the slit, and were rewarded by getting a spectrum with lines coinciding with some lines which we had mapped, in chloroform and ethyl-iodide, and a variety of organic compounds which we previously tried. Then, again, we tried ammonia, which is a combination between one nitrogen and three hydrogen atoms; there we found the lines again. Then we tried sulphuric acid, which is SO_4 and H_2; there we found the lines again and no bands. In water we found bands, but bounded by lines, which coincided with lines in the chloroform spectrum; so that you see by a process of elimination we were able to show that the lines, at all events, in the different spectra were due to the vibrations of hydrogen in these different molecules, and not to the carbon or the chlorine or the iodine.

What was the effect on oxygen when mixed with other substances? All the oxygen compounds we found had absorption lines and shaded bands, which always lay between two hydrogen lines. The meaning of this was clearly, that the oxygen simply blocked out the radiation between two hydrogen lines, and gave the absorption bands, and the shading was simply due to the step by step gradation between the different hydrogen lines as they were carried down the spectrum.

I have here a table showing the tabulated results of our investigations in regard to absorption :

Carbon, hydrogen, and a halogen . .	Sharp bands and fine lines.
Carbon, hydrogen, and oxygen . . .	Shaded bands and fine lines.
Carbon and chlorine ⎱ Carbon and nitrogen ⎰ Carbon and sulphur	. No bands or lines.
Hydrogen and oxygen	. Bands and lines.
Hydrogen and chlorine ⎱ . . Hydrogen and nitrogen ⎰	. Lines.

I will now show you another series of the Benzine group.

Benzine is $C_6 H_6$ (*Fig.* 3), the carbon and hydrogen being combined together in very curious forms. From a series of experiments with different derivatives of a group, we came to the conclusion that the absorption of every derivative contains what is called the Radical band; that is to say, you could tell what substance it was derived from by its having a particular band in a particular part of the spectrum. For instance, if I was to analyse any compound and find a band in the spectrum coincident with wave-length 866, I should know that I had some derivative of benzine. So with ethyl-alcohol : if I found I had a band about 900, I could immediately tell I had got the radical band of alcohol present, and that it must be some derivative of alcohol. So with all these different compounds—they all have their radical bands ; and if you find in a spectrum that particular radical band present, you may be quite sure that you have either that substance present itself or else some derivative from it. Thus, then, by this method of spectrum analysis we are able to state absolutely whether we have got the derivative of some body present or not.

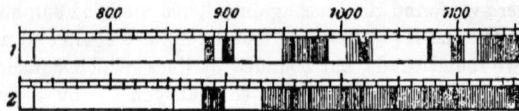

N° 1 Aldehyde
N° 2 Paraldehyde
Fig. 4.

I want to digress for a moment, and show you the effect that a different conglomeration of definite molecules has on a spectrum.

In this map we have the spectrum of aldehyde, which chemists tell us is a combination between carbon, hydrogen, and oxygen ; and par aldehyde, which contains exactly the same proportion of the three elementary bodies, but differs in that three molecules aldehyde are combined to form its one molecule. You will see there are certain common lines, but the molecular difference is shown by the difference in the absorption spectra of the two. Here we have two substances of identically the same chemical composition, and yet they give you perfectly different absorption spectra.

About a fortnight ago Professor Tyndall gave a lecture in which he showed that, when you put a millimetre of liquid ether in front of the thermo-pile, it absorbed exactly the same amount as it did when that same thickness was expanded into vapour; and from this he adduced the fact that the absorption took place in the molecules of the organic compound, and not in the ether in which these molecules were placed — a fact which he told as a novelty, but which we had published in January last. It was hardly a deduction to make from such slender evidence, but it is confirmatory of the evidence which I have the honour to bring before you to-night; for I think you will see that all absorptions which take place must take place inside the molecules. It may be the molecule, itself vibrating, gives the continuous absorption, but that point I do not enter into now.

After these researches had been finished, we compared what we had obtained in the absorptions of liquids with the linear absorptions with the solar spectrum. We found a variety of coincidences between the two. When we took ethyl-iodide and placed the solar spectrum above it, we found that there were lines at X_2 and also that the very broad line at 900 corresponded. Also, when we examined benzine, we found we had X_3, and X_3 was the exact position of that broad band of benzine which you saw upon the screen. Also we found that there were some other lines in the group Σ with which the benzine absorption spectrum was coincident, and therefore we were driven to the inevitable conclusion that we must have some derivative or another of benzine and ethyl present either in our atmosphere or in the sun.

Now, how were we to distinguish whether this absorption takes place in our atmosphere or in the solar atmosphere? The method is very simple. If you take the spectrum of the sun at a high altitude at mid-day, and also in the evening at sunset, there is always a greater absorption of certain lines caused by the atmosphere at sunset than at mid-day. We found that certain lines in the sunset photograph were blackened, and others were not, and amongst those which were not were the lines which coincided with benzine and ethyl. So that you see we were inevitably fixed to this, that we have a derivative of benzine and ethyl present, and that it was not present in our atmosphere; therefore, the only locality in which we could place it was in the solar atmosphere.*

A very curious remark was also made with regard to certain lines, that when you throw the image of the sun upon the slit of the spectroscope, so that the radiation from the limb and the centre of the sun were dispersed by the prisms, some lines were very much darker at the limb than at the centre. That tells us that at the limb of the sun there was a greater thickness of hydro-carbon present than at the centre. How could that be? I have a very rough diagram here which will explain to you how it is.

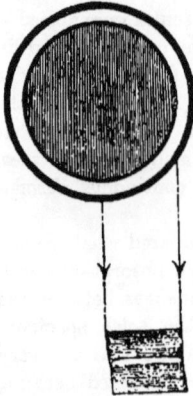

Fig. 5.

This ring is supposed to be a hydro-carbon ring. You will see at the top of the spectroscope it has to pass through a greater thickness of this ring than the centre, and the probable fact is that the absorption of this hydro-carbon is due to this. Mr. Lockyer made another suggestion, namely, that really when we were spectroscoping, that we were spectroscoping the corona. The corona is the solar halo of glory seen round the moon at an eclipse, and he supposes that you get the image of a thick layer of this halo of glory at one part of the slit, and only a very thin layer of it at another part.

There are two very remarkable lines, the A and B. Both have one particular form. They have a black nucleus and shaded bands on one side—that is to say, a fluted spectrum on one side of the black band. These lines have never been allotted to any substances. I am not going to allot them to any substance absolutely now, but I am going to show you the probability as to what they do belong. The A and B lines are very nearly alike, looked at in the spectroscope.

In the figure we have a drawing of the A line—a very beautiful line it is; and here we have a photograph of a drawing of that benzine band. I ask you to remark that they are drawn to the same scale, and also to note the coincidence there is between the two, the only difference being that the one is shaded, and in the other the shade is broken up into lines. The probability is that that remarkable A line, which

Fig. 6.

* Since this lecture was delivered, the author has made experiments which cause him to believe that it may also exist in space.

is the crux of spectroscopists, is due to some benzine derivative or some derivative which contains the same quantity of carbon and hydrogen.

What can that be ? When you come to examine different combinations, you find there is a certain substance called acetylene, containing two atoms of carbon and two of hydrogen. Benzine is $H_6 . C_6$; so that one has three times the weight of the other, and one has three times the amount of carbon and hydrogen in the molecules. It is curious that when you heat acetylene, it is converted immediately into benzine. As you diminish the atomic weight of the molecules in these different organic bodies, so the radical band mounts up towards the blue end of the spectrum. I have shown you that the benzine radical band is coincident with the X line, and therefore it is very highly probable—it being a very much lighter molecule—that the same species of radical band would be found only nearer the blue end of the spectrum, and probably that A line is due to acetylene instead of benzine. The B line has been proved to be an atmospheric line; and if so, and if it is due to a similar organic substance, it must be something lighter than acetylene. We do not know what it is, but it is said to be atmospheric, and, being so, must lie very near the limits of our atmosphere.

I have made a rough sketch to show you how acetylene and benzine can exist together.

The dark disc is supposed to be the sun, and the light shaded ring to be a ring of acetylene. The nearer you get to the sun the hotter it is; and therefore at a certain temperature three molecules of acetylene will be combined to form benzine ; and, therefore, you may have the existence both of benzine and acetylene in the same ring, one forming the shallow part, and the other the deeper part; and from the evidence we have, from the excessive sharpness of the benzine

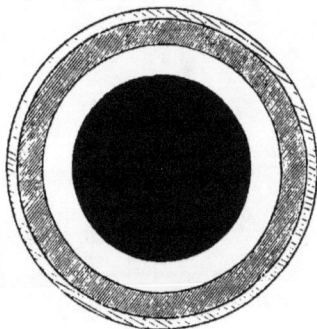

Fig. 7.

band, we are inclined to think the benzine band is not very deep, and from the fluted spectrum of the A line we are inclined to think the acetylene is of very great thickness.

I will, in conclusion, show you a photograph of the spectrum of the comet of this year, which Dr. Huggins has kindly lent me in order to bring before you. Long ago Dr. Huggins suspected that the spectrum of the comets was due to the light of a hydro-carbon. Here we have the spectrum of the comet as obtained by Dr. Huggins, photographed on a very sensitive plate. What he saw was this: he saw part of the solar spectrum as it were reflected, and then he saw bright lines which did not belong to the solar spectrum, but to the comet itself. Now, when you come to put things together, it is quite evident that the comet must be, comparatively speaking, a cool body, then how could it give rays which we have here in the violet part of the spectrum? Comets are supposed to be a conglomeration of meteors, and these meteors, knocking about one against another, there is a generation of vapour and also of electricity. Now, these bright lines, seen in the comet's spectrum, coincide with the bright lines seen from certain hydro-carbons when the spark is passed through them in a very attenuated atmosphere. Not only, then, do we have hydro-carbons in the sun, but it is also proved that we have hydro-carbon in cometary matter; it remains to be seen whether in the fixed stars we can also trace hydro-carbon.* There is no doubt whatever in my mind that, as spectroscopic science advances, so we shall be able to place more and more compounds in the stars, in the sun, and in cometary matter.

* Since this lecture was delivered, Dr. Huggins has shown the presence of carbon compounds in certain nebulæ.

PAPER X.

RAILWAYS FOR MILITARY COMMUNICATIONS IN THE FIELD.

By Colonel J. P. Maquay, R.E.

THIS Paper treats on the nature of plant to employ, and the most suitable method of making railways, for the supply of an army engaged in war in a country where such means of communication do not exist.

In most of the wars that England has undertaken during the past thirty years, attempts have been made to construct railways for the transport of stores and materials from the base of operations. This base must necessarily be on the sea coast, for a country situated as England is. These railways have not been successful, chiefly because, when war had broken out, such material was hastily got together as seemed most suitable to the occasion ; and further, the construction of these lines was not carried on with any system. It is not surprising, therefore, that our military railways were never completed in time to be of much use to the troops they were intended to serve.

In looking for the quickest and simplest method to make a railway for military communications in a strange country, and for the most suitable material and plant to use in its construction, it is well to have a description of the various gauges of which railways are usually made ; to study the powers and capacity of different locomotives and rolling stock for these lines ; and to consider the time, labour, and cost of making a railway.

Before commencing a study of these three subjects, a statement will be given of what has been done in making railways in war time, excluding any account of their construction for the same purpose in civilised countries, such as the case of the Prussians, who made a railway round the fortress of Metz, and at the destroyed tunnel of Nanteuil ; or the railways made by the Russians from Bender to Galatz, and from Fratesi to Zimnitza.

RAILWAYS THAT HAVE BEEN MADE IN WAR TIME.

After a season of great suffering to the troops engaged in the siege of Sebastopol, caused partly by the difficulty of communicating with their base at Balaclava, a railway was constructed of the ordinary gauge of 4 ft. 8½ in. About 21 miles of track were made of single line; civil engineers with a working staff of navvies were employed in its construction. The rolling stock consisted of five locomotives of 12 to 18 tons weight, and about 40 ordinary side-tip ballast trucks; one of the locomotives was worked as a stationary engine to haul trains up a short incline.

This railway never had the capacity for transporting all the supplies required by an army engaged in a siege. It did a fair amount of work at the re-embarkation of the troops on the conclusion of peace, but it would have been of no use if hostilities had been continued on a different line of operations.

It must not be attributed to any failing of the Army Works Corps that better results were not obtained from this line, for it was composed of a staff thoroughly practised in railway construction; the mistake was in having only one line of rails instead of a double line, which is indispensable to ensure uninterrupted traffic; and in the plant being cumbersome and quite unsuited for military requirements.

For the Abyssinian campaign materials for a railway were collected in India from the public works and other sources, and a works corps of natives for laying the line was raised in Bombay. In the month of November Government came to the decision of sending railway plant to Abyssinia; in the following January work was commenced at the landing place in the Red Sea, at Zoulla; and about the end of March 12 miles of the line were opened for traffic, giving a rate of progress in constructing of one mile a week. As the railway took so long to make it was not of much use to the expedition. The chief causes of delay in making this railway may be attributed to the materials having been shipped from India without any system, any transport vessel that could afford space being employed. The plant was all for the Indian standard gauge of 5 ft. 6 in., which was heavy and difficult to handle under unfavourable conditions of landing appliances; the rails were also of different sizes and weights, giving much additional labour and loss of time in laying. For rolling stock four contractors' tank locomotives, which had been much used, were supplied; half of them were constantly under repairs. The material for making bridges consisted of rolled-iron floor-joists for barrack buildings, which were procured from Aden.

One great advantage of a railway at a point of debarkation was noticed on this occasion—the saving of labour that was effected by being able to run the trucks on rails into the water, so that boats with stores from the transport vessels could be unloaded directly into the trucks.

For the war in Ashantee, where the objective was to force our troops over many miles of the wildest African bush country, some steam-sappers (road traction engines), adapted for running on rails, were sent from England, and light rails were shipped for making a railway of 4 ft. 8½ in. gauge. This plant could not be utilised for the following reasons : it was difficult to land heavy stores on a beach that had a surf constantly rolling on it; the amount of labour required to clear a track for so wide a gauge through the bush would have been excessive; and the period of fair season at the disposal ·of the General for the accomplishment of his enterprise was too limited for making a field railway of the full gauge of 4 ft. 8½ in.

A light portable surface tramway (such as is hereafter described), with light trucks that could have been pushed by manual labour, might have answered in Ashantee for transporting stores and pro-visions better than the swarms of carriers that had to be employed for supplying the force that went on to Coomassie. A tramway of this class could have been laid quite as fast as the troops cut their path through the bush.

These are the attempts that have been made by England to con-struct and utilise railways for troops in the field. They have not been very successful, owing to the plant used for them being unsuited for military requirements, and being hastily got together.

DESCRIPTION OF DIFFERENT GAUGES FOR RAILWAYS (PLATE I.).

The 4 ft. 8½ in. gauge of the ordinary permanent railways is adapted specially to heavy and rapid traffic ; its carrying capacity is greatly in excess of what is likely to be required for a force operating in an enemy's country. The plant is heavy, and it takes a long time to make a line of this gauge, which must be well and truly laid to take the rolling stock adapted for it. The rails should be 78 lbs. to the yard; a mile of line of single rails weighs 272 tons, and costs about £1,700. The ordinary platelaying gang of three superintendents, thirty platelayers, and forty labourers, can only lay a mile of this track in thirty hours.

A field railway is only a similar line to the above, with lighter rails of about 42 lbs. to the yard; it weighs 131 tons, and costs £737 to the mile. The same platelaying party can make a mile of field railway in twelve hours. In its construction nearly the same curves of large radius are required, and the gradients cannot be made steeper, while the rate of travelling on it is much slower than on a permanent line of the same gauge.

In India a metre-gauge has been adopted on some of the Government lines; it is 3 ft. 3⅜ in. wide; rails 36 lbs. to the yard may be used for it; the line weighs about 106 tons, and costs £590 to the mile. Railways of this gauge are made for quick traffic, and require to be laid nearly as well as wider lines. The rolling stock which is made in England and sent out to India, is of a heavy nature ; the locomotives weigh 16 tons, and the carriages, which are iron-framed, weigh about 3½ tons.

The United States have lately adopted the 3-ft. gauge in a great many lines, which answer their purposes just as well as the wider permanent railway. They can construct these lines with great rapidity, progressing as much as four miles in one day, including forming the earthwork. The Americans carry these light railways over the most difficult country, and up ravines and over mountain passes where it seems almost impracticable to make any sort of road.

There are portable railways made in England as well as in France, which possess all the requirements for a military line. They are of various gauges, but the 2 ft. 6 in. wide has advantages over the narrower gauges—such as the power and speed of the locomotives, the capacity of rolling stock, and the great simplicity of parts. These seem to point to this gauge being more suitable for military purposes than the narrower ones. The rails are of steel, of 30 lbs. to the yard, fixed in lengths of 12 ft. to the sleepers ; the sleepers are also of steel, made of various sections. The most convenient seems to be the U shaped (*Fig.* 5, *Pl.* I.) ; these can be placed at any distance apart to suit the nature of soil. One section of rails of this tramway of 12 ft. weighs 310 lbs., and forms an easy load for four men to handle in laying the line, which is intended to be a surface line. It can be laid very fast by inexperienced men—about nine miles in a day. It is easily taken up, removed, and relaid in another situation. The plant for the track is complete in all its parts, such as curves, points, and crossings ; it is also very compact for shipment.

Some very narrow gauge railways have been made in North Wales ; the line to Festiniog is 1 ft. 11½ in. wide ; passenger and mineral traffic have been running on it regularly for some time. This railway is 13¼ miles long and rises 700 ft. ; the gradients are from 1 in 70 to 1 in 180, and the curves of 2 to 30 chains radius ; the locomotives, which are of Farlie's pattern, weigh about 8 tons, and can draw trains of 120 tons at an average speed of 12 miles an hour ; the rails are 30 lbs. to the yard, and the sleepers are of wood.

At Dinas there is a similar railway, but with 35-lb. rails, and Cleminson's flexible wheel base to the carriages, which admits of their going round very sharp curves.

Railways of this very narrow gauge work well enough when the line is laid with care, and the rolling stock for these lines runs safely on an even road-bed; it would require modification to run on a roughly-laid surface line to this gauge.

Railways are made of an even narrower gauge—18 in.; they are much used in H.M. Dockyards and the Royal Arsenal. This gauge has been adopted in the service, for a tramway to run along trenches and parallels to supply the artillery and engineer requirements at sieges. There are two types of this tramway; one with rails on wooden sleepers, and the other of a portable description. The first is that which has been taken for the service; it is designed for laying down without noise at night, this being a necessary requirement in making a tramway in siege trenches; the sleepers are of wood, 3 ft. 6 in. long, 7 in. wide, by 3 in. deep; the rails are fixed to these sleepers by T-headed coach-screws (*Fig.* 4, *Pl.* I.). With rails of 24 lbs. to the yard, 14 men can lay 100 yards of trench tramway, *in the dark*, in an hour.

The other description of portable tramway of the same gauge * is made of steel rails, 18 lbs. to the yard, secured in lengths of 10 ft. to steel-plate sleepers (*Fig.* 6, *Pl.* I.); it is a handy line for laying on the surface of the ground, and is much used for agricultural and manufacturing purposes. Each section of 10 ft. of rails, with the sleepers attached, weighs about 180 lbs., so that two men can easily carry it; a party of 14 men can lay 400 yards of this nature of tramway in an hour. The end sleepers are made to lock, so that the joint at the rail ends is quite secure; with wooden sleepers, fishplates should be used to fasten the ends of the rails; this is very necessary on all roughly-laid lines.

It would be thought that this gauge of tramway would be suitable for all military requirements besides siege work; but it is only applicable on very flat sites, and the engines for it have so little power that they would not be equal to the wants of keeping uninterrupted communication for an army. They answer perfectly in the Dockyards and the Arsenal, and are admirably adapted for laying in a trench; the engines would, however, fail in the event of a long line being required, or one over a rough country.

Table I. gives the prices and weights of one mile of track plant for different gauges, and in Table V. will be found a comparison of the time it takes to lay a mile of these various gauges.

* Patent of M. Decouville Ainé, of Petit Bourg; the plant is procurable in England from Messrs. Fowler & Co., of Leeds.

TABLE I.

Plant for One Mile of Single Track of Different Gauges.

Gauge	Description of Material	Quantity	Weight	Measurement 40 ft. c.	Cost	Remarks
			Tons		£	
Ordinary Railway, 4 ft. 8½ in. gauge	Double-headed rails, 78 lbs. to yard	3,520 yards	122½	33	857	
	Fishplates, 24 lbs. a pair . .	503 pairs	5½	1	48	
	Bolts and nuts (hexagonal), 1¼ lb. each	2,012 No.	1	¼	17	
	Cast-iron chairs, 32 lbs. each .	3,520 ,,	50¼	15	402	
	Oak chair keys	3,520 ,,	½	¼	22	
	Sleepers, fir creosoted, 10 ft. long, 10 in. × 5 in. . . .	1,760 ,,	90¼	133	308	
	Oak trenails and spikes . .	7,040 ,,	2	½	46	
	Total . .		272	183	1,700	
Field Railway for Steam Sappers, 4 ft. 8½ in. gauge	Flanged rails, 42 lbs. to yard .	3,520 yards	66	13½	462	
	Fishplates, 15 lbs. a pair . .	503 pairs	3¼	1	30	
	Bolts and nuts (cup-headed), 1 lb. each	2,012 No.	1	¼	14	
	Sleepers, fir creosoted, 8 ft. long, 9 in. × 4 in.	1,760 ,,	60	88	220	
	Dog spikes, 4 in. × ½ in. . .	7,040 ,,	¾	¼	11	
	Total . .		131	103	737	
Metre gauge, 3 ft. 3⅜ in.	Flanged rails, 36 lbs. to yard .	3,520 yards	56½	10	396	
	Fishplates, 9 lbs. a pair . .	587 pairs	2½	½	21	
	Bolts and nuts (square-headed), 1 lb. each	2,348 No.	1	¼	15	
	Sleepers, fir, 6 ft. long, 9 in. × 4 in.	1,760 ,,	45¼	66	147	
	Dog spikes, 4 in. × ½ in. . .	7,040 ,,	¾	¼	11	
	Total .		106	77	590	
2 ft. 6 in. gauge	Flanged rails, 30 lbs. to yard .	3,520 yards	47½	8¼	330	
	Fishplates 6 lbs. a pair . .	587 pairs	1¾	¼	14	
	Bolts and nuts (cup-headed), ¾ lb. each	2,348 No.	¾	¼	11	
	Sleepers, fir, 5 ft. long, 9 in. × 3 in.	1,760 ,,	28¼	41	132	
	Dog spikes, 4 in. × ½ in. . .	7,040 ,,	¾	¼	11	
	Total . .		79	50	498	
Portable 2 ft. 6 in. gauge	Flanged steel rails, 24 lbs. to yard, in sections of 12 ft., fixed to 5 steel-plate sleepers . .	1,760 yards	61	17	541	
Portable 24-in. gauge	Flanged steel rails, 18 lbs. to yard, in sections of 12 ft., fixed to 5 steel-plate sleepers . .	1,760 ,,	45	12	460	
Trench Tramway, 18-in. gauge	Flanged rails, 24 lbs. to yards .	3,520 ,,	37	8¼	300	
	Fishplates, 4 lbs. a pair . .	503 pairs	1	1½	17	
	Bolts and nuts, ¼ lb. each . .	2,012 No.	¼	¼	10	
	T-headed coach screws . .	3,520 ,,	¾	¼	21	
	Sleepers, fir, 3 ft. 6 in. long, 7 in. × 3 in.	1,760 ,,	13	20	22	
	Total . .		52	30	370	

Systems of light tramways on structures raised from the ground have been suggested for the use of the army. One of these tramways, designed by Mr. Fell (*Fig.* 1, *Pl.* IV.), has been experimented with at Aldershot. It consists of rails on the edges of beams supported on trestles of various heights to overcome the inequalities of ground, the principle being to dispense with cuttings and embankments as far as possible, and to use trestles whenever the earthwork exceeds 3 or 4 feet in height. Mr. Fell has worked his scheme out still further, and suggests the adoption of iron lattice-girders on posts of similar construction for raising the track over hollows, or wherever the rails cannot be laid on the surface of the ground. There are advantages in this method of making a railway; the raised portions of the work keep the line above the influence of rains, and make the least disturbance of natural watercourses. It requires time, however, to put together elevated iron or wooden structures, and a great deal of material is necessary; for instance, one mile of wooden structure for this railway, with an average height of trestles of 3 ft. 9 in., takes 250 tons weight of material.

The results of the trials of Mr. Fell's railway, which was erected at Aldershot, were as follows: an engine, weighing 4½ tons, took 25 tons of load up an incline of 1 in 50; at a speed of 25 miles an hour trestles, 20 feet high, were quite steady. It was found that 500 soldiers could lay two miles of this class of tramway, after a little practice, in a day of 10 hours.

Another style of raised tramway has been designed by Mr. Hadden (*Fig.* 2, *Pl.* IV.). The structure can be made of wood or iron; it consists of a single upper rail or beam, fixed on posts 7 feet high, let into the ground 3 feet; there are also lower or grip rails made of wood, which are halved and let into the posts. These have saw cuts in them to admit of their bending to take curves in the line of 100 ft. radius. The breaking strength of the structure is estimated to be 20 tons. The materials for one mile of this tramway are stated to measure 40 cubic ft. and to weigh 80 tons. The rolling stock consists of pairs of boxes or panniers suspended on the upper rail or beam by means of central wheels or rollers with V-shaped tyres; they also have horizontal wheels acting on the lower or grip rail. These boxes are ingeniously contrived to take stores, horses, and passengers, and may be used as pontoons for taking loads across rivers. By employing long ropes, trains may be drawn by animals towing alongside of the raised tramway.

The locomotives to be used on this raised tramway are reported by Mr. Hadden to be capable of drawing a load of 100 tons up an incline of 1 in 10; they are said to gain the necessary power by acting on the

grip principle instead of by gravity and traction like ordinary locomotives. The driving machinery is on a carriage by itself, and the
power is applied to one pair of the horizontal wheels on one side of the
grip rail; the steam is generated in two boilers, in front and behind the
engine truck. It is further stated by the inventor that an endless rope
or chain attachment can be applied to all the wheels on one side of a
train, giving continuous grip power for ascending gradients and break
power for descending steep inclines. The draw-bars connecting the
trucks of a train are devised to work automatically on the driving
action of the wheels, increasing or diminishing their grip or break
power according as the strain on the draw-bar is augmented or decreased
by variations in the gradients the train is travelling over. Whether the
engine and the draw-bars can be perfected and made to perform these
various duties remains to be proved by experiment.

With regard to raised railways, it should be observed that they
obstruct traffic crossing them—this is objectionable in a military point
of view; they do not lend themselves to the drawing of loads by
manual labour or by animal power as favourably as surface lines;
sidings are not easily managed on raised structures; separate bridges
are required for the passage of rivers, when the carriages cannot be
run on rails on the roadway of pontoon or other field bridges; they
require a great deal of time to construct, and take much material;
and they are not so easy to take up and relay as surface lines, and are
more destructible.

LOCOMOTIVES (PLATE II.).

In treating of lines of railway for military purposes, the use of
locomotives upon them must be taken into consideration; for although
the line may at first be worked by horse or other means of draught, it
must eventually be adapted to engines to make it of any use for keeping up the supplies of an army in the field.

It will be advisable to look at the different natures of locomotives,
and to see which appear to give the best results of work under the
special conditions of service in a strange country. A reference to
Plate II. will show the sizes of the locomotives made for various
gauges with their relative weights and dimensions.

Taking the ordinary passenger or goods engine of permanent lines,
it will be seen to be a very heavy machine to handle, particularly in
situations deficient of appliances for landing such engines. They
possess great power and speed, but are too cumbersome to be used on a
light line; they require the railway to be laid with care and to be
nearly level, that is with gradients not exceeding 1 in 70; and they

cannot work round sharp curves, 15 chains being the maximum that can be safely got round with engines of this class. The weight on each pair of driving wheels is so great, 10 to 15 tons, that the rails require to be heavy to stand the traffic.

There are contractor's and tank engines which are very suitable to roughly-laid lines; they weigh about 16 or 18 tons; they seem, however, beyond the limit of weight that should be adopted for military lines.

The same remarks apply to the class of engines that are used for the metre-gauge lines; they weigh about 16 tons, giving 6 tons on each pair of wheels, and, like the others, are constructed for quick speed; they are also not easy to handle under difficulties.

The small engines made by Manning, Wardle, & Co., and which are extensively used in H.M. Dockyards and the Royal Arsenal, are not powerful enough to take a load up a steep gradient; they are very well adapted for the 18-in. gauge of rails on level sites; they will take sharp curves and have good speed; but the line for these locomotives must be well laid and almost level; that is the reason why such good results have been obtained from these engines in our Dockyards and the Arsenal, where the rails are generally cast in solid iron plates and the sites are perfectly level.

The Royal Engineer Committee designed an engine for the 18-in. trench tramway, which has some advantages over the locomotives last described. It possesses the following characteristics. The working weight of the locomotive is 8 tons (*Fig. 7, Pl. II.*); the driving wheels are on a rigid base of only 3 ft., admitting of its travelling on very sharp curves; the engine is furnished with a 'rail-clip' on the Handyside principle, and has a winding drum on the front part, with 400 yds. of steel wire rope worked by a distinct pair of engines to the ones required for driving the locomotive; the last two appliances enable it to get up a very steep gradient; by sending the engine up by itself, and then, by clipping the rails, it can draw the train after it by means of the rope.

In trials made with this locomotive, 25 tons were drawn on the level on a very roughly-laid surface line; up a slope of 1 in 25, 7 tons could be drawn by the engine attached in the ordinary way; this incline had a curve in it of 2.5 ft. radius; the engine could just steam up a slope of 1 in 11, and draw 10 tons up the same slope by means of the 'rail-clip' and the winding drum.

These trials were certainly satisfactory, and showed that the Royal Engineer Committee were working in the right direction in trying to design an engine that could run safely over roughly-laid surface lines, could take very sharp curves, and was capable of getting a loaded train up a steep incline.

The boiler of the first locomotive of this class that was made was too small, and placed too high from the rails, and there was not sufficient allowance made for carrying fuel and water; for instance, this engine could only carry fuel for five hours' steaming, and water for a four hours' run. The clips acted well on the rails, but the length of wire rope gives a limited power of ascent for the engine to get over.

There is, however, another method of applying winding power to an engine; it is a suggestion of Mr. Russell Shaw, C.E., and consists of a chain securely fixed at the top of an incline, and the locomotive is furnished with a clip-drum that can catch up the chain. The steam power generated in the boiler will serve to wind up a loaded train by means of this chain and drum, and, by reversing the action, the chain can be made to break the descent of the train down the same incline. It would be well to convert one of the Royal Engineer Committee locomotives to this system of haulage, so as to test the appliance.

The 'steam sappers,' or road traction engines, which have been adopted in H.M. service (chiefly used by the Royal Engineers), are made by the firm of Aveling & Porter, of Rochester. They can be used as locomotives on rails by changing their road driving wheels. There are two sizes of these engines in the service, one 6 tons and the other 8 tons weight; 80 per cent. of the weight is borne on the driving wheels.

The 'steam sapper' is specially made for drawing loads on roads and across country; on good roads they will draw three times their own weight up a slope of 1 in 12; when used on rails (at 4 ft. 8½ in. gauge), they can ascend a gradient of 1 in 20 with a load equal to their own weight; and they can go round curves of 2 chains radius. They are constructed to travel on road or on rails at two speeds, four miles and eight miles an hour.

Some of these 'steam sappers' have been provided with a crane equal to lifting and moving about with 5 tons weight; there are also some with a winding drum and 400 yards of steel wire rope, which enable them to draw loads up a slope of 1 in 2; the ones fitted with the crane are invaluable in Artillery Parks, being able to move about with a load suspended, and to deposit it in a fresh site.

These road traction engines are a valuable auxiliary to an army in the field. In the event of a railway having to be constructed for a military expedition, they can be advantageously employed in hauling the materials for the line to where they may be required over the open country, or as steam cranes at the point of disembarkation to land the heavier portion of the railway plant. 'Steam sappers' can also be used as winding stations at the tops of inclines, where the trains cannot be drawn up either by animal or steam power.

Road traction engines, made by the firm previously mentioned, and of almost exactly the same pattern as has been adopted in H.M. service, are used by France, Russia, and Italy in their army transport trains.

It is, however, desirable to confine these useful machines to the work they are specially designed for, that is, drawing good loads on a road or in open country, and for lifting weights; locomotives for traction on rails require particular construction to get all the work possible out of them.

Table II. gives details of locomotives for different gauges, with the weight and cost of each. By reference to this table it will be seen that a tank-engine for a 2 ft. 6 in. gauge railway puts only 4 tons on each pair of driving wheels, and therefore will work on much lighter rails than the passenger engines of either ordinary lines or the metre gauge; it is also of one-half the cost.

An engine with superior traction power, having a moderate speed, and capable of going up steep gradients and round sharp curves, could very well be designed and be made suitable to the special wants of military service. It is worth studying how such a locomotive could be made, chiefly with steel and malleable cast iron.

TABLE II.

Details of Locomotives for Different Gauges.

Nature of Engine	Gauge	Weight	Weight on Pair of Wheels			Rigid Wheel Base	Minimum Curve Radius	Cost	Remarks
			Driving	Leading	Trailing				
	ft. in.	tons	tons	tons	tons	feet	feet	£	
Passenger Locomotive, Ordinary Railway.	4 8½	31	15	9	7	16	660	3,500	Tender weighs 18 tons
Passenger Engine	Metre	16	6¼ on each pair	...	3½	11¼	330	2,000	Tender weighs 11 tons.
'Steam Sappers'.	4 8½	11	8½	2½	...	7¼	132	430	8-horse power.
Tank Engine	2 6	11	4 on each pair		3 on four bogie wheels	3	30	1,000	Special construction for Military Service, £1,500. Weight, 10 tons.
R. E. Committee, Handyside Pattern	1 6	8	2¾ on each pair	1½	1½	3	20	860	
Royal Arsenal Pattern	1 6	6	3 on each pair		...	3⅓	20	480	

203

ROLLING STOCK (PLATE III.).

The rolling stock for a light railway must be of such a nature that it is easily drawn on the line either by animals or by steam power.

In *Plate* III. are shown various passenger carriages for different gauges drawn to the same scale, so as to be able to make a comparison of their bulk. It will be readily seen that the 4 ft. 8½ in. gauge carriage, which is built to stand the heavy wear and tear of a permanent line traffic, is much too heavy for drawing by horses, except for short distances, as in shunting. The metre-gauge carriages are built with iron frames for India; they are heavy and could not be taken any very great distance by horses or mules. The permanent line passenger carriages weigh about 3½ tons, and the metre-gauge ones about 2½ tons.

The simplest description of wagons for transporting military supplies on rails to an army in the field are long platforms fitted on bogie trucks; they are capable of taking almost any sort of load; they require to be furnished with movable sides, so as to make these platforms into box trucks at pleasure. For the transport of men and horses regular passenger and goods vans would have to be supplied, but it is for the stores chiefly that a military railway would have to be constructed.

For a gauge of 2 ft. 6 in. the width of the passenger carriages would be 5 ft. 9 in.; they could be made 24 feet long, or even longer, without difficulty, if fitted to bogie trucks; they would weigh about 2 tons, and take loads of 6 tons dead weight, or 80 cubic feet by measurement; this gives a working load on the rails of 2 tons on each pair of truck wheels. Such wagons, with freight, could be drawn by horses or mules at a speed of 4 miles an hour; the draught animals should be worked by stages or relays of 8 or 10 miles.

'Ambulance' wagons for a 2 ft. 6 in. gauge railway can be made 30 feet long (*Fig.* 5, *Pl.* III.), divided into two end compartments for six patients sitting in each, and a centre compartment for five patients lying down on stretchers, leaving a passage in the middle of this compartment for the attendants. Railway communication with an army operating in the field affords a ready means for taking to the hospitals established at the base all men falling sick and the wounded; the trains returning from taking forward supplies to the troops would be available for bringing to the hospitals the non-effective men from the front.

Well-appointed ambulance wagons on springs and bogie trucks reduce the sufferings of the patients in removal to a minimum ; and the advantage of railways for transporting the wounded and sick is that they save a great number of effective soldiers being taken from the front to be employed in attendance on these sick men, to escort them and remove them in stretchers and wheeled ambulance wagons along roads and by short stages.

To afford means of crossing wide rivers with a tramway, steel boats of the same description as were advocated by General Sir Lintorn Simmons, G.C.B., could be employed as pontoons for a floating bridge. The locomotives would have to be taken over the water on rafts made of these steel boats, for use with trains on the opposite side of the stream, as it is doubtful whether they could be steamed across a river on any sort of floating structure. As floating bridges for a double line of rails would have to remain some time in position, the steel pontoons advocated would be more suitable than the service pontoon bridge, and besides, the pontoon train would have their own functions to perform in the front with the troops. An idea of the sort of steel pontoon tramway wagon on bogies is given in *Fig.* 4, *Pl.* IV. The boats are made to rest on the frame which forms the longitudinal bearers or superstructure of the bridge for the rails of the tramway ; when the boats are not required to form a bridge, they would thus be available for freight wagons.

Whatever kind of rolling stock is adopted for military service, it is absolutely necessary that every carriage should have its break to render perfectly safe the drawing of wagons individually by animal draught, and also to have complete control over a train descending inclines. The 'Heberlein' continuous break is well suited for this purpose. It can be applied by the engine driver of the train or by the guard, and can also be put on by a person on the side of the wagons.

It should be observed that, though the bogie-truck system is recommended for military rolling stock as being the safest to travel on roughly-laid lines, and as giving the power to make sharp curves on a railway, there is another plan of 'flexible wheel base,' invented by Mr. James Cleminson, which has all the advantages of bogies. By this method the defects of a rigid wheel base are overcome, the carriages travel smoothly and safely round sharp curves, and the rolling stock can be made much lighter in weight than ordinary railway carriages. They have been constructed to take ten passengers, or three tons to every ton weight of the carriage, giving about two tons on each pair of wheels on the rails.

The rolling stock that has been approved for the trench tramway is on the same principle as is advocated for military railways ; it consists of platform wagons 18 feet long, which are well suited for transporting the requirements of troops at sieges, such as fascines, rails, and timber for gun platforms and splinter proofs. These platform wagons run on bogie trucks, they are easily drawn by men and by a horse pulling at the side of the wagon, and are made low so as not to be seen by the enemy over the earthwork of the parallels. Trucks for siege purposes have been made for the transport of artillery to the batteries; they are particularly suitable for this work, saving the very heavy labour to the artillery of arming their batteries by transporting the guns over the open country during the night. The weights of the siege guns of the present day would make this operation one of great difficulty if a tramway in the parallels were not available.

The ammunition, too, can be readily supplied to the magazines on these platform wagons; and now that the main artillery magazines have to be established at a much greater distance from a fortress than formerly was the case, a very great saving of labour is made by moving the heavy shot and shell on tram-trucks, instead of the old trench cart.

Wagons also for siege work have been designed that make ambulances for wounded men, and can take them from the trenches to the rear with ease and comfort; the platforms that are used for general work are capable of being converted into ambulances so as to utilise the empty return trucks. These trench tramway wagons weigh only 1½ ton, and are equal to a load of 3 tons.

In *Figs.* 6 to 8, *Pl.* III., are shown the three sorts of trench wagons, one for ammunition, for transporting the wounded and sick, and for carrying guns in arming the batteries.

Table III. gives the weight and cost of carriages and the number of passengers they will accommodate; the 2 ft. 6 in. gauge here has advantages in price and weight on the rails.

TABLE III.

DETAILS OF ROLLING STOCK FOR DIFFERENT GAUGES.

Class of Carriage	Gauge	Load	Weight of carriage empty	Weight on pair of wheels or carriage loaded	Cost	Remarks
			tons	tons	£	
Passenger Carriage	4' 8½"	32 First 40 Second 50 Third	11	6	570 430 350	Ordinary 4-wheeled rolling stock.
Covered Goods	..	8 tons	6	7	100	
Open Goods	..	8 tons	5¼	7	80	
Passenger Carriage	Metre	18 First 24 Second	3¼	3	200 240	Iron-frames, 4-wheeled carriages.
Covered Goods	..	6 tons	3½	4¾	85	
Open Goods	..	6 tons	3	4¾	85	
Passenger Carriage	2' 6"	24 First 32 Second	3	1½	250 200	Carriages on bogie trucks.
Open Goods		6 tons	2	2	60	
Passenger Carriage	2' 0"	30 First 42 Second	4	2¼	325 225	Carriages on 6 wheels, with 'Cleminson's' flexible base.
Open Goods	...	8 tons	3	4	95	
Open Goods	1'6"	3 tons	1½	1	40	Platform wagons, with iron frames, on two bogie trucks.

RELATIVE COST OF PLANT FOR DIFFERENT GAUGES.

In considering any special appliance for military service, its original cost must be studied, as well as the expense of working it, in comparison to other means of transport. Taking, as an example, a force of 20,000 fighting men of all arms, in the field in a strange country, and having to operate a distance from its base, in many circumstances a railway would be of the greatest possible assistance to place on the communications of this force. If a light railway of 2 ft. 6 in. gauge were sent out with the expedition, it would probably cost the following sum for 100 miles of *double* track, with rolling stock, for that distance :

TRACK PLANT.

	£	Tons
100 miles of DOUBLE LINE of portable tramway plant of 2 ft. 6 in. gauge . .	108,200	12,200
Sidings and points for ditto. . . .	5,410	610
	113,610	12,810

ROLLING STOCK.

	£	Tons
15 Locomotives of special make . .	18,000	150
20 Wagons fitted up as ambulances .	4,000	50
100 Platform wagons on bogie trucks .	4,000	150
30 Steel pontoon trucks . . .	3,000	75
20 Spare bogies	200	50
	29,200	430

WORKING PLANT.

	£	Tons
6 'Steam Sappers' of 8 h.p. . . .	2,580	66
24 Roar-tenders	1,920	48
Machinery for 2 complete workshops .	2,200	40
Materials for ditto.	1,000	16
Station accessories	2,000	10
Platelayers' tools, 40 sets . . .	400	10
	10,100	190

Making the total cost of 100 miles of double railway, of 2 ft. 6 in.

gauge line, with rolling stock suitable for the length of the line, and with workshop plant for its construction and maintenance, £152,910, and the weight 13,430 tons, say £1,530, and 135 tons to the mile. It would cost £4,500 a mile for plant to suit the 4 ft. 8½ in. gauge, and for metre-gauge plant the cost of one mile would be £1,850.

It is almost impossible to give an estimate of what the ordinary transport for an army in the field costs the country; its expense is influenced by the price at which transport animals can be procured and despatched to the scene of action; the distance which the transport has to cover tells upon its cost, and further the climate and season, whether a good one or disastrous to baggage animals, materially affects the expense.

Taking the case of the quantities given in Table IV., where different means of transport for 100 tons of stores are noted, wagons and horses for this amount of stores would cost £15,000, and pack animals for about the same weight, £30,000, presuming they cost £25 a head to get them to the field. Now, tramway plant for the same load would only cost £10,760; besides, the railway would be capable of doing twelve times the amount of work that the ordinary means of transport can perform; that is, if the load of 100 tons had to be taken 200 miles, the train would do it in 16 hours, while the animals, whether draught or pack, would be 10 and 13 days respectively at least over the journey.

Looking at it in this light, £1,530 a mile would provide railway plant capable of moving 600 tons a day if necessary (exclusive of freight to the site, and the cost of laying the line); the same sum would purchase 60 pack animals a mile (not including the expense of making the roads, establishing forage depôts, or the cost of their attendants), and they would not be able to take more than about 6 tons.

In making a comparison between transport by wheeled wagons and by means of a railway, the quantity of forage and fuel for the two systems must be taken into account. The conditions under which forage may be procured vary greatly with the different localities; but in most cases transport columns must move with a certain number of days' forage for the draught or pack animals employed, and in the same way a locomotive must take its fuel along with it. The forage may be collected in the country in which an army is operating, or it may have to be sent from England; the steam coal will certainly have to come from home.

Taking, as an example, the transport of 100 tons of stores for 200 miles, the following Table shews approximately the quantity of fuel, forage, and time that would be required. The calculations of this table are based on the employment of general service wagons, taking 2½ tons, 4 horses to draw, and 2 drivers to each wagon, with proportion of non-commissioned officers; for the pack animals the load is taken at 200 lbs. for good horses, with one attendant to 6 horses, and non-commissioned officers in proportion. The trucks for the railway are loaded to 6 tons, and the road wagons of the 'steam sappers' to 4 tons.

The column of gross weight is estimated on the load of 100 tons with the weight of the wagons, the horses, the locomotives, the trucks, and the forage or fuel, according to the numbers and quantities in each case. To the railway means of transport has been added the weight of the plant that is necessary for making the railway; if 2 ft. 6 in. gauge is employed, the weight of 100 miles of single line is 6,100 tons.

TABLE IV.

QUANTITY OF STORES TO BE CARRIED, 100 TONS—A DISTANCE OF 200 MILES. THE FORAGE OR FUEL TO BE STORED AT STATIONS 20 OR 23 MILES APART.

Means of Transport	Horses or Mules	Drivers or Attendants	Wagons or Trucks	Time			Weight of Forage or Fuel	Gross Weight	Remarks
				Days' March	Halts	Number of days			
				Miles		Total	Tons Forage	tns.	
Horse draught	180	80	40 G.S. Wagons	8	2	10	30	252	25-mile march.
Pack Animals	1,200	220		10	3	13	Forage 120	820	20-mile march.
Steam Traction on Railways }	..	8 {	2 Locomotives 18 Trucks }	⅔*	..	⅔	Steam coal 5	6290	{ *At 15 miles an hour.
Steam Sappers	..	25 {	5 Steam Sappers 25 Road Wagons }	2½†	..	2½	Steam coal 20	225	{ †At 4 miles an hour.

Table V. gives the conditions for the construction of railways of different gauges; by reference to this table will be seen at once the great advantages that a 2 ft. 6 in. line has over others, and more particularly the portable class of line of this gauge.

TABLE V.

CONDITIONS OF CONSTRUCTION OF RAILWAYS OF DIFFERENT GAUGES.

Nature and Gauge of Railway	Minimum Curve Radius	Steepest Gradients	Speed per Hour		One Mile of Plant for Track			Rolling Stock to carry 100 Tons			100 Miles of Double Line		Remarks
			On the Level	Up steepest Gradient	Time to lay	Weight	Cost	Engines and Carriages	Weight of Train	Cost	Weight	Cost	
	Feet		Miles	Miles	Hours	Tons	£	No. and Nature	Tons	£	Tons	£	
Ordinary Railway: Permanent Way, 4 ft. 8½ in. gauge	660	1 in 150	30	20	30	272	1,700	1 Locomotive 6 Covered Goods 8 Open Goods	100	4,740	40,260	374,000	This includes workshop plant, stations, sidings, &c.
Field Railway for 'Steam Sappers' 4 ft. 8½ in. gauge	132	1 in 20	8	4	12	131	737	5 Steam Sappers 25 Road Tenders	105	4.150	28,820	162,140	
Metre gauge, 3 ft. 3⅜ in.	330	1 in 100	20	10	20	106	590	2 Locomotives 8 Covered Goods 10 Open Goods	90	5,330	23,320	129,800	The bogies.
Portable Railway, 2 ft. 6 in. gauge	66	*1 in 30	15	5	4	61	541	2 Locomotives 18 Open Goods	58	3,080	13,220	109,206	'Clemison's' flexible base carriages.
Railway, 2 ft. gauge	20	*1 in 30	12	3	2	45	460	2 Locomotives 14 Open Goods	54	3,330	9,900	101,200	
Trench Tramway, 18 in. gauge	15	°1 in 30	6	2	8†	52	370	5 Locomotives 30 Open Goods	85	5,500	11,440	81,400	Tramway laid on wooden sleepers, not the portable class, which can be laid as quickly as the 2 ft. gauge.

* Without any special appliance for hauling up on steep inclines.

† Same platelaying party in each case, 3 superintendents, 30 platelayers, 40 labourers.

CONDITIONS FOR A MILITARY RAILWAY AND THE MOST SUITABLE PLANT.

Having now studied the various descriptions of plant that are made for different gauges of railway, it is easy to select from these detailed accounts what will answer best the purposes of a military railway. First, let the conditions required for such a line be distinctly stated.

A double line should be laid, as a single line is worse than useless if any check on it occurs.

The material must be simple, so that any *unskilled* labour can lay the line.

The sleepers should be of iron or steel, without any fastenings.

The rails should not exceed 30 lbs. to the yard in weight.

Each length of pair of rails and sleepers should not exceed 440 lbs., to be carried by four or six men.

The carriages should all be of the same type, that is, on bogie trucks.

Powerful and simple breaks to all rolling stock.

The line to be for traction by *horses, locomotives,* and *men.*

The bridges to be of the same construction as are used in the field on service for the passage of rivers.

The following are the chief points that must be attended to in selecting a serviceable plant for military purposes:

Simplicity.—In order to dispense with skilled and civil labour in laying out and working the line.

Stability.—In order that a great amount of work may be done, therefore, it would not be prudent to have too light or too narrow a line.

Portability.—In order that the maximum quantity of railway may be transported in the minimum quantity of space, and that it may be easily moved from place to place.

Efficiency.—So that the line may answer fully and in all respects the purposes for which it is designed.

The above conditions would be fulfilled by a railway of which the following is a short description.

Gauge.—The gauge to be 2 ft. 6 in.; the best authorities on narrow-gauge lines agree that a more efficient engine can be made for a 2 ft. 6 in. line than for smaller gauges; further, the trucks could be made with more overhang when carrying the same load as a 2-ft. or 18-inch line, and the curves would be equally sharp.

Rails.—These should be of steel, and not exceeding 30 lbs. to the yard, as this weight in 3, 4, or 5-yard lengths is most convenient for handling by two, four, or six men. Such rails are sufficiently strong for their purpose, and present every advantage for freight, landing, &c., while nothing would be more cumbersome than too heavy a rail.

Sleepers.—These also should be of iron or steel, and be attached to the rail. 'Legrand's'* patent (*Pl.* I.) seems the best suited of all plant made with iron sleepers, as the sleepers require no keys, spikes, or chairs, and have no loose parts; they can be taken off the rails for shipment and can be again attached to the rails, being interchangeable in all their parts. They have the great advantage of establishing the gauge permanently, that is, they fix the rails to the true distance apart and avoid constant use of the 'gauge' to test the work of laying. Wooden sleepers take up too much room to transport, and take time to prepare; they are always liable to be used as fuel.

Points and Crossings.—To be of the simplest kind, and be put together in one piece, and made all to the same angle, as nearly as possible. Thus the permanent way consists of two parts only, and the work of laying would never be stopped in consequence of the want of some part being left behind and not coming to the front where the line was being laid.

Double Line.—A military railway from any base of operations must be a double line. A single line is no line at all; the slightest hitch on the latter and the whole of the traffic is stopped. If double, both lines can be used in either direction, as was done in the Franco-German war. The movement being mostly in one direction, it would go on night and day. With a proper system of signals two lines can be worked in any way one wishes, and any quantity of materials be brought forward; whereas, with a single line, the limit is at once reached, and this is one of the principal reasons why military railways have never been a success.

Laying the Line.—The rails and sleepers being landed and the rolling stock ready, in order to lay the line it should be traced by engineers without any elaborate survey, and the line carried forward as fast as possible, following a contour line, with gradual maximum ascents, say 1 in 30. When crossing mountains all the steep gradients should be gathered in one place, so as to reduce the difficulties to that one spot, instead of distributing them over the whole line, entailing thereby cuttings, embankments, bridges, &c.

The great point to be aimed at is to get the line through, leaving

* Messrs. Shaw Brothers, Cambridge Street Buildings, Birmingham, are the agents for this patent in England.

all improvements such as gradients, curves, and ballasting for after-wards.

Rolling Stock.—The whole of this should be on the bogie system; they should be platform wagons capable of being made into box waggons. If a better description of carriage is required according to the circumstances, the carriages to be made so as to be easily and readily converted into ambulance wagons. Every carriage must have its own break; the 'Heberlein' break is well adapted for trucks that may be used for draught by animals or steam. The principle of this break is that the rotation of the wheels themselves is the power which is used to stop a carriage, and that the breaks are always *on* unless purposely taken *off*, thus preventing such a thing occurring as a run-away train or single carriage breaking loose. Letting go a cord puts the break *on* and winding it up takes it *off*.

Locomotives.—These should be specially designed for military ser-vice; they should be of the greatest possible power in proportion to the gauge and the weight of rail. An arrangement might be applied to them to enable heavy loads to be taken up steep inclines, either by 'Handyside's' system of clipping the rails and winding the train up-hill, or by Mr. Russell Shaw's suggestion of having a chain anchored at the top of the incline that would be clipped by a special drum on the engine and hauled upon, or paid out for descending steep gradients.

Such a line could be worked by horses, mules, bullocks, or even men, for limited distances, and would be equally adapted to traction by steam-power. Practically there is no limit to the work that can be got out of this line. As stated before, the great point is to have a railway plant that will enable communication to be established in the shortest time possible, and that, if necessity requires it, can be removed to a fresh site and worked there.

Another advantage of the nature of plant here advocated is that the whole of the railway can be laid by *unskilled labour*. This cannot be done with full gauge railway plant of 4 ft. 8½ in., or with metre-gauge lines. And again, these heavy railways cannot be used with horses or mules for drawing the trucks.

Had light railway plant been readily procurable, and lines laid where practicable during the Affghan war, we would not have lost tens of thousands of baggage animals. They would probably have been saved to have done good work in advance of the lines of railway. The troops which had to hold an advanced post at the termination of the first stage of that campaign would have been better supplied if they had had railways to the foot of the passes, or part of the way from the base; and when the forces had to push forward a second time, they would have done so more readily and with greater security had their communications been established by that means, instead of having to delay for the purpose of organising fresh transport.

In South Africa, 200 miles of portable railway would have given two separate lines of reliable communication for the supply of our troops; and would have saved the immense cost of hiring country wagons and spans of oxen. Such a light railway could have been constructed quite as fast as our troops were able to get over the country. The tramway would have been useful to the colony at the termination of the war.

It is generally thought that metre-gauge plant can be procured in the open market; this is not the case: there is no reserve kept by any firms for a sudden call of rails or rolling stock. The 2 ft. 6 in. gauge has been laid in several places in Europe, so that the nature of plant is well known and made to order by several firms.

It is in peace time that we should study what is best suited to our army in war; thus one of the requirements for our troops is plant for a light railway, and this wants thinking out. When we have made experiments with the view of finding the most efficient locomotive, and made patterns for it, the rolling stock and other plant, it is simple enough to get what we want from our manufacturers; it is merely a matter of time and money.

Troops, however, should be accustomed to the use of railways, their construction, and maintenance; for this purpose lines of the sort that would be used in the field should be laid where our troops would see them constantly at work; for instance, between all our depôts of stores and at our great camps; they should also be employed on our fortifications that are completed or in progress at home and abroad; and in our colonies, where light railways would be a financial success as against the cost of making full-gauge railways, the adoption of the plant selected for military service should be encouraged as much as possible.

By these means a quantity of the plant that is suitable for military purposes would always be in hand, and when wanted, might at once be collected and sent to accompany any military expedition in any part of the world.

J. P. M.

SLEEPERS, & FASTENINGS.

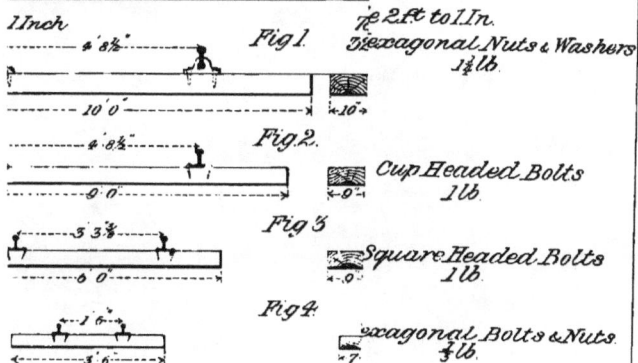

1 Inch

2 ft to 1 In.

4'8½"   **Fig 1.**   *Hexagonal Nuts & Washers*
1¼ lb.

10'0"   *10"*

4'8½"   **Fig 2.**

9'0"   *9"*   *Cup Headed Bolts*
1 lb.

5'3⅜"   **Fig 3**

6'0"   *9"*   *Square Headed Bolts*
1 lb.

1'6"   **Fig 4**

3'6"   *7"*   *Hexagonal Bolts & Nuts*
¾ lb.

PORTABLE TRAMWAY.   BLE TRAMWAY.

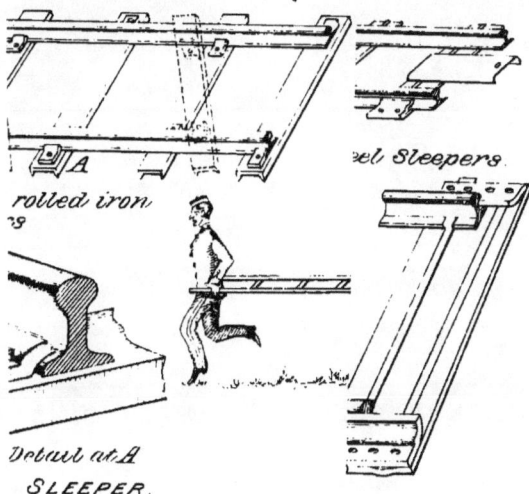

A

rolled iron

el Sleepers

Detail at A

SLEEPER.

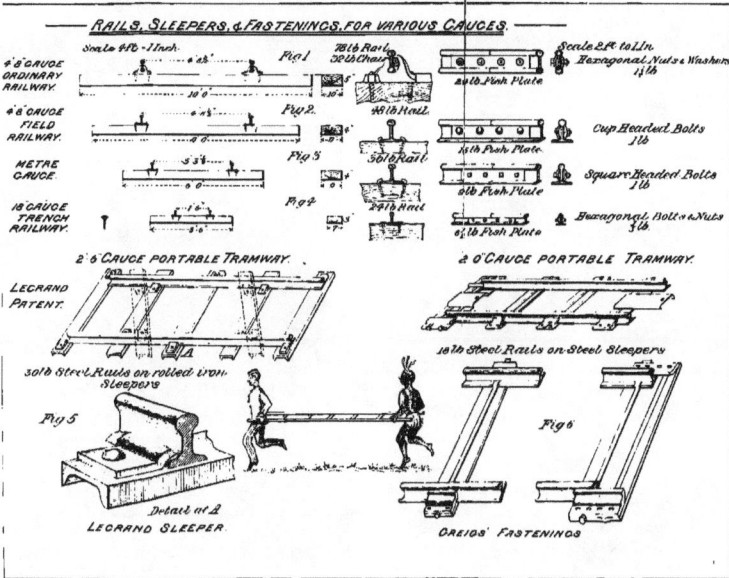

RAILS, SLEEPERS, & FASTENINGS, FOR VARIOUS GAUGES.

2'6" GAUGE PORTABLE TRAMWAY.

2'0" GAUGE PORTABLE TRAMWAY.

LEGRAND PATENT.

30lb Steel Rails on rolled iron Sleepers

18lb Steel Rails on Steel Sleepers

Fig 5

Fig 6

Detail at 2
LEGRAND SLEEPER.

GREIGS' FASTENINGS

—— *LOCOMOTIVE*

LOCOMOTIVE & TENDER.   *(3'3⅞)"*

ngine 31 Tons, of Tender 18 Ton·s 9 Tons, of Tender 11 Tons

Fig 1.

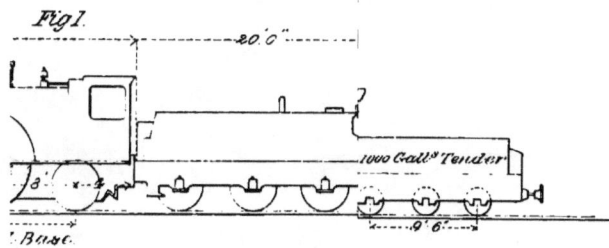

1000 Gall^s Tender

Base.

M SAPPER.   *8 HORSE POWE: LOCOMOTIVE.*

3 Tons·,   *ON ROAD W^t· 11 Tons.*

Fig 4

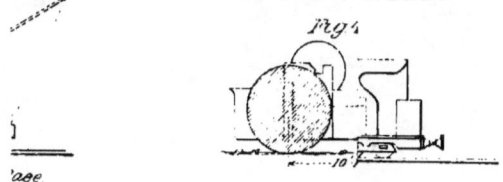

·ase

·COMOTIVE.   *SIEGE CUN MOTIVE.*

Tons   *Weigh·up & Winding Drum.*

            ·ltern.) Weight 8 Tons.

         Fig 8

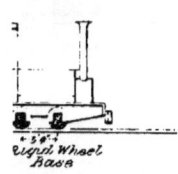
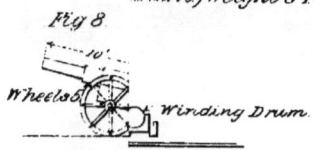

Wheels5   *Winding Drum*

Rigid Wheel Base

LOCOMOTIVES FOR VARIOUS GAUGES.

6'8⅝" GAUGE LOCOMOTIVE & TENDER.
Weight of Engine 31 Tons, of Tender 18 Tons.

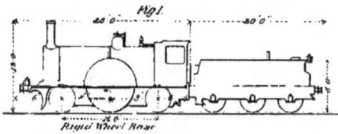

MÈTRE GAUGE (3's 8¾")
Weight of Engine 16 Tons, of Tender 11 Tons

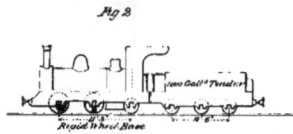

Fig 1.

Fig 2.

6 HORSE POWER STEAM SAPPER
On 6'8⅝" GAUGE. Weight 8 Tons,

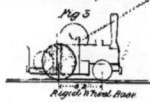

Fig 3.

8 HORSE POWER STEAM SAPPER
ON ROAD Weight 11 Tons

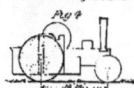

Fig 4.

2'6" GAUGE TANK LOCOMOTIVE.
Weight 11 Tons

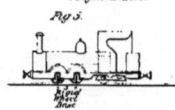

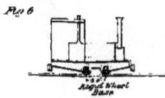

Fig 5.

18" GAUGE LOCOMOTIVE.
Weight 6 Tons

Fig 6.

SIEGE GUN ON CARRIAGE.
Weight 5 Tons

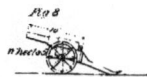

Fig 8.

18" GAUGE LOCOMOTIVE.
with Handyside Grip & Winding Drum.
(R.E. Committee Pattern.) Weight 8 Tons

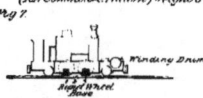

Fig 7.

CARRIAGES FOR VARIOU

ge.

Mètre
Gauge
Fig 2.

2.' Gauge
Fig. 4.

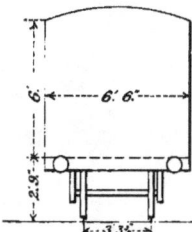

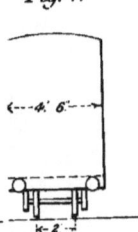

ons.   2½ Tons.   1½ Tons
Passengers   18. Passengers 10 Passengers
do.   24.   do.   12   do.

AMBULANCE CARRIAGE 2

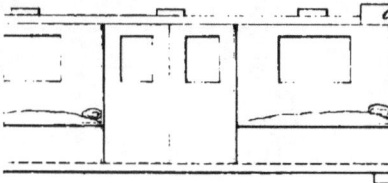

ght of Carriage 6 Tons
ing 30 Passengers or,
or Wounded. 12 Sittings
n Stretchers.

18" GAUGE TRENCH T

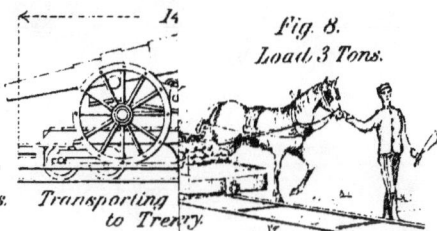

14

Fig. 8.
Load 3 Tons.

ed Men from Trenches.   Transporting
g. 6.   to Tren'y.

CARRIAGES FOR VARIOUS GAUGES.

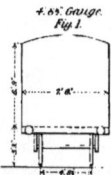

4.85" Gauge.
Fig 1.

Metre
Gauge
Fig 2

2' 6" Gauge.
Fig. 3.

2' Gauge.
Fig. 4

2' 8"

6' 6"

4' 6"

4' 6"

6' 6"

3.16

2' 6"

3' 3"

Weight = 3½ Tons.
1st Class, 24 Passengers
3rd Class, 32 do.

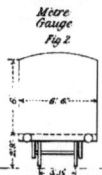

2½ Tons
18 Passengers
24 do.

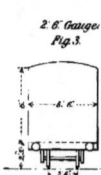

2 Tons
12 Passengers
16 do.

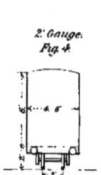

1½ Tons
10 Passengers
12 do.

AMBULANCE CARRIAGE 2' 6" GAUGE on BOGIES.

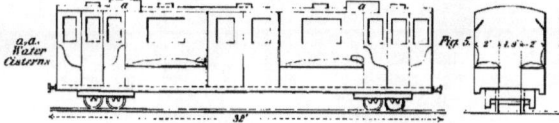

G.d.
Water
Cisterns

Fig. 5.   2'   1.6"

Weight of Carriage 6 Tons
taking 30 Passengers or,
Sick or Wounded, 12 Sitting
5 on Stretchers.

32'

18" GAUGE TRENCH TRAMWAY TRUCKS.

18'

14'
Fig. 7.

Fig. 8.
Load 3 Tons.

18"

Removing 8 Wounded Men from Trenches.
Fig. 6.

Transporting Siege Gun
to Trenches.

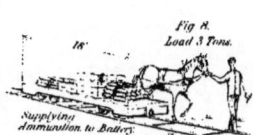

Supplying
Ammunition to Battery.

VARIOUS EXPED.

Fig.2.

Hadden's
Tramwo *Sapper Road Wagon*
on Rails.

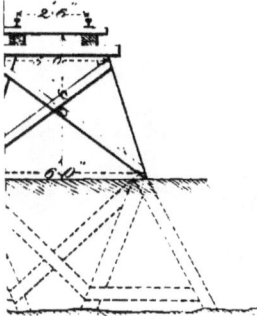

Fig.3.

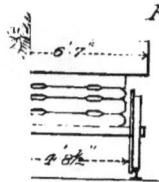

Weight 1¼.Tons.
Load   3. do.
(Length 14')

Steel Boats on Bogies *Section.*

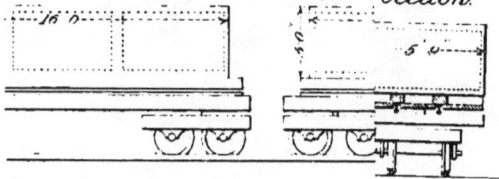

Superstructure
for Bridge.

...itary Carriages on 2' 6" gauge *...eserve guns.*

Fig 5

General Servi...
Wagon load...

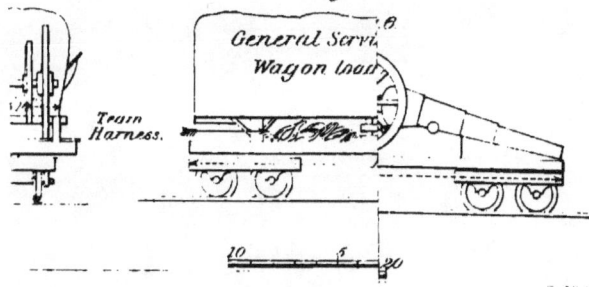

Train
Harness.

VARIOUS EXPEDIENTS FOR MILITARY TRAMWAYS.

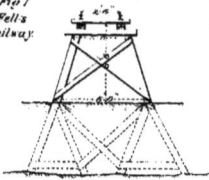

Fig 1
Fell's
Railway.

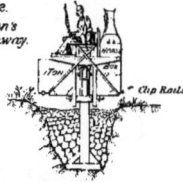

Fig. 2.
Hadden's
Tramway.

Clip Rails.

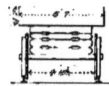

Steam Sapper Road Wagon
on Rails

Fig 3

Weight 1¼ Tons.
Load 3. do
(Length 14')

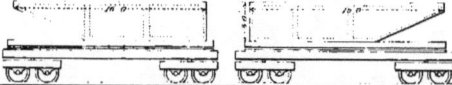

Steel Boats on Bogies 2'6" gauge

Section

Fig 4

Superstructure
for Bridge

Military Carriages on 2'6" gauge Bogie Trucks.

Fig. 5

General Service
Wagon loaded.

Team
Harness

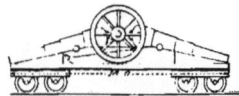

Transport of Reserve guns.

Fig. 6

Scale of Feet

Shrapnel shell.		CASE SHOT.		Charge.		Projectile, weight.	Muzzle velocity.	Muzzle energy.	armour-plate.	
				Weight.	Description of powder.				At 1000 yards.	At 2000 yards.
lb.	oz.	lb.	oz.	lb.		lb.	f.s.	ft. tons.	ins.	ins.
0	8^m	......		11·0	"	90	1165	847	...	...
0	8^m	......		10·0	"	90	1165	847	...	...
0	3^l	40	13½	5·0	"	40	} 1180	386	...	...
0	3^l	40	13½	5·0	"	40		386	...	...
...		20	9¼	2·5	"	21·6	1130	191	...	...
...		20	9¼	2·5	"	21·6	} 1000	149	...	...
...		20	9¼	2·5	"	21·6		149	...	...
0	0¼	11	7	1·5	"	1125	1239	119	...	...
0	0¼	8	13	1·2	"	8·5	1055	63	...	...
...		6	2	0·75	"	5·4	1046	41	...	...
0	5	70	0	34	P	80	1881	1962	8·4	6·8
0	7	100	0	42	P²	100	1900	2503	10·1	8·4
0	3	25	0	13	P	25	1930	...	...	...
0	3	25	0	3¼	RLG^e	25	1180	...	...	...

ht.

Number of Grooves.	Length of Rifling.	Charge.	Bullets.
	ins.	grs.	
7	29·0	85 RFG²	480 grs. "
7	28·1	270 "	3 oz. 4 drs.
7	30·1	85 "	480 grs.

special ·45 gatling cartridge has been issued for India, charge 80 grs. R.F.G², bullet 410 grs.

LIST OF SERVICE RIFLED ORDNANCE.

MUZZLE-LOADING ORDNANCE.

BREECH-LOADING ORDNANCE.

SHELL.					SHOT.						
	Bursting charge.										
Naval.	Common shell, L.G.	Diaph., shrap. RFG FG or pistl.	Mortar, Shell, L.G.	Naval, Shell, L.G.	Case.		Grape.		Solid.		
lb. oz.	lb. oz.	drs.	lb. oz.	lb. oz.	lb.	oz.	lb.	oz.	lb.	oz.	
...	0 7	24	...	...	16	15½	......		12	8	
...	...	18	...	...	13	9	......		9	4	
...	...	10	...	...	8	6	......		6	3	
...	...	...	...	...	4	7	......		3	1½	
...	...	...	...	...	4	7	......		3	1½	

TABLE OF SMOOTH-BORE ORDNANCE.

[Corrected up to 1st July, 1882.]

		ORDNANCE.[1]						CHARGE.[m]		SHELL.								SHOT.		
		Service.	Weight.	Length.	Bore.		Preponderance.	Exercising and saluting.	Service.	Empty.				Bursting charge.						
					Calibre.	Length.		Blank, RLG. or L.G.	L.G.[n] or RLG.[2]	Common.	Diaph. shrapnel.	Mortar.	Naval.	Common shell, L.G.	Diaph. shrap. RFG FG or pistl.	Mortar, Shell, L.G.	Naval, Shell, L.G.	[f]Case.	Grape.	Solid.
			cwt.	ft. in.	in.	ft. in.	cwt.	lb. oz.	lb. oz.	lb. oz.	lb. oz.	lb. oz.	lb. oz.	lb. oz.	drs.	lb. oz.	lb. oz.	lb. oz.	lb. oz.	lb. oz.
Bronze. Guns.	12-pr. ...	L	18	6 6	4·623	6 2¼	2·3	2 0	4 0	8 9	10 3	...	...	0 7	24	...	...	16 15¼	......	13 6
	9-pr. ...	L	13½	5 11·4	4·2	5 7·74	1·5	1 8	2 8	...	7 12¼	...	...	...	18	...	...	13 9	......	9 4
	6-pr. ...	L&S	6	5 0	3·668	4 9·47	0·75	1 0	1 8	...	5 0	...	...	...	10	...	...	8 6	......	6 3
	3-pr. ...	L	3	4 0	2·913	3 10	......	0 12	0 12	...	...	...	...	...	...	...	...	4 7	......	3 1½
	" ...	L	2¼	3 0	2·913	2 10	......	0 10	0 10	...	...	...	...	...	...	...	...	4 7	......	3 1½
Bronze. Howitzers.	32-pr. ...	L	17	5 3	6·3	5 1½	2·0	2 0	3 0	22 6	28 3	...	...	1 5	50	...	...	21 7	......	......
	24-pr. ...	L&S	12½	4 8·6	5·72	4 7·15	1·0	1 8	2 8	16 12	21 0	...	...	1 0	40	...	...	13 13	......	......
	12-pr. ...	L&S	6½	3 9·2	4·58	3 7·8	0·5	1 0	1 4	8 9	10 3	...	...	0 7	24	...	...	7 14	......	......
	4⅖-in. ...	L	2½	1 10	4·52	1 6·86	0·5	0 4	0 8	8 9	10 3	...	...	0 7	24	...	...	8 1	......	......
Bronze. Mortars.	5½-in. royal	L	1¼	1 3·1	5·62	0 11·94	......	....	0 7	16 12	...	...	...	1 0	...		...	......		......
	4⅖-in. coehorn	L	¾	1 1	4·52	0 10¼	......	....	0 5	8 9	...	...	...	0 7	...	...	...	......	......	......
Cast-iron. Carronade.	68-pr. ...	L	36	5 4	8·05	5 2	2·3	....	5 0	47 4	..	..		2 9	..	...	...	46 1¼	56 8¼	......
	42-pr. ...	L	22	4 3	6·84	4 7	1·0	....	3 3	29 11	...	..	...	1 12	..	...	...	35 6	38 8	......
	32-pr. ...	L	17	3 11·71	6·25	3 11⅞	0·5	....	2 11	22 6	...	...	...	1 5	...	...	...	22 1½	28 4	......
	24-pr. ...	L	13	3 8	5·68	3 7¼	0·3	....	2 0	16 12	...	...	...	1 0	...	...	...	17 11	16 10	......
Cast-iron. Guns.	68-pr. ...	L	112[a]	10 10	8·12	10 3½	10·8	8 0	18 0	47 4	60 5	...	...	2 9	80	...	...	50 8	65 9	66 3
	" ...	L&S	95[a]	10 0	8·12	9 5·9	10·5	8 0	16 0	47 4	60 5	...	47 13	2 9	80	...	2 9	50 8	85 0	66 3
	10-in. ...	L&S	66[c]	9 4	10·0	9 1·33	9·0	8 0	12[j] 0	79 4	...	...	79 13	6 12	...	...	6 5	82 0	81 7	......
	8-in. ...	L&S	65[b]	9 0	8·05	8 9·27	8·0	6 0	10 0	47 4	60 5	...	47 13	2 9	80	...	2 9	50 3	65 9	......
	" ...	L&S	60[b]	8 10	8·05	8 7½	6·2	6 0	10 0	47 4	60 5	...	47 13	2 9	80	...	2 0	50 8	65 9	......
	" ...	L&S	54[a]	8 0	8·05	7 9¾	6·7	6 0	8 0	47 4	60 5	...	47 13	2 9	80	...	2 9	50 3	65 9	......
	42-pr.° ...	L	84[d]	10 0	6·97	9 6¾	9·0	6 0	14 0	29 11	37 14	...	...	1 12	60	...	...	44 6	48 11	41 6
	" ...	L	67[a]	9 6	6·935	9 0¾	9·0	6 0	10 8	29 11	37 14	...	...	1 12	60	...	...	44 6	48 11	41 6
	32-pr. ...	L	63[b]	9 7	6·41	9 3	5·25	6 0	10 0	22 5	28 3	...	...	1 5	50	...	...	36 12	36 12	31 6
	" ...	L&S	56[b]	9 6	6·375	9 0·65	6·0	5 0	10 0	22 5	28 3	...	22 6	1 5	50	...	1 5	36 12	36 12	31 6
	" ...	L&S	58[c]	9 6	6·41	8 11·2	5·0	5 0	10 0	22 5	28 3	...	22 6	1 5	50	...	1 5	36 12	36 12	31 6
	" ...	L&S	50 A[d]	9 0	6·375	8 7·08	7·0	....	8 0	22 5	28 3	...	22 6	1 5	50	...	1 5	36 12	36 12	31 6
	" ...	L	48 or 50[bg]	8 0	6·41	7 7	4·5	....	8 0	22 6	28 3	...	...	1 5	60	...	...	36 12	36 12	31 6
	" ...	L&S	45 B[d]	8 6	6·35	8 1¼	6·0	....	7 0	22 5	26 3	...	22 6	1 5	60	...	1 5	36 12	36 12	31 6
	" ...	L&S	42 C[d]	8 0	6·35	7 7·2	5·7	....	6 0	22 5	28 3	...	22 6	1 5	50	...	1 5	36 12	36 12	31 6
	" ...	L	40[ck]	7 6	6·35	7 0¼	3·5	....	6 0	22 5	26 3	...	...	1 5	50	...	...	36 12	36 12	31 6
	" ...	L	39[ce]	7 6	6·375	7 1	3·5	....	6 0	22 5	28 3	...	...	1 5	50	...	...	36 12	36 12	31 6
	" ...	L&S	32[ce]	6 6	6·3	6 0¾	3·2	....	5 0	22 5	28 3	...	22 6	1 5	60	...	1 5	36 12	36 12	31 6
	" ...	L&S	25[a]	6 0	6·3	5 7·64	3·5	....	4 0	22 5	28 3	...	22 6	1 5	50	...	1 5	36 12	36 12	31 6
	" B. L. converted Mark I.[p]	L	42	8 1½	6·3	7 2	3·5	....	3 0	...	...	...	...	...	...	...	...	36 12	......	......
	24-pr. ...	L	50[e]	9 6	5·823	8 11·41	4·5	3 0	8 0	16 12	21 0	...	...	1 0	40	...	...	24 12	25 0	23 8
	" ...	L	48[e]	9 0	5·823	8 5¼	4·5	3 0	8 0	16 12	21 0	...	...	1 0	40	...	...	24 12	25 3	23 8
	" ...	L	20[e]	6 0	5·823	5 7½	2·5	3 0	2 8	16 12	21 0	...	...	1 0	40	...	...	24 12	25 3	23 8
	18-pr. ...	L	42[c]	9 0	5·292	8 5·75	3·5	3 0	6 0	12 10	15 15	...	...	0 12	30	...	...	19 0	18 13	17 12
	" ...	L	38[c]	8 0	5·292	7 6	3·5	3 0	6 0	12 10	15 15	...	...	0 12	30	...	...	19 0	18 13	17 12
	12-pr. ...	L	34[c]	9 0	4·623	8 6½	3·5	2 0	4 0	8 9	10 3	...	...	0 7	24	...	...	16 15¼	12 15	12 4
	9-pr. ...	L&S	28[c]	8 6	4·2	8 0½	2·7	1 8	3 0	...	7 12¼	...	...	...	18	...	...	13 9	10 12	9 2
Cast-iron. Howitzers.	10-in. ...	L	42[b]	5 0	10·0	4 9½	5·0	....	7 0	79 4	...	...	...	6 12	...	...	...	82 0	......	......
	8-in. ...	L	22[b]	4 0	8·0	3 9¾	2·5	....	4 0	47 4	60 5	...	...	2 9	30	...	...	34 0	......	......
Cast-iron. Mortars.	13-in. ...	L&S	100	4 3	13·0	3 3	......	....	20[j] 0	...	...	195 3	...	...	...	10 15	...	......	......	......
	" ...	L	36[b]	3 3·65	13·0	2 8·5	......	....	9 0	...	...	195 3	...	...	...	10 15	...	......	......	......
	10-in. ...	S	52[c]	3 10	10·0	2 11	......	....	9 8	...	...	87 2	...	...	...	5 4	...	......	......	......
	" ...	L	19[h]	2 5	10·0	2 1	......	....	4 0	...	...	87 2	...	...	...	5 4	...	......	......	......
	8-in. ...	L	9[h]	2 1·23	8·0	1 8	......	....	2 0	...	...	46 1	...	...	...	2 9	...	......	......	......

a Dundas's. b Millar's. c Blomefield's. d Monk's. e Bored up. f The weight of shot for bronze guns includes the riveted bottoms. l The maximum charge to be used when firing carcasses from the 13-inch S.S. mortar is to be 15 lbs., and from the 10-inch gun 8 lbs. j Dickson. h Congreve gun. k 100-pr. wrought-iron guns are in the service for coastguard and training ships. Those natures marked with * are only retained in the service until replaced by rifled guns. m Service cartridges to be of serge; exercising to be of silk cloth. n L.G. is retained for S.B. mortars (see List of Changes, ¶ 3760). p For defence of flanks.

www.ingramcontent.com/pod-product-compliance
Lightning Source LLC
Chambersburg PA
CBHW030907270326
41929CB00008B/609